THE ENCYCLOPEDIA OF

EUROPEAN HISTORICAL WEAPONS

THE
ENCYCLOPEDIA OF

EUROPEAN HISTORICAL WEAPONS

Text by Vladimír Dolínek and Jan Durdík

Translated by Petr Nykrýn

Photographs by Pavel Vácha and Dagmar Landová

Line Drawings by Petr Moudrý

HAMLYN

ACKNOWLEDGEMENTS

The photographs of the individual items have been reproduced by the kind permission of the following museums, galleries and institutions:
Berlin: Museum für deutsche Geschichte; *Bítov:* Státní zámek; *Cracow:* Muzeum Narodowe; *Dresden:* Historisches Museum; *Frýdlant v Čechách:* Státní zámek; *Hluboká nad Vltavou:* Státní zámek; *Konopiště:* Státní zámek; *London:* Royal Armouries HM, Tower of London; Wallace Collection; *Mnichovo Hradiště:* Státní zámek; *Munich:* Bayerisches Nationalmuseum; *Orlík:* Zámek; *Paris:* Musée de l'Armée; *Prague:* Muzeum hlavního města Prahy; Národní muzeum; Uměleckoprůmyslové muzeum; Vojenské muzeum; *St Petersburg:* Hermitage Museum; *Stockholm:* Livrustkammaren; Statens historiska Museer; *Tábor:* Muzeum husitského revolučního hnutí; *Vienna.* Kunsthistorisches Museum; *Warsaw:* Muzeum Wojska Polskiego; *Žleby:* Státní zámek.

Text by Vladimír Dolínek and Jan Durdík
Translated by Petr Nykrýn
Photographs by Pavel Vácha, Miroslav Ciunowicz, Jaroslav Guth, Jürgen Karpinski, Dagmar Landová and Josef Šechtl
Line drawings by Petr Moudrý
Graphic design by Pavel Helísek
Designed and produced by Aventinum

English language edition first published in Great Britain 1993 by
Hamlyn, an imprint of Reed Consumer Books Limited, Michelin House, 81 Fulham Road, London SW 3 6 RB, and Auckland, Melbourne, Singapore and Toronto

Copyright © 1993 Aventinum, Prague

ISBN 0 600 57538 1
A CIP catalogue record for this book is available at the British Library
Printed in Slovakia
2/13/03/51-01

CONTENTS

INTRODUCTION

The history of arms development represents an integral part of the story of human society. The weapon is considered first of all as a product of human society at the various stages of its evolution. From this point of view weapons reflect production and technology standards at any given stage of development. They also reflect the aesthetic views and the potential of art and craft decoration of material in the period in question.

Arms were probably first designed for hunting, i.e. providing food. The hunting weapon was also gradually adapted for sporting purposes or entertainment. The object of military-oriented historiography is represented by weapons used for combat — and as a tool of military and political evolution.

The history and evolution of weapons helps in understanding the past. This branch of scientific study is of considerable importance to those who may share the increasing interest in collecting weapons.

The present work endeavours to satisfy this interest by dealing with European weapons from the Early Middle Ages till the end of the 19th century. The prehistoric era and Classical times will be just touched upon here because the origin of weapon evolution begins there. As to the upper limitation, we believe that at the turn of the 19th and 20th centuries the present period of weapon evolution began, the epoch of technology and automation. Legal standards and regulations, too, mostly put the dividing line separating antique arms from those at the end of the 19th century.

As to the factual scope of the present work, it has been limited to weapons in the proper sense of the word, i.e. to objects classified as *Trutzwaffen* in German and arms in English. We have omitted everything dealing with armour for, in our opinion, this study represents a separate part of the history of arms, calling for a considerable and specific knowledge and approach.

We are therefore following the evolution of edged weapons and firearms, leaving aside war machines, artillery pieces or other weapons which needed to be operated by several people.

Specific features of both the main groups of weapons and their evolution have meant that there has to be a different approach to their treatment. While firearms represented a basically unified evolution, the problem of edged weapons is somewhat more complicated. They represent a whole system of individual types with common basic features of historical evolution, where, however, the evolution of the individual style is far from being unimportant. This has resulted in our complementing the short chronological survey with a more extensive section dealing with types and details.

It would not have been possible to achieve this goal without co-operation with a number of institutions, first of all the museums both in the Czech Republic and abroad. We are deeply indebted to all of them. Our thanks belong in particular to Dr. E. Šnajdrová from the Archaeological and Historical Department of the National Museum in Prague, to Dr. L. Letošníková, and to Mr. V. Červinka, Director of the Frýdlant Castle in Bohemia.

EDGED WEAPONS

DEFINITIONS OF EDGED WEAPONS

Under the term edged weapons we include a wide range of objects produced in historical sequence ou of varied materials such as stone, wood or metal and designed to be wielded by the muscular powe of their user. They were used for combat in man-to-man direct confrontation, hunting and later on fo sporting purposes. The decisive feature of edged weapons is their effective application achieved through cutting, thrusting or striking.

According to the style of use we define: cutting weapons (the basic sword types, the broadsword the falchion, the axe), thrusting weapons (the dagger, the rapier or smallsword, the lance or the spear) and the striking weapons (the mallet, the mace, the club or the combat flail). It must be pointed out however, that there never existed any real distinction between these categories. The function of mos swords, broadswords and some falchions, too, included not only cutting, but thrusting as well. On the other hand, some rapiers were intended both for thrusting and cutting (the so-called *Haudegen*) Moreover, we can mention weapons with a purposely combined function. Combinations of the thrust ing point of the pike and lance with the cutting edge of an axe are represented by poleaxes, halberds and other staff weapons.

Arms can also be classified according to the way of wielding them. First there are weapons used exclusively in one hand (*Griffwaffen* in German), which, following the way they were carried, can be at the same time mostly included among side-arms. Another category is represented by weapons provided with a staff where mostly both hands are required for wielding them. They are called staff weapons. There also exist exceptions. The two-handed sword is intended to be used with both hands yet it is not a staff weapon. It is not a side-arm either, since, due to its length, it was carried on the shoulder. On the other hand the basilard, a long thrusting weapon of the 15th — 16th centuries, was wield ed by one hand, but because of the length could not be classified as a side-arm; it was suspended from the saddle. Battleaxes with short handles were intended for one-handed use, but there were axes on a long staff which were wielded in both hands. Such a possibility of dual interpretation can also be encountered with some striking weapons, such as war hammers and clubs with short handles for the equestrian warrior or with a long pole for men on foot. Not even the concept of edged weapons being close hand-to-hand combat weapons holds true. The spear was a kind of projectile weapon, no matte that the distance was limited by the muscular strength of the warrior. In a similar way, the throwing axe was used in the late Middle Ages.

It is apparent, then, that the topic of edged weapons is quite extensive. The evolution in the course of centuries was subject to considerable alterations as to the materials used for making them, their type and application.

CHRONOLOGICAL SURVEY

THE ORIGINS OF EDGED WEAPONS

The origin of edged weapons lies in the Palaeolithic era. The wooden club or the hand-axe of the mammoth hunter was the beginning of the evolution which continued through the Gothic sword and the Renaissance rapier. Shaping the stone into a more effective form represented a step forward. In such a way the stone axe originated, bound to the wooden handle with animal sinew and tendons. During the Neolithic period the axe head was provided with an opening to accept the handle. By splitting the flint man could achieve shapes suitable for knives, spear-heads or heads for arrows discharged by the bow. These weapons, which at the same time could be working tools, were first of all intended for hunting, but could be used as well for combat between the groups of primeval peoples or Neolithic peasants. The dual designation of these weapons — or, better, objects, intended both as hunting tools and weapons, continued in use for a long time to come.

The discovery of metallurgical technology and the connected social and property-ownership development created the need for objects specifically designed for hand-to-hand combat. At the end of the Stone Age, in the late Neolithic, the first metal weapons appeared in Europe. In the first half of the 3rd millennium B.C., copper daggers and axes appeared. The period of copper use was of a comparatively short duration. Knowledge of bronze spread from the area of the Aegean Sea at the end of the 3rd millennium B.C. Bronze represented a far more suitable material for weapon manufacture.

1   Stone mallet, Neolithic, c. 3000 B.C.
Two stone axes, Late Neolithic, c 2000 B.C.

2 Bronze dagger, the people of Únětice, 1900—1500 B.C.
Copper dagger, the people of bell-shaped goblets *c.* 2000 B.C.

Bronze, an alloy of about 90 per cent copper and 7—10 per cent tin with some additional ingredients, was a hard material yet fairly pliable in the hands of master casters. If copper brought about the dagger as its contribution to the evolution of edged weapons, then the sword represented the greatest contribution of the Bronze Age to this process. The bronze sword underwent substantial evolution in the course of more than a millennium.

3 Copper axe, the people of bell-shaped goblets, *c.* 2000 B.C.
Ritual bronze sword, the people of Bylany, 900—500 B.C.

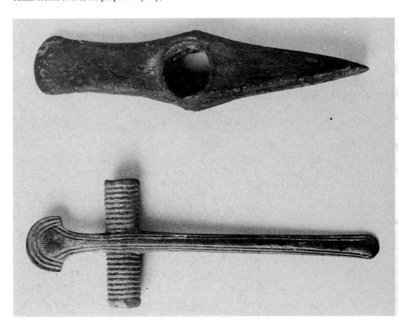

4 Bronze sword, the people of Bylany, 900–500 B.C.

ronze sword,
00–750 B.C.

ronze sword (Antennen-
hwert), 900–750 B.C.

Early swords had a long, primarily thrusting blade but later on they had straight or leaf-shaped blades suitable both for cutting and thrusting. In the later Bronze Age the swords were cast in one piece including the grip and most often had a flat pommel of diverse shape. The antenna (or voluted) swords represent a particular phenomenon with their pommel branching out into two symmetrical scrolls — perhaps as a representation of a human figure with raised hands. Bronze daggers basically preserved their leaf shape, but were generally of larger dimensions.

Side by side with swords, axes, too, appeared over most of Europe. The earliest ones featured a groove on their head into which a curved handle was then inserted and fixed by a narrow leather strap or animal tendon or sinew. The other type, frequently with a loop on the blunt side, is provided with a shallow opening at the rear into which a bent handle was inserted. Still another type had, as in the Neolithic period, a round opening in the thickened, central part of the head to accommodate the handle. The last type,

5 Bronze axe with groove for insertion and fastening of an angled handle, c. 1000 B.C.
Bronze axe with an eye on the facing socket for insertion of a bent handle, c. 1000 B.C.

11

6 Leaf-shaped head and conical ferrule of a bronze lance, ▶
the people of Bylany, 900–500 B.C.
Head of iron lance, ritually bent, beginning of Christian era.

◀ 7 Celtic iron sword in scabbard, 1st century A.D.

Roman sword, 2nd–3rd
century A.D.

probably of ritual character, features a rather small curved blade and elon
gated rear section. A barrel socket protruding in both directions was inten
ded for attaching the handle.

Other Bronze-Age weapons known from archaeological finds in grave
were lance-heads with a ridge and socket and in some cases also a conica
ferrule at the base of the haft.

At the time when the evolution of bronze swords culminated in the lat
Bronze Age, metallurgy of another material suitable for production of tools
but particularly for manufacture of weapons, had already been known for
long time. Although isolated specimens of iron swords had already ap
peared towards the end of the 3rd millennium B.C. in the Near East an
later on, in the 14th century B.C., in Egypt, the main period of iron weapon
falls within the first millennium B.C. The weapons of the Hallstatt type, s
called after the Austrian archaeological site where the first examples wer
excavated, were for a long time both of iron and bronze, and did not diffe
much typologically from earlier weapons. The sword and the lance change

8 Bronze and iron spear-heads with prominent ridges, 3rd—1st century B.C.

only slightly. But the properties of iron facilitated some changes in typology. Hallstatt swords with relatively long blades (up to 90 cm) were often provided with bronze hilts or later on with pommels and grips of ivory, inlaid with amber, and sometimes with gold. On daggers, and sometimes on swords, too, there also appeared the branched antenna pommels already encountered on Bronze Age weapons.

At about the middle of the lst millennium B.C. the Hallstatt period of the Iron Age was superseded with the La Tène period (so named after the archaeological site in Switzerland), connected with the upsurge of Celtic tribes in Western and Central Europe. Early La Tène swords were somewhat shorter than their forerunners and were intended both for cutting and thrusting. Later, towards the end of the period, the blades were lengthened again and their most frequently rounded points indicate a primarily cutting function. The lance-heads were of diverse shapes, most frequently however they were of broad leaf-shape with a central ridge. In some areas there appeared curved knives sometimes wrought with bronze.

Ancient Greece and, later on, Rome, fall within this period. The equipment of the principal warriors of the Greek phalanx, the hoplites, included first of all javelins (*dóra*). There were usually two of them for each warrior, a heavier one and a lighter one, and they were used for commencing the combat at a distance. In close combat first of all the sword (*xíphos*) with its pointed blade came into play, since the sword was primarily intended for thrusting, although cutting was possible. The Greek expression *spátha*, which might have been the denomination of another cutting sword, provided the basis for naming the weapon, not only in Latin, but also in many other languages. In the Hellenic period the Macedonian infantrymen were using a long lance (up to 5 m) called a *sarissa*.

A sword called a *gladius* was the principal weapon of the Romans, a relatively short sword with a two-edged blade capable of both thrusting and

13

9   Late Roman sword, the circular pommel inlaid with yellow metal, 2nd—3rd century A.D.

cutting. Later on, during the early Empire, a cutting sword appeared, the already mentioned *spátha*, used mainly in the cavalry. Late Roman swords of the 2nd and 3rd centuries A.D. often had circular pommels with a central opening. The name of the Roman dagger — *pugio* — was preserved in a number of languages, particularly in those of the Romance group. In a way similar to the Greeks, Roman legionaries used a spear known as a *pilum*, often with a long neck and socket running down all the way to the middle of the staff. The pilum was primarily a throwing spear. The long spear called *lancea* was the origin of the later medieval horseman's weapon and the name itself was incorporated into a number of languages.

THE MIDDLE AGES

Following the development of feudal society, weapons typical of the equipment of tribal warriors began to lose some significance. The German sax and the *framea* throwing spear, and later the battleaxe typical of German and Slavonic warriors and favoured by the Vikings, were gradually abandoned. Riders equipped with sword and lance became the basic unit of the armed forces. Production of iron and iron weapons in the early feudal era was developing, above all in the Franconian Empire, especially on some estates or in monastery workshops and on the sites of old Roman towns. Franconian sword blades were even exported to the north where they were provided with hilts of local origin. Viking swords appeared between the 8th and 10th centuries practically all over Europe from England to Russia. Not even frequent acts banning exports (such as decrees by Charlemagne) could prevent the widespread use of Franconian blades. The development of metallurgy, however, enabled manufacture of swords in many localities following the Franconian patterns.

An upsurge of medieval towns as centres of production and commerce began in the 12th century in the west and from the 13th century and later in Central and Eastern Europe, and provided, among other things, conditions for the development of weapon production. Specialization by craftsmen brought improved quality standards. Grinders, polishers and finally the sword-makers added finishing touches and created the overall appearance of the weapon. In the late Middle Ages we find makers of edged weapons in every large town. In Prague in the course of the 14th century 13 blade-makers and 20 sword-makers were working and other specialists participated in the manufacture of edged weapons, such as the hastator (maker of lances) and the fletchers who made arrows.

In the large towns of the Holy Roman Empire (like Frankfurt-am-Main) such specialization was even more pronounced. In this period there originated important production centres which then kept their place in production of edged arms for long periods to follow. The town of Passau in Germany falls within this category. Its mark, the Passau wolf, derived from the town's coat-of-arms, was still used as late as the 17th century, even though, particularly in the later period, it was often copied. In the late Middle Ages the foundations of the important production centre at Solingen were laid. Production of blades was maintained there up till the 20th century. Moreover, numerous sword- and blade-makers could also be found in Nuremberg and other German towns in the late Middle Ages.

The origins of sword-making activity in Italian centres, above all in Milan, Brescia and Genoa, fall within this period. Sword-making also developed in

10   Lance head with triangular wings, the neck and the socket decorated with engraved lines, 9th – 10th century.

11 Sword with thrusting blade, Dětenice, Bohemia, *c.* 1400. In the groove of the blade, a cross inlaid with yellow metal on a formalized heart; the pommel of circular shape is provided with a circumferential groove.

Spain. Sword-makers were operating in Toledo as early as in the period of Moorish dominance (8th—11th centuries) and after the Reconquista production continued to develop on the old foundations and traditions.

Weapons of the late Middle Ages were undergoing changes both typologically and in their shape. The effectiveness of rather narrower but longer swords increased, and their dual function — both cutting and thrusting — grew in importance. In connection with the gradual spread of plate armour, blades designed mainly for thrusting appeared and in the 14th century the number of thrusting swords, forerunners of the later rapier, increased. The horseman's lance acquired a slimmer outline with a shorter, but better penetrating point and a longer socket. Tournaments brought special shapes and types of armour, as well as particular types of lance intended just for this kind of sporting application.

Creation and widespread use of gauntlets consisting of articulated plates necessitated lengthening the sword grip. Thanks to it the weapon became more manageable. From the 13th century on, the dagger became an inseparable part of a feudal knight's equipment. In the 14th and 15th centuries the dagger developed into a variety of diverse shapes. In the course of the 15th century the sabre, a weapon with a single-edged, curved blade and a hilt similar to that of the sword, became more common. It is a weapon of indisputably Eastern origin, and combat with the Turks on the battlefields of Eastern Europe from the 1440s on probably had a substantial influence upon its spread.

The growth of towns as centres of production and trade was closely followed by accumulation of human resources there, which necessitated better protection of their growing wealth. This in turn emphasized the significance of foot soldiers and their equipment. Firearms, whose discovery and gradual evolution were inseparably connected with towns, were not yet really significant. The long-bow and the crossbow kept their dominance. Pikes for infantry developed separately from the rider's lance and were provided with larger, longer and wider heads. Other types of staff weapons appeared, too, both thrusting and cutting. The Flemish *godendag* falls within this category, a weapon used by the town of Flanders in their victorious confrontation with French knights at Kortrijk in 1302. There was also the Swiss halberd which asserted itself in battles waged by Swiss infantry against Austrian knights at Morgarten and particularly at Sempach in 1386.

From the 13th century on, particularly in contemporary illustrations, we encounter weapons with a shorter blade widened in its lower section, with a greater or lesser curved cutting edge. These weapons, pictured mostly in biblical illustrations in the hands of the pagans, were evidently widespread over most of Europe. The name *storta* is connected with them in Italy, perhaps *badelaire* in France, but more frequently *fauchon*, known in England, too, where later on it developed into falchion. In Germany and Central Europe they appeared under the name of *malchus*.

Combat on foot is naturally connected with the foot soldier's sword (*gladius pedestris*) which emerged towards the end of the 14th century in Switzerland. It spread in Germany as well as in neighbouring countries in the early 15th century.

In the period of the Hussite Wars firearms were first used on a larger scale and the Hussites also developed infantry tactics utilizing battle-waggons against the knightly cavalry. Other types of arms, primarily striking weapons, were utilized as well. The Bohemian flail, known in German sources of the period as *der behaimische Drischel*, remained an infantry weapon for a long period not only in Bohemia, but also in the countries bordering it. The flail was mentioned as late as the 16th century in the inventories of Saxony, Poland and other countries. The Bohemian partisan of the 14th and 15th centuries represented the other development line of the halberd.

Both the Swiss and later the German Landsknechts played an important role in the development of infantry combat tactics. In both cases infantry was formed into densely packed formations of several thousand people whose decisive force was represented by warriors equipped with staff weapons. Soldiers equipped with firearms represented only 7—10 per cent of Swiss units of the first half of the 15th century, but the percentage grew to 25—30 per cent by the end of the century. The Landsknecht formations, too,

12 Landsknecht's sword (*Katzbalger*), 16th century (the blade of a later date).

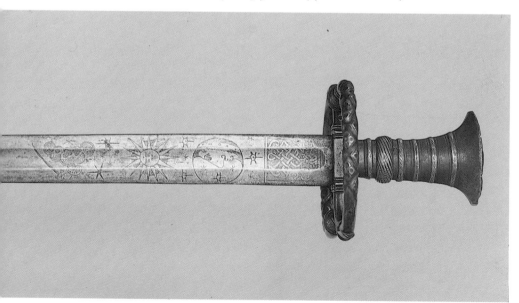

included only about 30 per cent or more warriors with firearms at the end of the 15th century, the main force being represented by halberdiers and pikemen with long pikes. They formed the core of a unit capable of defence against both cavalry and infantry as well as of attack. But at this point we have already passed the end of the Middle Ages.

THE PERIOD OF MERCENARY ARMIES AND RENAISSANCE WEAPONS

The fighting tactics and organization of close formation were still prevailing during the first decades of the 16th century, in which the principal role was played by pikemen along with halberdiers and Doppelsoldners armed with two-handed swords. For hand-to-hand combat after the enemy formation was penetrated, the short Landsknecht sword called *Katzbalger* was particularly suitable. Soldiers equipped with firearms still represented a relatively small percentage of infantrymen, and their task was to commence the combat.

The formidable Landsknecht square formation of several thousand men, although effective both in defence and attack, was difficult to manoeuvre. Spanish infantry tried to solve this problem by dividing the formation into so-called *tercios*, smaller square-shaped formations of pikemen surrounded with rows of musketeers reinforced at the corners of the formation. The chess-like arrangement of the *tercios* (usually there were five of them) facilitated easier manoeuvrability in the course of the battle.

The two-handed swords began to disappear about the mid-16th century from infantry armament, and later on, more and more, the halberds. Both of them, however, became weapons of heralds and palace guards and often developed into rather sophisticated shapes with rich decoration. Cutting down the weight of firearms in the course of the 16th century permitted an increase in the number of musketeers in battle formations, so that in the early 17th century the numbers of musketeers and pikemen were equal. This process continued and during the Thirty Years' War the Swedish army of Gustavus Adolphus had only one-third pikemen and two-thirds musketeers, organized in independent shallow formations of six rows. In such a way not only the firing capacity of infantry increased, but the manoeuvrability as well. The advantage of the Swedish system over the Hapsburg and German Catholic League *tercios* at the battle of Breitenfeld in 1631 was so evident that these armies, too, abandoned their deep formations and organized their infantry in ten-row formations. This trend went on, and when, at the end of the 17th century, the bayonet, which could be fitted to the musket, was introduced, pikemen and their long pikes began to disappear from the infantry.

The partisan continued to be used as a sign of authority by officers and NCOs and later on it became much flimsier and as a spontoon was pretty well incapable of any combat application. Neither the pikemen nor the musketeer could do without a side weapon, essential for hand-to-hand combat after the formations clashed. For this reason swords or rapiers were a must in infantry equipment for much of the 17th century.

Regular cavalry set aside lances in the early 17th century. The Polish heavy cavalry represented an exception for a long time as did light cavalry in Eastern Europe. Edged weapons used by cavalry were represented by a weighty sword; single-edged broadswords started appearing later on, and in some areas (Poland, Hungary), the curved sabre was gaining in popularity. Increased numbers of hand-protecting elements are typical of most side-weapons. This gradually led to the creation of a more or less complex hilt (*Gefäss*). Over a period individual parts of armour were discarded. In the early 16th century armour fully covered the body of a heavy cavalryman but by about the mid-17th century only the helmet, breast and backplates were

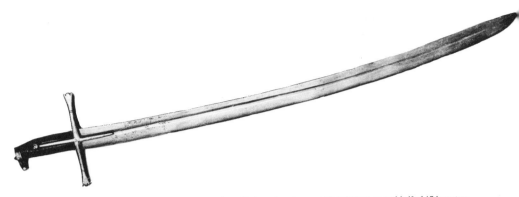

13 Hungarian-type sabre with drop-shaped cap and long langets, second half of 17th century.

worn. The two plates formed the cuirass after which one type of heavy cavalry was named — the cuirassiers. On the other hand the equipment of cuirassiers and riders was complemented with wheellock firearms, a pair of pistols and a shorter gun called the arquebus which was superseded by the still shorter carbine in the course of the 17th century. The carrousel represented a typical feature of cavalry tactics in the first third of the 17th century. In the course of charging, the individual rows carrouselled in front of the enemy while firing their pistols. Then they attacked with drawn weapons.

Fencing exerted considerable influence upon the design of edged weapons in the 16th century. Its origins reach far back into the past. Combat of two individuals using an identical type of weapons — the duel — appeared first as a sort of judicial procedure (ordeal by combat) as early as in the late Middle Ages. In the later phase of this period methods of combat between two individuals always equipped with the same type of weapons were summarized in an instructive way, documented in illustrations by Johann Talhoffer in his *Fechtbuch* of the years 1443, 1459 and 1467.

However, in the first decades of the 16th century fencing and duels along with it, or perhaps duels and theories of fencing derived from them, took on a quite new, different appearance. This social phenomenon was undoubtedly connected with the upsurge of duels which accompanied the Renaissance among the aristocracy in Italy, France and even in other countries of Europe. The rapier, primarily a thrusting weapon, became their basic weapon. Maybe thousands of noblemen fell victims to this fashion of duelling because they had drawn their weapon for reasons so petty-minded that in many a case nobody but themselves could appreciate it. Mastering the weapon thoroughly was a vital prerequisite for taking part in a duel. For this reason fencing schools originated first of all in Italy where master fencers published a number of books on the theory and practice of fencing. The first of them was published in Modena in 1536 by Achille Marozzo; then followed books by Agrippa (1553), Grassi (1570) and in the same year the first work was produced north of the Alps by Joachim Mayer from Strasbourg

An academy of fencing originated in France in 1567, and in 1573 the instructive work by H. de Saint Didier was issued.

The development of the sword and the rapier from the early 16th century on was concerned particularly with protecting the hand, a development that we have previously encountered. The use of the weapon for thrusting necessitated holding the weapon with the index finger grasping the cross guard from beneath. For this reason protective elements moved down below the cross-guard and a complex system of arms developed to protect the hand. A specific type of rapier, the so-called cup-hilt rapier, was developed in Spain, but in the 17th century it gained favour elsewhere in Europe.

The dagger was frequently used in the Renaissance, and its styling assumed new shapes. In fencing there also originated a new type — the left-hand dagger used when fencing with the rapier in the right and the main-gauche in the left hand.

The endeavours of Renaissance noblemen and princely courts to display their wealth, their longing for luxury and splendour, all led to an upsurge of artistic styling and decoration of weapons and their components. This holds true also for swords and rapiers, daggers and falchions or for other hunting equipment. Carving, gilding, etching, engraving, relief carving in iron appeared on weapons. Prominent goldsmiths and enamellers co-operated and took part in the decoration. Their metalwork was often based on patterns by the foremost artists of the period.

STANDING ARMIES, WEAPONS OF THE BAROQUE AND THE ROCOCO

The Thirty Years' War was the last major conflict waged mainly by mercenary armies hired by owners of regiments or by important military entrepreneurs like Albrecht of Wallenstein.

The second half of the 17th century in all major European countries was a period of absolutism and gradual organization of standing armies financed, equipped and maintained by state bodies. An upsurge of production, both private and state-owned, facilitated a relatively large-scale production of standardized weapons. This can be seen in Prussia at Potsdam, France at Klingenthal, in the Hapsburg monarchy at Pottenstein, in Russia at Tula, and in Sweden at Arboga and later Eskilstuna. However, it took several decades before conditions had been created for the introduction of unified regulation arms and uniform for soldiers of all regiments of the same branch of an army. At the same time it is necessary to bear in mind that officer weapons still remained individual purchases for a long time to come, as for example in Austria regulation weapons for infantry officers were not introduced until 1798 and 1811.

There originated specialized units both in infantry and cavalry. Dragoon guns, musketoons and carbines with French-style flintlocks were introduced for the cavalry everywhere. Heavy cavalry, the cuirassiers and the dragoons too, were using broadswords. The curved sabre was the prime weapon of the

14 Jan van Huchtenburg, Battle of Turin, 1706, copper-plate.

15 Heavy-cavalry broadsword Model 1700/1705, Austria. The hilt with a thumb-ring, the scabbard metal-framed.

light cavalry including hussars who had originated in Hungary but were adopted by many other European armies during the 18th century. Long lances reappeared on the battlefield in the hands of such units as the uhlans who had been copied from the Polish lancers.

Side by side with the infantry equipped with matchlock or flintlock mus-

16 Prussian hussars at the battle of Týn in 1744, engraved by J. S. Ringck after L. Wolfe, copper-plate.

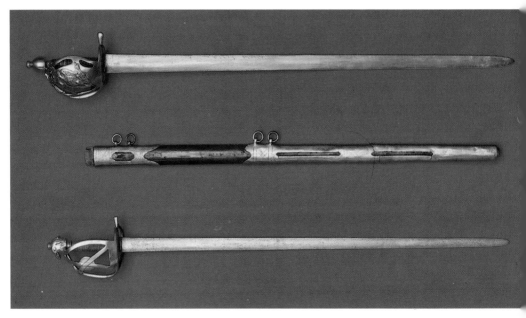

17 Prussian dragoon broadsword of the year 1735 with scabbard and cuirassier broadsword Model 1732.

kets, the musketeer, there developed special units such as fusiliers, grenadiers and skirmishers. The introduction of the bayonet had made it possible
to eliminate the pike from the armament but in most armies, however,
side-arms remained part of infantry equipment; only in the Austrian Hapsburg army was infantry left without side-weapon until 1765.

Side-arms — sabres or falchions — were also used by the jaegers, artillerymen and by the technical units of pioneers, miners and others. In the
latter category there also existed weapons with saw backs. It goes without

18 Confrontation of a hussar (sabre) with an uhlan (lance), coloured copper-plate, late 18th century.

saying that armies could not do without carpenters, yet few army axes have been preserved.

Linear tactics dominated the 18th century battlefield, with the infantry forming three or more ranks and then firing volleys. The exchange of fire was often followed by a bayonet charge and hand-to-hand combat. The heavy cavalry made massed charges with drawn weapons whilst the light cavalry specialized in raids, reconnaissance and chasing a routed enemy.

On civilian weapons brass and bronze were sometimes used to decorate the hilt and other fittings on smallswords. The hilts and furniture were simplified compared with their Renaissance forerunners, but their artistic concept was changing. Ornamental or high relief was more pronounced and battle scenes were often depicted. The following Rococo period further refined the overall aesthetic concept of the smallsword which gradually gained the character of a jewel-like accessory of a rich costume.

A similar style trend can be followed on hunting gear, falchions and carving knives. Where the sabre was a part of a nobleman's costume — in Russia, Poland and particularly in Hungary, the above-mentioned style changes made themselves felt in the appearance and styling of the weapon.

19   General Vandamme taken prisoner in the battle of Chlumec in 1813, engraved by C. Ruhl after J. A. Klein, coloured copper-plate.

AFTER THE FRENCH REVOLUTION

The victorious French Revolution created, after 1789, an army differing considerably from the previous armed forces of absolutist feudal states. The French revolutionary army employed its own brand-new tactical organization against invading armies still using the old rigid linear tactic. There originated divisions combining infantry, cavalry and artillery. Their core was represented by assault columns in deep formation screened by light skirmishers, often armed with rifles, who harried the enemy before the two formations clashed. After preliminary artillery bombardment the column moved forward and by sheer weight of numbers often broke the enemies' shallow formation. Cavalry complemented the attack by destroying and pursuing the adversary. This tactic was not original, for its individual elements had already appeared somewhat earlier. Utilization of sharpshooters is associated with the American War of Independence of the 1770s. Employment of columns in bayonet attack appeared in the Russian army under Suvorov in the war against Turkey — also in the last quarter of the 18th century.

Coalition Wars experience led many European powers to dispense with linear tactics and to copy both the army organization and the combat tactics created by the French Revolution. These lasted, with some modifications, for a long time to come. The modifications included changing the original battalion columns into company ones in order to achieve better manoeuvrability. This way of waging battles came to an end only after armies were equipped with effective breech-loading repeaters. The old columns then disintegrated and lines of riflemen were created.

The new infantry tactics influenced also the style of cavalry combat. The infantry column in closed formation could hold and disperse enemy cavalry by volley firing. Only a column disrupted by artillery and rifle fire represented a suitable target for attack by closed formations of cavalry, which in such a way still could decide the fate of battles. To a certain degree this was the case of the 1870—71 Franco-Prussian War. Towards the end of the 19th century and in the early 20th century, when repeating weapons were becoming more common and machine-guns were introduced, the cavalry's principal role changed to reconnaissance, protection of other army units or pursuing a retreating enemy.

Armies were expanding from tens of thousands to hundreds of thousands, and the demand for arms was increasing accordingly. New production centres were added to the old ones already operating. In Great Britain there were in Birmingham companies turning out a considerable share of the nation's output of edged arms and later Sheffield became another major centre of this production. In France, state manufacture was organized in Versailles after 1792, and in the 1830s state-owned production was transferred from Klingenthal to Châtellerault. In Germany, too, new production centres originated, like Amberg in Bavaria or Oberndorf in Württemberg. Orders by the Prussian state placed with sword-making companies from Solingen provided the basis on which, along with the introduction of new types of steel and machine-based production, a number of new industrial companies were founded over the following decades. In Austria, Fischer in Vienna was the principal supplier in the first decades, later on Jung and others. In Russia, Tula was complemented with another manufacture — Zlatoust — in 1814. The latter, specializing in edged weapons, was later turned into a modern factory and remained the principal supplier for the whole 19th century. The activity was not limited to regulation military weapons at Zlatoust. Quite the contrary, for the local masters executed a number of outstanding luxury weapons with rich decoration.

Side by side with large-scale manufacture and industrial production private sword makers continued working, though in many cases they were just assemblers, using factory-made blades. Not even this could stop the decline of their craft (in much the same way as in other crafts) and the number of sword makers gradually decreased and their workshops ceased operating.

At the beginning of this period it was first of all France which set the pace. A rich assortment of diverse-type edged weapons ranged from heavy cavalry broadswords through sabres of the general cavalry to weapons used by mounted jaegers, grenadiers, lancers and hussars. Moreover, in the Napoleonic army more prestigious weapons for the various types of cavalry existed, especially for the Imperial Guard. To a lesser extent, these trends made themselves felt also in the armies of Prussia, Austria, Russia and other European countries.

The variety of edged weapons diminished along with the changing function of cavalry. In 1845 Austria introduced a single standard sabre for all types of cavalry. It had been the first country to introduce the broadsword in the past and also the first one to put it aside. However, in some armies weapons with a straight blade survived till World War I, as in France, Germany and Italy. Austria was also the first country to remove the lance from cavalry equipment. On the other hand, a new type of all-metal lance formed from a steel tube was introduced in Germany in 1893.

Another trend made itself felt in the infantry. Along with the development of spring-clip bayonets the number of infantry side-weapons — sabres and falchions — was decreasing. Then the bayonet with a grip became a side weapon as well. A new weapon type appeared in the trench warfare of World War I, a shorter assault knife.

Along with the growing significance of pioneer units, heavy falchions were introduced often with their back edge as a saw-blade, thus combining a weapon function with that of a very useful and much needed tool.

Navies were using special kinds of edged weapons. Boarding sabres and other weapons intended for hand-to-hand combat on board ship are of very specific shape and stayed in use into the 20th century. As the number of steam-powered and armoured warships carrying long-range artillery pieces was increasing, boarding weapons were disappearing. Navy officers carried swords different from those of the army, most often bearing the symbol of an anchor. For on-board duty tasks where the long sabre would hinder free movement, short smallswords (dirks) were introduced from the late 18th century on. It goes without saying that these weapons, too, featured naval symbols. The officers' weapons of the Napoleonic armies also represented a wide range differentiated according to the type of unit. However, all of them had something in common — the prominent element of the Empire style with a strong bias towards the antique design. In other countries the differentiation involved officers' weapons for heavy and light infantry, weapons for general infantry officers, officers of grenadiers or jaeger officers. However, unification was taking place gradually.

The civilian smallsword as a costume accessory surviving from the past lost its playful Rococo outline and even before the end of the 18th century adopted the stricter concept of Neo-Classicism. Neo-Classicism was soon superseded by the Empire style. The era of the smallswords as an accessory to the costume of males belonging to the upper strata of society was ended with the beginning of the Burgher style period — Biedermeier — *c.* 1780. This type of weapon, however, and sometimes the sabre, too, became a part of uniforms worn by civic or state officials of all kinds. Not only police or gendarmerie officers, but professors and administrative officials as well as dignitaries of the postal or railway services wore uniforms with side weapons. This trend was common in Russia, Austria, Germany and other countries.

Duels waged by edged weapons still occurred in the 19th century. Starting in the mid-19th century, fencing was turning into a genuine sport and as such governed by exact rules in which it was no longer the case of injuring or killing the opponent, but rather of proving one's greater experience, adroitness and general capability in wielding the weapon. Special sporting weapons with pliable blade and blunted point originated just for this particular application.

Moreover, in the course of the 19th century there also appeared a special sporting sabre with a slightly curved blade and a basket-hilt with an arched shell protecting the hand. Fencing using modern sporting equipment instead of actual weapons has continued and has also developed as an Olympic discipline.

World War I had a considerable adverse impact on the role of cavalry and edged weapons. Although the major combatants commenced World War II with cavalry as a part of their armed forces, only Poland preserved the uhlan lance in cavalry equipment. Evolution and the upsurge of tanks and other combat vehicles inevitably led to the gradual elimination of cavalry in all armies. Edged weapons have mostly preserved their ceremonial role only; their present application is limited to ceremonial units, parades and similar festive occasions. Only the assault knife remained for actual combat. In such a way edged weapons have been deprived of their role, having become a historic survival.

CATEGORIES OF EDGED WEAPONS

SIDE-ARMS

The first major category of edged weapons is represented by side-arms, predominantly wielded by one hand (*Griffwaffen*). We divide them into cutting weapons and thrusting weapons. Our comments will start with the cutting group including the sword, the broadsword, the sabre and the falchion.

CUTTING SIDE-ARMS

The Sword

The sword is a weapon with straight blade sharpened on both edges, with a point in line with the centre of the blade and provided with a cross-guard, a grip and a pommel. It is above all a cutting weapon; however, thrusting is

20 Empire sabre, early 19th century.
Light cavalry sabre, the blade blued, early 19th century.

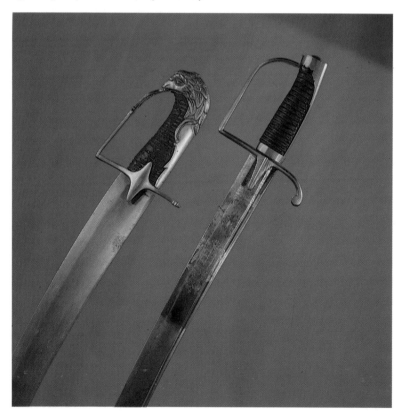

Sword
1 Pommel of the grip
2 Grip — tang
3 Cross-guard
4 Blade
5 Fuller
6 Sharp edge
7 Point

21 Viking-type sword, 9th—10th century. The pommel and the cross-guard covered with silver (a copy).

Spatha, 7th—8th century

not excluded. Its origin in primeval times and fate in antiquity have already been outlined in the preceding section.

The first significant type of early historic sword is the *spatha*. The name is of Greek origin, the weapon itself being derived from the earlier sword, perhaps of Celtic origin, used under this name by Roman mounted troops. *Spatha* appeared during the migration of peoples (end of 4th century A.D.) and stayed in use till approximately A.D. 700.

The relatively quick evolution from the 7th or 8th century led to the creation of a basic sword shape which was then further improved in the Middle Ages. It was the so-called Viking sword which in the course of the 8th—10th centuries spread over almost all Europe from England to Russia. From the typology point of view it is a series of variable shapes. In 1920, Jan Petersen needed the whole alphabet for their classification. Its homeland was Scandinavia, Norway in particular. Swords of this type were widespread as a result of Viking expansion. Their common characteristic feature is always represented by relatively broad two-edged blade with wide fuller. In the early period there also appeared, though rarely, single-edged blades. The short oval or oblong cross-guard is rather massive as a rule, the pommel is quite often, especially on earlier types, lobe-shaped, with the base and three or more lobes. Among extant swords there are a number of luxury specimens with pommels inlaid or overlaid with precious metal, silver, gold or copper. On the most luxurious ones the whole cross-guard, grip and pommel were overlaid with wrought gold plate. Towards the end of the period there also appeared simpler cap- or mushroom-shaped pommels of solid iron which already foreshadow further stages of evolution.

22 Sword with moon-shaped pommel, Blansko, Moravia, second half of 13th century.

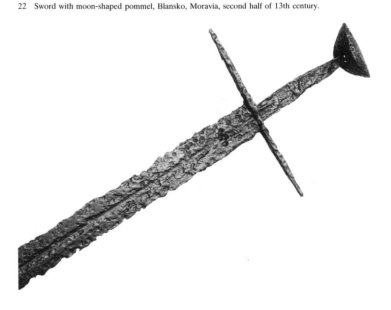

Sword, 9th—10th century

Sword, 10th century

23 Sword with mitre-shaped pommel, Bohemia, 13th century.
The cross-guard bent.
Sword with dome-shaped pommel, Bohemia, 13th century.
The cross-guard missing.

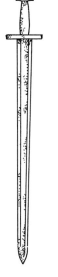

10th — 11th century

In the 12th — 13th centuries, apart from types surviving from the past, swords with pommels fashioned like a Brazil nut represented the prevailing type. The shape of cross-guard changed considerably, having been lengthened into a relatively narrow bar 18 — 21 cm long of square cross-section. The upper part of the sword represents the shape of cross and this was a feature which remained for centuries.

Silver-incrusted inscriptions or groups of letters may be encountered on the blades of these swords, most frequently abbreviations and symbols with a religious content, again connected with the idea of fighting for Christianity (e.g. *IN NOMINE DOMINI*).

From the Brazil-nut shaped pommel the outline resembling the third phase of the moon was derived which appeared in the 13th and 14th centuries. Besides the pommel-shapes already mentioned, from the 11th till the 13th century there also appeared triangular-roof outlines. The geographical spread of this shape in Europe is witnessed by finds in Northern Europe and in Central Europe as well. Swords with mitre-shaped pommels are evidently of somewhat later origin. Trapezoid pommels rounded at the bottom undoubtedly still belonged to the 13th century.

In the time of the late Middle Ages, the sword remained an important weapon in the hand of the mounted knight. However, some changes materialized both in shape and function of the weapon. The evolution of armour from the 13th century on, in the course of which mail was complemented with plate-defence elements, made it necessary to look for

24 Sword with circular pommel and straight cross-guard, Bohemia, 14th — 15th century.

31

25 Luxury sword possibly belonging to Siguinus, Archbishop of Cologne (1079–89). The pommel fashioned as Brazil nut and the cross-guard inlaid with silver, copper and yellow metal (gold?) depicting motifs from the Old Testament (the tree) and the New Testament (the fish). On the blade the inscription *SINGVINAIS* in the channel originally inlaid with iron wires.

means to thrust between the joints of the armour. For this reason, from the 13th century on there appeared, side by side with blades of primarily cutting character, sporadically at first but more frequently later on, blades which were somewhat narrower and tapered sharply towards the point. These thrusting swords were the early forerunners of the later rapier.

The development of gauntlet in the early 14th century necessitated lengthening the rather short grip which up to that time had been suitable for a hand in a glove of mail. The grip was gradually extended to the length of one and a half hands.

The need for balancing the lengthening blade also led to changes in the pommel. As early as about 1200 a circular pommel appeared fashioned as a relatively massive flat disc. Up till the 15th century we can find sword pommels derived from this basic shape, as a circular flat pommel with a groove around its circumference or a similar oval pommel. Another variety is represented by a circular pommel markedly thickened towards the centre and flattened about the circumference so that it creates an impression of two superimposed cones without tips. The pommel is sometimes enhanced by a rounded recess on the central flats, often provided with a symbol (such as a rosette, equal-armed cross or sometimes even the owner's coat-of-arms) punched or inlaid with non-ferrous metal.

Swords in the basic shape of the cross with round or oval pommels had spread over almost all Europe in the 14th and early 15th centuries. They

Hilt of the same sword, detail.

26 Relic sword with trapezoidal pommel and straight cross-guard. Bohemia, 13th century.

27 Sword, circular double-conic pommel with finial, Bohemia, end of 14th – early 15th century.
Sword with octagonal pommel, Roudnice nad Labem, Bohemia, 14th – 15th century. Nine-lobed rosette punched in the hollowed centre of the pommel, thrust blade.

28 Sword with pommel shaped as half-lily, thrusting blade, mid-15th century.

were found in Austria, Bohemia, and on the territory of modern Germany as well as in England. From circular or oval pommels there was just a slight step to the shape of two superimposed octagonal pyramids with flattened tops and often a round recess therein as well. However, the shaping of pommels showed considerable diversity at the turn of the 14th and 15th centuries. Polygonal flat-nosed double pyramids set vertically on the end of the tang were more and more common.

The cross-guard, still quite often four-faced in cross-section, became

29 Luxury sword, Central Europe, mid-16th century.
The blade with gilded, engraved and chased ornament. The hilt, with guard bars, is gilded.

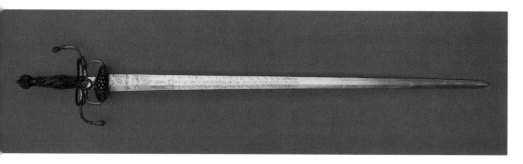

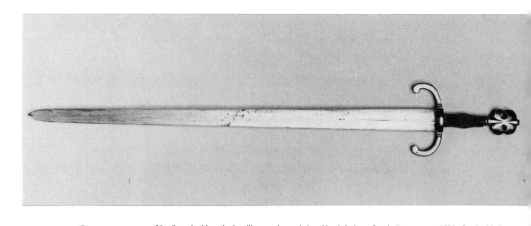

30 Sword with arched quillons and guard ring, North Italy or South Germany, c. 1500. On the blade, copper inlaid sceptre and engraved snake.

more complicated, polygonal and somewhat thickened towards the end, sometimes also with slightly drooping quillons.

The claymore represents a somewhat different type. The sword apparently was of Scottish origin and appeared in the later Middle Ages. Short cross-guards with quillons tilted down obliquely are its typical feature.

31 Sword with hilt typical of the Swiss sabre,
Switzerland, early 17th century.
The hilt carved in relief.

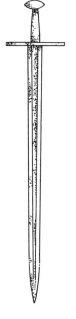

11th—12th century

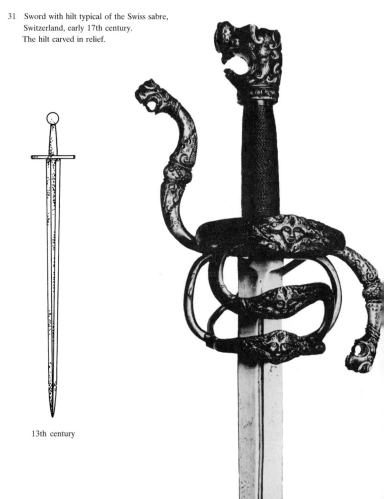

13th century

34

13th century

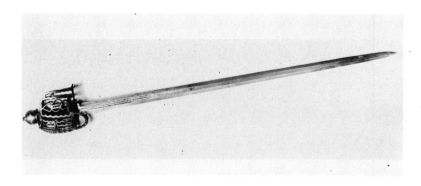

32 Scottish basket-hilted sword, 18th–19th century.

In the course of the 15th century there appeared other shapes of pommel, notably a flat shape fashioned as the upper part of a stylized lily. Pear-shaped pommels, sometimes smooth, sometimes grooved, usually belonged to swords with one-and-a-half hand grips, which often have an unusually long blade and belong to the category of swords for combat on foot. The left hand laid on the pommel facilitated easier balancing and wielding of the sword. From the second half of the 15th century on there also occurred a square-shaped pommel, relatively flat, with a vertical rib in Central Europe or with a circular projection in the Venice area. This style of pommel is often connected with cross-guards shaped as horizontally S-shaped quillons of a relatively wide iron band sometimes profiled with parallel grooves.

About 1500, hand-protecting elements developed. At first this was just a simple horizontal ring in the centre of the cross-guard. Later, along with the development of the rapier, down-sloping rings or bars were added, and the S-shaped quillon was developed into the knuckle-bow. Gradually other elements, ribs and bars were added on one or both sides of the grip during the evolution towards the complex basket. Some early 17th-century Swiss swords feature a peculiar styling of furniture (hilt) — taken from the Swiss sabre.

The complex basket hilt reached its fully developed stage on the so-called *schiavona* swords, weapons originally typical of Venetian mercenary cavalry, largely consisting of Dalmatians, i.e. people of Slavonic origin (*Schiavoni* — from where the name of the weapon probably originated). The hilt basket is constructed using wider or narrower bands or bars in a characteristic arrangement and covers the entire hand.

Several stages can be traced in the complex-basket evolution. In the earliest stage the individual bars grew in a fan-shaped pattern towards the

11th–13th century

33 Sword with basket of skittle-ended rods, J. Hoppe, Solingen, after 1650. The blade marked with five shields showing crossed arrows and inscribed *INRI I. HOPPE ME FECIT SOLINGEN.*

35

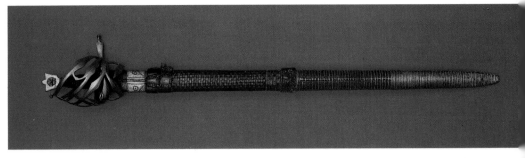

34 *Schiavona, c.* 1600. Single-edged blade with the mark of the running wolf, brass inlay. The pommel of brass with carved lion's head. The basket of earlier type; the scabbard of woven leather straps.

Sword, 14th century

peripheral band. Later on an insert with a row of openings running parallel with the peripheral band was placed in between the circumferential band and the fan-arranged bars. Earlier specimens feature two- or even three-row inserts. The pommel, often of bronze or brass, is flat with two projecting corners and a central lion-head mask in relief. Plain troopers' swords have iron pommels with a smooth cone-cap shaped protrusion.

Other sword types with the hilt fully covering the fist developed in Scotland roughly at the end of the 16th century and quickly spread all over the British Isles. This sword, called a basket-hilted broadsword, is characterized by its considerably wide blade with two or more fullers. The basket of early specimens of the 17th century was composed of bars often crossing at the front; later specimens (from the 18th century on) used to have open-work plates inserted between the bars. Protection of the hand was further improved in the 17th century with an inner lining of leather, replaced later on by coloured cloth. This weapon is still carried by officers of certain Scottish regiments.

On the Continent the position of the sword was still significant in the second half of the 17th century. Relatively wide blades were coupled with baskets featuring a simple knuckle-bow often complemented with outer ribs and the shell placed under the cross-guard or level with it.

Swords ranked among the characteristic equipment of the cuirassiers of the period — with baskets of skittle-ended round bars and shells either in open-work or wrought in a simple ornament. In the Austrian Hapsburg army this type prevailed well into the 18th century.

It goes without saying that sword-type weapons remained in army equipment even longer. 17th-century *schiavona* swords used to employ double-

35 Landsknecht sword (*Katzbalger*), Germany, first quarter of 16th century. The blade apparently Italian with narrow groove, three punched marks on the bridge. The hilt with octagonal cross-guard.

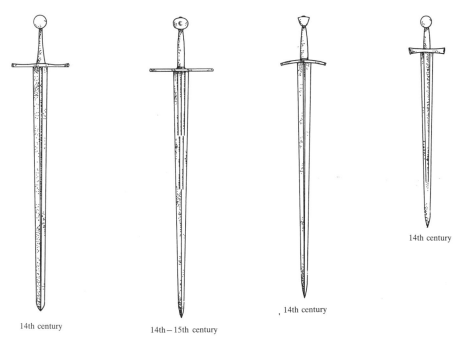

14th century

14th — 15th century

, 14th century

14th century

15th century

edged blades side by side with the single-edged ones. A similar situation is encountered among other army weapons, particularly in the 18th century. For example, regulation Prussian broadswords Model 1732 for cuirassiers, and Model 1735 for dragoons, continued to use double-edged blades until 1797 when the use of single-edged blades was approved. French regulations, too, permitted the use of double-edged blades on regulation broadswords as late as 1735.

In the course of time some special sword variants developed, differing from the basic type both in shape and dimensions. The so-called *Katzbalger* Landsknecht sword was a typical side-weapon of German mercenary in-

36 Ceremonial sword presented by Pope Paul IV to Ercolo d'Este as 'gonfaloniere' of the Church in 1556. The blade gilded in its upper part and inscribed *PAVLVS IV. PONT. MAX. ANNO II.* The pommel probably original, the cross-guard provided with shells most probably from early 17th century.

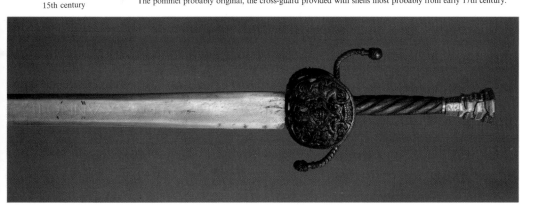

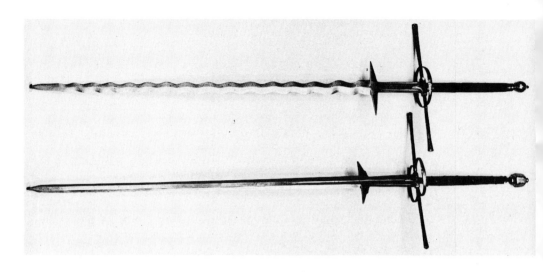

37 Two-handed sword with wavy blade, Central Europe, after mid-16th century. Straight cross-guard with horizontal guard-rings, the pommel with incrustation of silver wire.
Two-handed sword, on the blade inscription *JESVS./MARIA*, Central Europe, first half of 16th century.

fantry in the first half of the 16th century. The blade is shorter (up to 75 cm), but relatively wide, the cross-guard is of the typical horizontal S-shape almost entirely closed and the grip widened towards the pommel.

The two-handed sword represents another variety, having been a typical infantry weapon. The earliest specimens appeared in the course of the 14th century. However, it was only the increasing significance of infantry on the 15th-century battlefields which provided an impetus for its further development. The earliest extant specimens represent nothing but enlarged cavalry swords of the period. However, at the turn of the 15th and the 16th centuries, when on the battlefields thousands of infantrymen in close formations were with their long pikes hindering the attacks of the enemy, two-handed swords gained in significance. Mercenaries, German Landsknechts in particular, wielding these weapons often managed to cut through into the enemy formation having demolished the pikes first of all. It is no wonder that those mastering two-handed swords ranked among so-called Doppel-soldner who were entitled to double pay.

The 16th century, and its first half in particular, was the heyday of two-handed swords. The double-handed sword has a long (100−140 cm) and relatively wide (5−6 cm) blade with a long ricasso often covered with leather. At the transition between the ricasso and the blade proper there often appeared triangle-shaped, straight or slightly drooping flukes intended to catch the adversary's blade. The long cross-guard tends to be straight on earlier types, provided with guard rings in the middle. The grip is extended towards its middle part and most often covered with leather; pommels are of diverse types, circular-, pear- or barrel-shaped, sometimes adorned with channelling, other times with encrusted silver wire.

Specimens with wavy edges were known and it was thought that this shape provided a longer cutting edge. However, they appeared more frequently only with later specimens, from the second half of the 16th century on, for which, moreover, arched cross-guards with volutes and more sophisticated rings are typical. The grip, sometimes covered with velvet or

38   Two-handed thrusting sword, A. Picinino, Milan, 1584. Marked with a crowned tower and inscription *ANTONIO PICININO ME FECITE* (!) *IN MILANO 1584.*

other textile material, and sometimes fitted with decorative fringes, attested to the ceremonial nature of such specimens. The two-handed thrusting sword dated 1584 and coming from the workshop of the Milanese sword-maker Antonio Picinino represents an exceptional specimen both as regards length (overall length 249.1 cm, blade-length 165.1 cm) and shape. Its possible combat application was as a substitute for the pike.

Attention should be paid to the fact that there were a great number of imitation two-handed swords made in the 19th century which are now in both public and private collections. They were weapons made for traditional swordsmanship events using two-handed swords which originated in the 16th century and which were still being held in some towns well into the 19th century. These imitations, at times very good, were a romantic fashion of the last century. The nouveaux riches raised to the nobility were decorating halls in knightly style in their residences, and since original weapons were scarce, they had to settle for copies. Besides these quality imitations a lot of fakes came into being, intended simply to provide their makers with the chance of a share in the romantic fashion boom. Evaluating whether the specimen in question is an original weapon or not calls for great effort and knowledge, not only of literature, but above all of original specimens.

Sometimes the opinion will be encountered which maintains that two-handed swords were executioners' weapons. It is an example of a stubbornly surviving mistake; the executioner's sword is not only of quite different dimensions, but also of a different type. Although its blade is also wide, it is substantially shorter with the tip rounded and often pierced with three so-called blood openings or fullers. On the 17th- and 18th-century blades there used to be engravings of gallows, an executioner's wheel, sometimes statues of Justice or of the Crucifixion. Inscriptions and verses are frequent. The cross-guard of these executioners' swords is always straight, not too long, simply profiled. The pommel, too, is usually simple.

Swords which served as a symbol of the criminal court are very rare. They were not used for executions but were just hung up — most often on the town-hall — to indicate that a criminal court was in session.

39   Executioner's sword in scabbard.

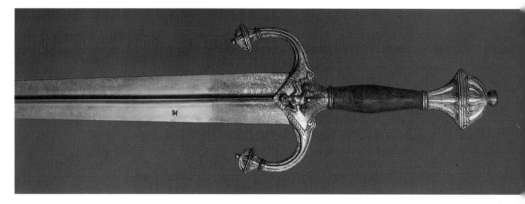

40   Decorative sword, northern Italy, *c.* 1520. The blade provided with central ridge, in the upper part gilded surfaces with engravings and the mark of a stylized tower. The hilt is gilded.

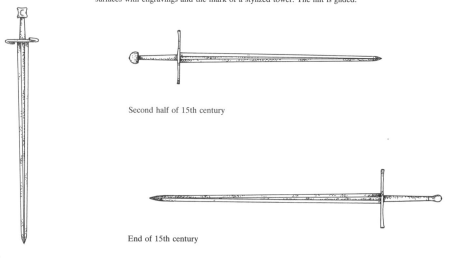

Second half of 15th century

End of 15th century

Second half of 15th century

41   Decorative sword of Venetian type, Venice, *c.* 1570. The blade with three grooves, the hilt gilded and rich decorated in relief.

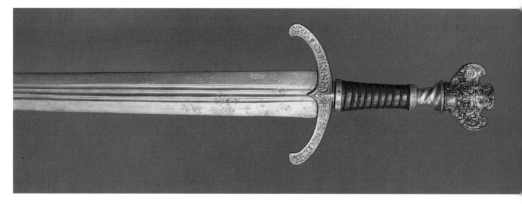

42 Boar-sword, the hilt with horizontal guard-ring, Central Europe, 17th century.

Below:
Two-edged blades
in cross-section.

Lenticular, smooth

Hexagonal, flattened

Rhomboid, smooth

Rhomboid with concave sides

Lenticular with a broad channel (hollow) on each side

Lenticular with a groove on each side

Lenticular with obliquely placed grooves

Lenticular with two grooves on each side

A special group consists of ceremonial swords which are not actual weapons in the proper sense of the word, but rather symbols or reminders of certain persons or events. Coronation swords which were a part of the ceremony of crowning a sovereign ruler also belong to this category. Examples are the coronation sword of Frederick II from the 13th century, the Polish *sczierbiec* from the 14th century, the so-called St Wenceslas' sword (Prague, St Vitus' Cathedral) from the period of Charles IV (14th century) and the sword of Frederick the Bellicose of 1426 with the pommel of mountain crystal.

Collections of the world contain a number of richly adorned specimens, especially from the Renaissance period. Swords presented to rulers by popes are particularly famous. In this category we will mention the sword presented by Pope Paul II to Vladislav Jagiello, King of Bohemia and Hungary, and the sword presented by Pope Paul IV in the second year of his pontificate (1556) to Ercolo II d'Este (probably due to the latter's having been named by him the 'gonfaloniere' of the region, i.e. commander-in-chief of the papal armed forces).

Swords were also used as hunting weapons. Many are short bladed and can be ranked among the falchions, but very different is the boar-sword. The blade is usually rather long and its main section (from two-thirds to three-quarters) of its length is of square section and so represents an extension of the ricasso. Only the double-edged section near the point represents the blade proper designed for thrusting into the wounded prey. The furniture of boar-swords was generally of iron and is of the usual type of the period, i.e. 16th- and 17th-century swords.

The Back-Edged Sword

Side-by-side with the double-edged sword, there had been for centuries weapons with single-edged straight blade. They originated in the short single-edged cutting weapons of Germanic tribes which, due to their size, fall between a long knife and the short sword called a sax. Single-edged straight-blade weapons enjoyed the longest history in northern Europe, and several specimens from the 8th—9th centuries have been preserved. They are very similar in form to the Viking swords but for the long single-edged blade. However, in the centuries to follow the double-edged sword generally predominated.

It was not before the turn of the 16th and 17th century that weapons with single-edged, long blades reappeared first in eastern Europe, where they became known as the pallach. The term itself may be of Turkish origin which, through the intermediary of Hungarian (*pallos* — sword) first entered the Slavonic languages and then gradually spread into other European countries as well. It must be pointed out, however, that the term and description of the pallach are far from being uniform. The old Polish terminology distinguished between a straight-bladed pallach and a curved-bladed pallach.

The classical straight-bladed pallach has a rather robust straight blade relatively wide and single-edged, with a sharp edge on the one side and blunted back-edge. At the point — most frequently a central one — there used to be a rather long double-edged section. It is an effective cutting weapon, but one on which the point also enabled a thrusting attack.

Towards the end of the 16th century and in the early 17th century, there appeared in Hungary pallaches with furniture identical with that of Hungarian sabres of the period. Increasingly it is the case of an open-work hilt without the knuckle-bow, a long straight cross-guard and equally long rectangular guards. The hilt used to be finished with a cap of almond shape. On top of this simple furniture there also appeared cross-guards bent rectangularly in the front and coming into an open hand-guard, foreshadowing the basket. Such a basic shape, richly fashioned, though, can be seen on both the broadswords of so-called Hungarian sets (according to Hungarian fashion), as executed in 1610 and 1612 by Johann Michael, a Prague goldsmith, for Maximilian, Duke of Bavaria, and Christian II, Elector of Saxony. A similar, though simpler, furniture can be seen on a Polish broadsword dating to the second half of the 17th century.

43 Polish broadsword, Poland, second half of 17th century. The blade, with three grooves at the back edge inscribed *GENOA* in between two engraved half-moons, apparently an imitation of a Genoese mark.

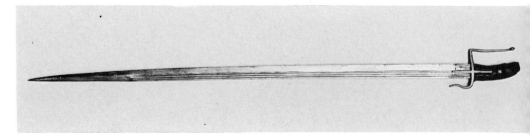

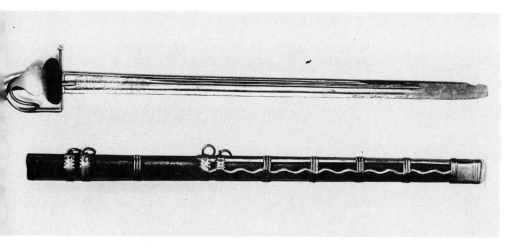

44 Broadsword of Austria Hapsburg army Model 1716 with scabbard. The blade with two channels in the central part and two grooves at the back edge; the inscription *VIVAT CAROLUS VI.*

Along with the extended broadsword application there appeared new styles of furniture. We can find the closed *schiavona* basket not only on weapons with two-edged blades, but also on specimens with single-edged blades. The most common cuirassier's weapons of the second half of the 17th century, too, with their baskets, were fitted with both types of blade.

45 Cuirassier's broadsword with basket of globose-ended rods, Central Europe, after 1711. On the blade, engraved cuirassier and inscription *VIVAT CAROLUS VI.*

43

46 Sabre for grenadiers of cuirassier and dragoon regiments, *c.* 1730—40. On the blade, engraving of a rider and inscription *VIVAT CAROLUS VI.*

Hapsburg army broadsword for cavalry troopers, Model 1763. The blade from a Prussian broadsword of the year 1732 (spoils); on the outer shell, the *MTJ* monogram (Maria Theresa, 1740—80, Joseph, 1780—90) executed in relief. The scabbard with frame-type metalwork.

Broadsword of the Austria Hapsburg army, *c.* 1730—40. The hilt of brass with fluted shell.

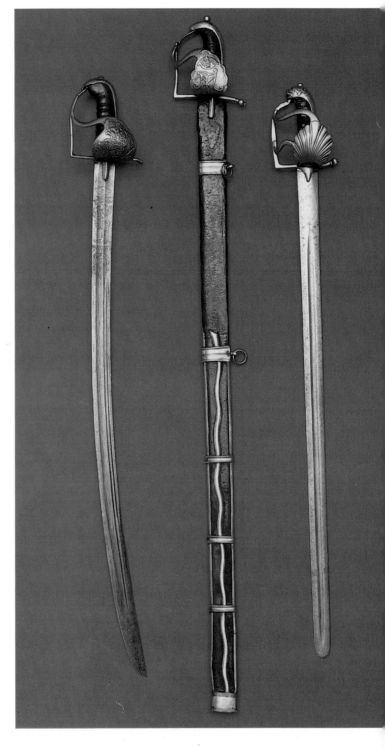

47 Broadsword of Hapsburg cavalry officers, Model 1763.
Part of blade only, pierced *MTJ* monogram on the hilt.

The basket provided relatively good protection for the weapon-holding hand.

The broadsword as a regulation weapon was first specified in the heavy cavalry equipment of the Central European Hapsburg monarchy. The broadsword, introduced in 1700 (or 1705 according to other sources), still had a hilt corresponding to that on sabres of the period, a grip with a cap, a simple narrow knuckle-guard with cross-guard, langet and thumb-ring. Hilts were either of brass (for the regiments using yellow buttons on their uniform), or of iron (for regiments using white buttons). Quite frequently, the blade is engraved with a rider with drawn weapon and inscriptions which may facilitate dating. A broadsword with the inscription *VIVAT ERZ-HERTZOG JOSEPH* can be dated before 1705 (when the Archduke became the Emperor as Joseph I). The inscription *VIVAT CAROLUS VI* dates the weapon to the period after 1711.

The experience gained in the course of the War of the Spanish Succession as well as in campaigns against the Turks in the early 18th century might

48 Austrian heavy cavalry broadsword for sergeants, Model 1769, brass hilt.
Model 1769 for troopers, iron hilt, the upper end of the grip-guard fashioned as lion's head, with scabbard Model 1775. On the blade, engraving and the Schönborn coat of arms.

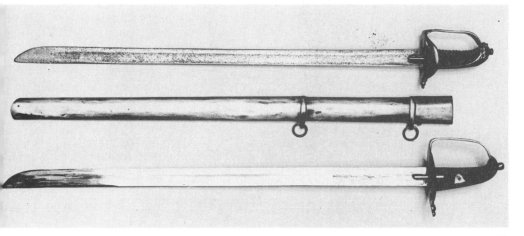

45

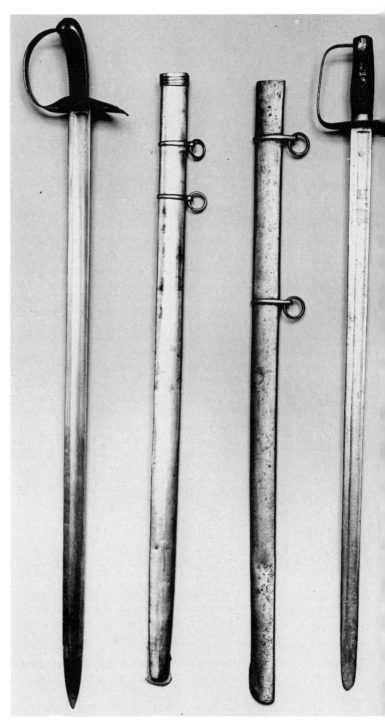

49 Austrian broadsword of the year 1803 with scabbard. On the blade, *F II* monogram (Francis 1792–1835), marked *Fischer* (a Viennese sword-making enterprise).
Austrian dragoon's broadsword Model 1798. On the blade, *F II* monogram, marked *Fischer*. The hilt provid with pivotable attack guard held by a spring device.

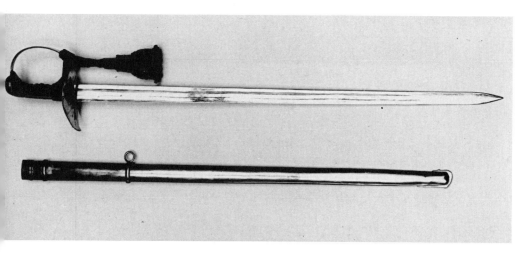

50 Austrian cuirassier officer's broadsword Model 1837. The following inscriptions on the blade: *Schütze die Unschuld — Schone den Besiegten. Sei fruchtbar dem Feinde.*

have proved that simple, narrow, knuckle-guard hilts of the stirrup sabre-type did not provide adequate protection for the hand. Although the Hapsburg broadsword of the year 1716 can also be found with the hilt of brass or iron, the execution of the hilt is quite different: an outer rib and a vertical guard plate having been added; this initial shape underwent a number of modifications, however; from the 1730s the hilt was only produced in brass until 1769.

It is worth mentioning, too, that companies of mounted grenadiers were incorporated in cuirassier and dragoon units of the Hapsburg army during 1711—40. In contrast to the other troopers of the regiment these were equipped with sabres instead of broadswords. Their sabres, however, were fitted with hilts corresponding to those of regulation broadswords of the period. As to officers' weapons, double-edged blades had been permissible until 1769.

The Chevauleger broadsword Model 1763 of the Hapsburg army features the *MTJ* (Maria Theresa — Joseph) initials on the guard-plate. For troopers, they were executed in simple relief; in the case of officers' weapons the initials pierced and within an ornamental framing.

The scabbards of Austrian army broadswords were of wood, covered with leather, framed by brass or iron metalwork including mounts decorated with wavy bands in the central and lower part. In the nomenclature of the monarchy these weapons were called *schwere Säbel* (heavy sabres). Initially, the regulation of 1769 introduced the name of *pallasch* or *pallach*.

The regulation of 1769 also introduced a new broadsword to the heavy cavalry units of the Hapsburg monarchy which foreshadowed further changes. The knuckle-guard is of a single narrow band extended gradually into an almost round cross-guard plate with pierced openings and also with slits for the sword-knot at the rear. The hilt is of iron in the case of troopers' weapons, of brass (in a somewhat more subtle dimension) on NCOs' weapons. At first these broadswords were equipped with scabbards of the earlier type; in 1775, however, a new scabbard was introduced with its wooden

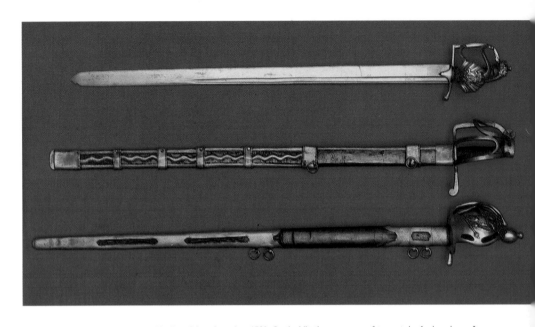

51 French broadsword, *c.* 1730. On the hilt, the monogram of two entwined mirror-image Ls.
Bavarian broadsword, early 18th century. The basket of iron bands, the scabbard with frame-type fittings.
Prussian cuirassier's broadsword Model 1732 with scabbard.
The blade marked with Prussian eagle and *POTZDAM* inscription.

core entirely covered with sheet iron and featuring two mounts with suspension rings. The blade is grooved on both sides with the engraved Imperial eagle in the upper part and frequently with the Pottenstein manufacture on the back edge under the cross-guard plate.

This particular broadsword type was of decisive importance for further evolution. Through its modification only the broadsword of the year 1798 originated (with a more subtle hilt and a smaller cross-guard plate), and later, Model 1803 (sometimes referred to as Model 1801) where the cross-guard plate was slightly reduced on the inner side, thus rendering the hilt asymmetrical. Five years later this model was modified in such a way that the solid guard, hitherto bent a little, was made a straight plate.

In addition to the basic type there appeared, in 1788, a broadsword for light dragoons featuring a narrower cross-guard plate and a pivoting lateral guard secured by a spring catch. Pierced openings of the cross-guard plate are of rectangular shape. Modifications in the years to come were generally marginal in character. It was not until 1837 that Austria's last broadsword model was introduced, an officer's weapon based on earlier models, but with a narrower, somewhat dished cross-guard plate.

The regulation of the year 1845 abolished all broadswords and substituted the standardized cavalry sabre Model 1845. However, broadswords remained in use in some regiments till as late as 1851.

Hilts with lateral solid shells were typical of most broadsword-type weapons of European armies over a considerable part of the 18th century. The

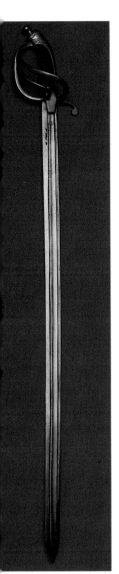

French broadsword of the 1730s featured the initials of Louis XV on its shells, two entwined and mirrored L's. In a similar way, two entwined F's stand for Frederick V, King of Denmark (1706—66), on the Model 1750 broadsword. Above the rulers' initials, lateral shells often feature the country's coat-of-arms.

This kind of weapon was called *Haudegen* in the Prussian army. It was

53 Russian dragoon's broadsword Model 1761 with scabbard. On the blade, a *P* mark in Cyrillic, the pommel fashioned as a lion's head. The scabbard of leather with brass metalwork.
Prussian dragoon's broadsword of the year 1735. The pommel shaped as an eagle head.

Wedged-shaped	Flattened wedge-shaped	Fullered on the outer side	Fullered on both faces	Single-fuller by the back edge on both sides

One-edged blades (sabres, broadsword, falchions) — cross sections (above on pp. 50—51).

introduced for the cuirassiers in 1732, with the two-edged blade marke
with a tiny punching of an eagle and often also with the Potsdam manufac
ture mark. The brass hilt featured a massive, slightly oval cap with a finia
The shell had the motif of a Prussian eagle under a king's crown. The thum
ring used to be positioned on the inner side. The scabbard of wood had
shorter upper mount, and the lower one reached as far as the middle and wa
pierced twice. Doubled rings are typical of this model.

A dragoon broadsword was introduced into the Prussian army in 173!
with two-edged blade. The grip was formalized as an eagle head in the uppe
part, and the brass hilt was asymmetrical with a front and side guard connec
ted with two diagonal bands. The scabbard was of leather with a short uppe
mount of brass with the suspension hook and a brass chape. The Russia
broadsword Model 1761 for dragoons was identical with its Prussian coun
terpart except that the top of the grip was a formalized lion head. This mode
stayed in use till the early 19th century. Both the Prussian models wer
changed to a single-edged blade in 1797 and were given the name of *pallac*
along with it.

In the army of Russia, too, the broadsword was used. In addition to th
above-mentioned dragoons' weapon there was the heavy cavalry broad
sword which appeared *c.* 1762 and featured a two-headed tsarist eagle o
the lateral shell. The Russian broadsword of the year 1809 was taken ove
and introduced in Prussia as Model 1819. The hilt has two outer ribs and th
shell is almost rectangular in outline and circularly recessed at the corners
It saw service until 1874, when the French broadsword Model 1854 — fo
dragoons — was introduced into the German army as booty captured in th
course of the 1870—71 Franco-Prussian campaign. The German broad
sword of the year 1889, too, had a single-edged blade with an asymmetrica
hilt of iron featuring engraved and partially pierced arms of the Empire, i
some cases along with symbols of other German territories.

The broadsword played a significant role in the French cavalry, too. A
weapon dated to the first years of the 18th century had a simple knuckle
guard and heart-shaped horizontal shell, a two-edged blade on which wa
engraved the royal coat-of-arms and *VIVE LE ROY*. Another weapon from
the 1730s has already been mentioned in this chapter. The broadsword

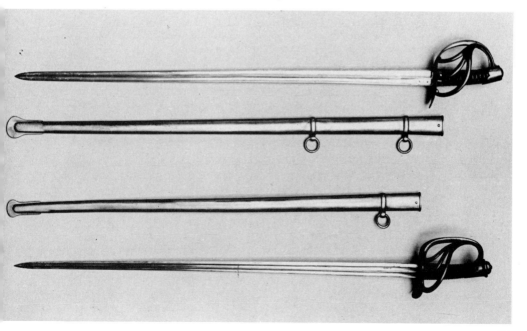

ıllered and single-grooved
the back edge on each
le

Double-grooved by the back
edge on both sides

With a quadrangular
projecting rib on either side

With a cylindrical rib

however, played an important role in cavalry equipment in the course of the French Revolution as well as during the whole 19th century. The broadsword Model AN IX (1800–01) is rather rare; Model AN XIII (1804–05) can be met more frequently. The blade has two fullers on each side, the hilt is of brass with three lateral counter-guard bars. There is no back strap on the grip which is topped with a brass cap — a typical feature — and the scabbard of iron is provided with two mounts. Dragoon broadsword Model 1854 differs from it only in the shape of the knuckle-guard and counter-guards, and the cap is of a more complicated shape, too. The scabbard has just one mount with a ring. With the modification of 1882 it stayed in service until the end of World War I. The modification concerns first of all the blade which is

54   French heavy cavalry broadsword Model AN XIII (1804–05).
The back-edge of the blade marked *Manuf(acture) Imp(ériale) du Klingenthal, Janvier 1815.*
French dragoon's broadsword Model 1854. The blade marked *Manufacture d'Armes de Chat(ellerault) Juin 1882 M(odèle) 1854.*

provided with a wide fuller at the flat edge on both sides; the brass hilt has a front knuckle-guard and the outer counter-guards are arched more widely. Model 1882 for general cavalry is provided with a considerably longer blade whose point is rather narrow; the hilt with three counter-guards is set on more vertically.

The Belgian cavalry broadsword Model 1849 was also derived from French models, the hilt shaped following the Model AN XIII. The Dutch heavy cavalry broadsword resembled French models in its hilt and grip cap executed, however, in iron. Bilaterally placed rings on the scabbard follow the British way of wearing the sword.

Broadswords saw service as late as World War I and in other European armies, such as Spain's. The British Model 1908 sword features a bulky hilt with a bowl reaching as high as the middle of the grip. The scabbard characterized by two suspension rings positioned symmetrically on both sides of its upper part under the mouthpiece.

The Swiss broadsword for cavalry sergeants Model 1867 has a simple basket of iron with the Swiss cross. The Italian officers' cavalry broadsword from *c.* 1900 has an interesting blade cross-section with a ribbed back-edge. The grip with oval cap has a flat back rib with chequering. The bulky basket

55 Saxony guard broadsword, *c.* 1830. On the blade, engraved and gilt arms and the *AR* monogram (Anthony 1827–37). The gilded hilt of brass with index-finger ring.
Baden cuirassier officer's broadsword, second half of 18th century. On the basket, a lion holding the arms Baden, on the blade the *CF* monogram (Carl Friedrich, 1738–1811) and the Baden arms.

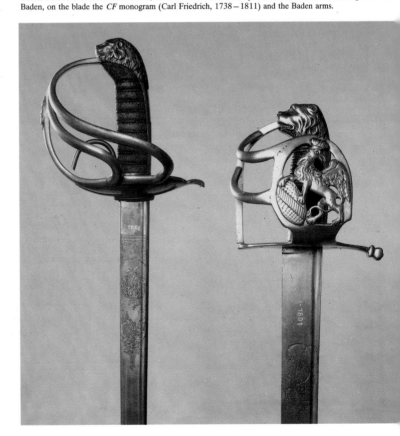

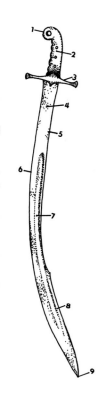

of iron bands with three wide arms is provided with a thumb recess at the rear.

The Sabre

The sabre is primarily a cutting weapon. Its characteristic feature is the more or less curved single-edged blade, which is two-edged in its lower part and sometimes also widened in this section. The curved blade not only provides considerable cutting effect, but offers a longer cutting edge if compared with a straight blade of the same length. The weapon is of oriental origin, in the past closely connected with the nomadic horsemen's style of combat. The earliest archaeological evidence in Europe comes from the burial grounds of Avar warriors, mostly on the territory of the then Pannonia, where the Avars settled on their penetration of the West in the second half of the 6th century. It was from there that they undertook devastating raids targeted at the Franconian and Byzantine Empires. When, following heavy defeats, the Avars started losing power in the second half of the 7th century, the curved blade of the sabre disappeared along with them.

Somewhat later, towards the end of the 9th century, history repeated itself to a certain extent. Hungarian tribes penetrated the Danubian lowlands from the East and settled there permanently. Swift Hungarian riders, in whose equipment the sabre appeared again, carried out ferocious raids not only in the neighbouring Slavonic territories, but also far west — into the East Franconian Empire. However, influenced by the other European countries, the Hungarian soldiers came to prefer the straight-bladed sword which then pushed the sabre out and into the background in the period of the late Middle Ages.

Only the Turkish expansion from the 14th century and from the 1440s, in particular, provided a major impetus for the widespread use of weapons with curved sabre blades in Central Europe, especially in Hungary and Poland. The surviving specimens of sabre-type weapons dating to the second half of the 15th century are not numerous in Central European collections. They differ from swords of the period only in their curved blade; otherwise they most often had a sword-type hilt, a grip with a rectangular pommel featuring a central rib and sometimes a hemispherical protrusion, and horizontally S-shaped quillons.

56 Danish heavy-cavalry broadsword of the year 1750. On the basket, two entwined mirror-image F's (Frederick V. 1706–66).
French broadsword (sword = *épée* in French), early 18th century. It has a double-edged blade, the royal arms and the inscription *VIVE LE ROY*. The *à la mousquetaire* hilt is of brass.

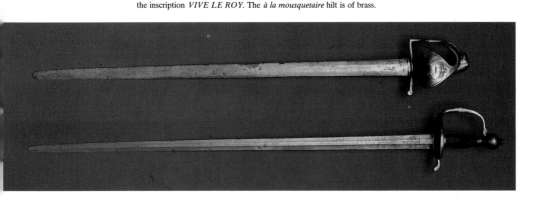

Some experts use the term *Krummschwert* to describe these weapons, considering their straight sword-type grip to be the decisive feature, while true oriental sabres have the grip slightly forward-tilted. In such a way, the grip along with the curved blade form a slightly S-shaped curve. The original way of grasping may enable a somewhat better use of the weapon's cutting function; however, the difference cannot be substantial. In our opinion, the type of blade is the decisive feature. The length and curve of the blade determine the characteristic properties of the weapon. Moreover, the evidence that the term sabre was used in written records in Central Europe as early as in the 1460s attests to the fact that their bygone users called them this.

In addition to the above-mentioned specimens with sword-type hilt we come across late 15th- and early 16th-century long weapons with a curved blade, sometimes provided with a widened double-edged lower part. They feature a straight grip with hafts and a beak-shaped pommel is frequent. The cross-guard is simple, straight or, later on, slightly arched. These sabres,

Eastern Europe, 9th—10th century

57 Central-European sabre with hafted grip (*Zweihändersäbel*), end of 15th century. The blade with extended double-edged lower part, the cross-guard slightly arched with buttons at the ends of the quillons.

called *Grosse Messer* or also *Zweihändersäbel*, are quoted as typical weapons of Czech or Moravian mercenaries in the service of Maximilian I in 1490 during the liberation of Vienna and Lower Austria. They are also encountered in the equipment of Landsknechts of the first half of the 16th century.

From the 16th century on the use of sabres was spreading more and more. They provided a weapon for light cavalry in particular, above all in Central and Eastern Europe. In the course of the 16th and 17th centuries some basic sabre types took shape.

A) Open type without any basket to protect the hand.
1 Polish-Hungarian type probably based on Turkish patterns. The blade used to be curved, often with prominent double-edged section; the straight cross-guard of considerable length was provided with long langets in the middle. The oblique grip, usually covered with leather, generally ended in a simple cap, most frequently of almond shape. In some cases we find a chain connecting the cap with the front of the cross-guard, thus substituting for the knuckle-bow; these specimens represent a transition to weapons of the basket type.
2 Polish *karabela* sabre, also derived from eastern designs. It used to have a grip or beak-shaped at the upper end. The grips of ordinary sabres were of horn or sometimes even of wood (*karabela czarna*). Luxury

Germany (Central Europe), end of 15th century

54

Polish *karabela* sabre,
17th century

Central Europe, second half
of 15th century

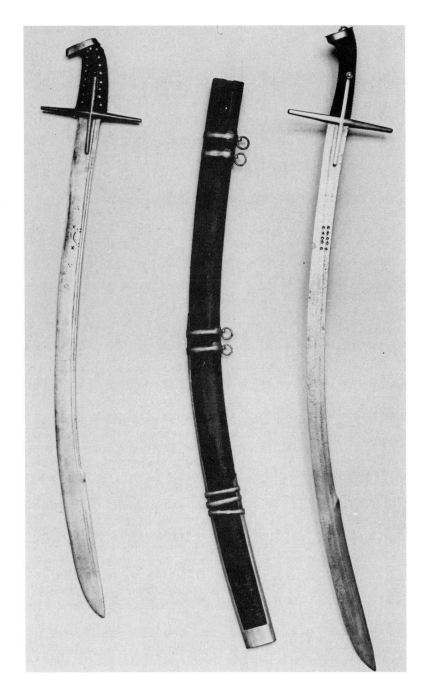

58 Hungarian-type sabre, second half of 17th century. The blade with two grooves at the back edge and a
half-moon sign.
Hungarian sabre, turn of 17th and 18th centuries.
The blade extended in the lower part, the scabbard with frame-type metalwork.

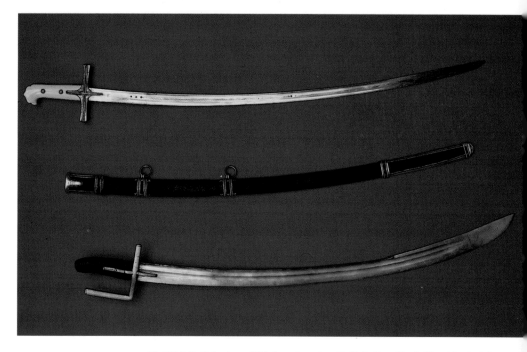

59 Polish *karabela* sabre, *c.* 1700. An eagle mark on the blade, the scabbard with metalwork of silver.
Polish sabre with rectangular open hilt and the blade extended in the lower part, second half of 17th centur

specimens feature metalwork in niello-decorated silver. A very shor
cross-guard may be encrusted or overlaid with silver in a similar way t
the mounts of the wooden, leather-covered scabbard. The *karabela* i
typical of the 17th century in particular but sometimes of the 18t
century as well.

   B) Closed type with basket-hilt.

1   Sabres with a simple, slender, hand-guard of bands or bars, most ofte
of rectangular shape, sometimes open at the upper end. They appeare
in Poland and Hungary from the end of the 16th till the end of the 17t
century. Polish specimens sometimes display wider knuckle-bow an
blades featuring in decoration or inscriptions, King Stephen Báthory
(1576–86). However, only a few sabres of this type, called *batorówk*
in Polish, actually originated during his reign. The majority are of a late
date; evidently it is a case of the Polish political and historical traditio
of the period.

2   Swiss sabre usually with the blade just slightly curved. The cross-guard
of early specimens are often horizontally S-shaped and the basket i
composed of two or three profiled arms while on later examples th
basket is composed of bands. Pommels of the earliest specimens used t
be fashioned in the same style as on the swords of the period; later o
they were shaped as lions' or birds' heads. Sabres of this type appeare
from the end of the 15th century, but mostly in the 16th and als
occasionally in the 17th century.

3   Sabres of Central European type, sometimes described as sabres from
the Austro-Hungarian borderland or as *Deutschgefaßte Säbel*. Their
characteristic features include curved blades, sometimes with a widene

Swiss sabre, 16th century

56

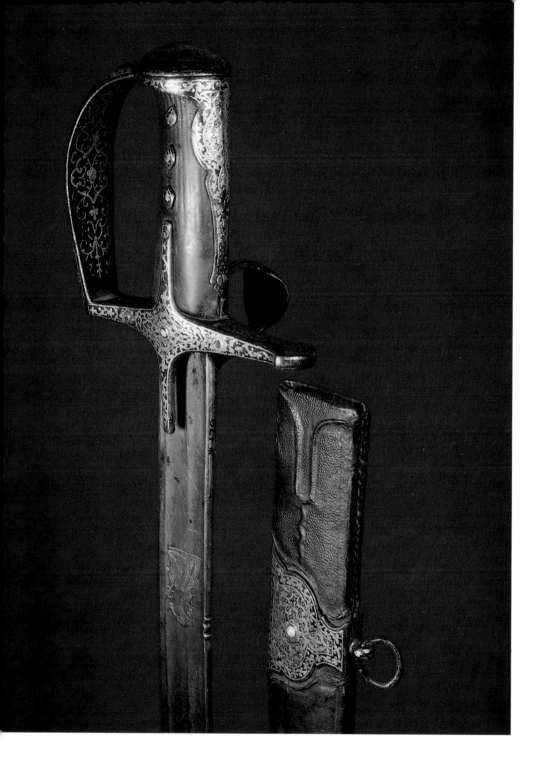

60   Polish *batorówka* sabre, early 17th century. On the blade, gilded portrait (bust) of the king and the inscription *STEPHANUS BATORI REX POLONIAE* (!). The hilt and the metalwork incrusted with gold.

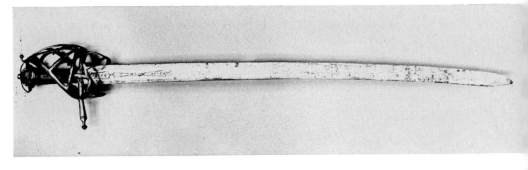

61 Central-European sabre, early 17th century. The blade decorated with engraving, the pommel hexagonal complex basket of entwined rods.

double-edged lower part, pommels shaped as low pyramids and profiled particularly on later specimens, and baskets providing rather elaborate protection of the hand. Sometimes the basket is composed of bands, at others of bars and in many cases provided with a shell on the outer side, quite large and bent upwards.

Weapons of this type appeared after the mid-16th century and stayed in use roughly until the mid-17th century. The principal area of their occurrence can be reconstructed according to extant specimens preserved particularly in collections in Central Europe. It was the area including territories of today's Bohemia and Moravia, Austria, part of Hungary and South Germany. Their Austrian or South German origin emphasized by the literature is not explicit. They spread as far as the north of Europe. At the turn of the 16th and 17th centuries, King Christian IV of Denmark bought a large number of these weapons which were then used as equipment for Norwegian peasants. It is remarkable that they were called *thisack, tesack* (or variations of these names — Seitz, 1962) in Norwegian, i.e. expression undoubtedly derived from the Czech term 'tesák'. Evidently, their connection with Czech lands should be considered.

62 Hungarian hussar's sabre, first half of 17th century. The blade marked *FRINGIA*, the simple hilt of brass.

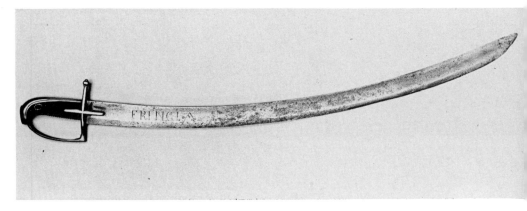

Sabres were increasingly incorporated into light cavalry equipment in the course of the 17th century; in Poland, however, they were used also by heavy armoured cavalry called *hussaria*. Anywhere else the term 'hussar', a word of Hungarian origin, is used to describe someone serving in light cavalry. At the same time the sabre was becoming a prestige item or status symbol, and quite often elaborate specimens complemented a nobleman's costume in Poland and in Hungary, but also in Russia and other countries. As an example we can mention the richly decorated sabre from the so-called Hungarian set (cf. also the chapter on the broadsword — The Back-Edged Sword) made on the order of Christian II, Elector of Saxony, in 1612. The fact that the rulers of Saxony favoured luxury sabres can also be attested to by the ostentatious specimen from the Dresden collection created by Thomas Kapusin in Cluj in 1671.

The equipment of Hungarian units serving in the army of the Central European Hapsburgs provided the starting point for the evolution of light cavalry sabres. Although standardization of heavy cavalry weapons was already going on from the very beginning of the 18th century, sabres were included in the process considerably later, in connection with the trans-

63   Hungarian hussar's sabre. On the blade, the inscription *G. BELEZNAY* in ornamental frame, the hilt of brass. Hussar regiment of this name was established in 1740.
Hungarian hussar's sabre, mid-18th century. On the blade, engraved hussar and incription *VIVAT HUSZAR*. The grip guard with profiled edges.

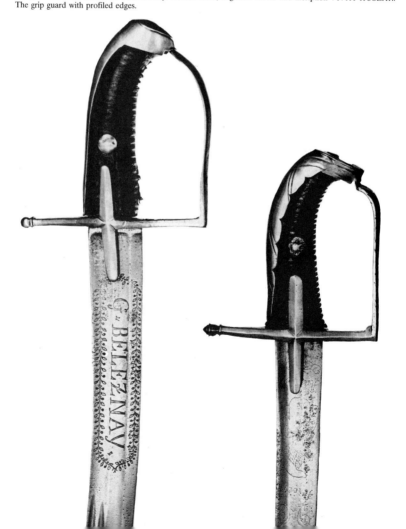

64   Hussar sergeant's sabre Model 1768/1775. The hilt of brass with the pommel shaped as a lion's head.

formation of irregular light cavalry units into hussar regiments. The first hussar regiment was organized as early as 1688, but the main evolutionary process belongs to the first half of the 18th century. For a long time the choice and shape of weapons was left to the user's discretion or to that of the commander of the regiment. For this reason the curve of blades, their length or cross-section are so diverse on sabres datable to the first half of the 18th century. Sabres bearing the *FRINGIA* inscription were highly appreciated. The meaning of this inscription has not been satisfactorily explained in current literature. In the same manner as engravings on a broadsword depicting a cuirassier, the decoration of light-cavalry sabres often included an engraving of a hussar with drawn sabre and the inscription *VIVAT HUSZAR*.

Between 1739 and 1748, the four already existing hussar regiments were complemented by twelve new ones. Hussar sabres of the period usually feature hilts of brass with a simple basket consisting of a slender hand guard, cross-guard and langets. The blades often show the Hungarian coat-of-arms and sometimes even the name of the commander of the regiment. Maria Theresa's accession to the throne in 1740 was celebrated in inscriptions like *Maria Theresia Regina Hungariae* and sabres with these inscriptions started appearing from 1740 on. The relatively wide blades with the engraving of the Holy Virgin and inscriptions invoking her as the patron saint of the Hungarian Kingdom may also have originated in this period. They continue to appear for a long time to come, till the mid-19th century, on sabres – sometimes on army models, but first of all on specimens which were a part of Hungarian magnates' costumes.

Sabre hilts of the mid-18th century are usually of brass (but sometimes of iron) and as a rule feature a back strap with a cap, a simple knuckle-bow and a straight cross-guard. Langets of considerable length extend from the middle of the cross-guard in both directions and their lower part fits into a recess in the upper mount of the scabbards. These were of wood, covered with leather and commonly fitted with tripartite mounts, the upper and the lower part of which are of considerable length. With sabres with an acute curve the upper part of the mount has a slot at the back, 15—20 cm long, following the Turkish pattern; this arrangement was to facilitate drawing the sabre

60

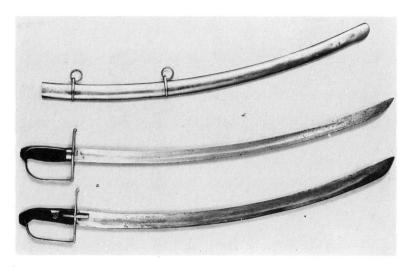

65 Austrian sabre for light cavalry, sergeant's Model 1803, with scabbard. The blade marked *Fischer 1825*, on the scabbard a punched anchor and date 1825.
Austrian light-cavalry sabre Model 1798. On the blade, engraved double-headed eagle, marked *Pottenstein* on the back edge.

66 Austrian officer's sabre with Order of Maria Theresa, from the property of General Schlick, 1837—49. On the blade, engraved names of battles he took part in.

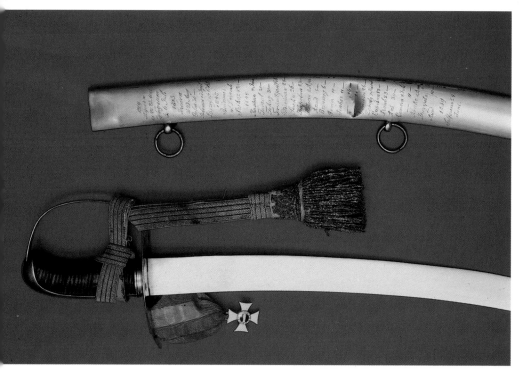

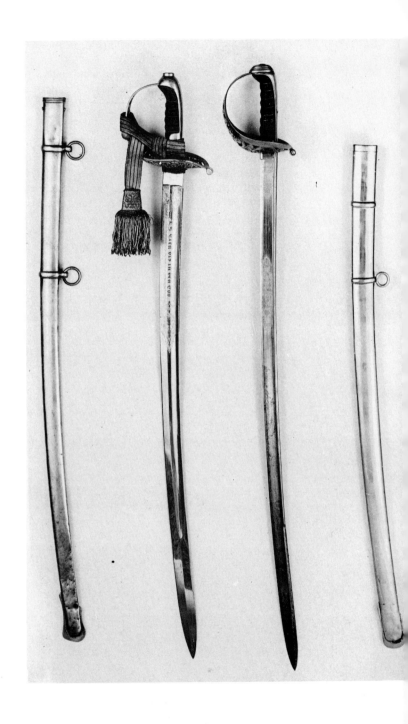

67 Austrian cavalry officer's sabre Model 1869, with scabbard. On the blade, etched ornament and marking *Weyersberg et Stamm, Solingen; .. Carl Grasser Wien.*
The basket pierced, featuring the figure of St George.
Austrian uniform sabre for cavalry officers Model 1845, with scabbard. On the blade, etched decoration and marking *I. H. Hausmann k. k. Hofschwertfeger.*

The regulations of 1748—68 specify the dimensions and shape of the blade. The length was to be from 79 to 84 cm, the height of curvation 5 cm and the blade was to be provided with shallow fuller on each side. The hilt was again left to the regimental commander's discretion. Typologically it did not differ much from the hilt of the previous period and, apart from a few exceptions, it was of brass.

Full standardization of light-cavalry sabres did not begin until the regulations of 1768 which, however, were not enforced until 1771. Sabres of this model have 84-cm-long blades, as a rule decorated with the Imperial two-headed eagle engraved in the channel, and the mark of the manufacture, usually Pottenstein, on the back edge. The hilts are of brass in case of NCOs' sabres, of iron for troopers; the same goes for the mounts of the scabbard. Starting in 1775 the light cavalry also introduced a wooden scabbard covered with iron sheet. The hussar sabre of this model was also prescribed for the then originating uhlan units after 1784. The regulation of 1794 abolished hilts of brass and stipulated a standard sabre for the light cavalry. Initially it still featured the langets, which, however, were missing on Model 1803; this one has a smooth back strap of iron ending in a cap and a slender guard where the back arm of the cross-guard is bent up rectangularly forming the knuckle-bow.

The last model designated especially for the light cavalry of the Austrian army was Model 1827 for uhlan and hussar officers. The blade was heavily curved (the height of curvature 9.5 cm), a slightly bent knuckle-bow and a pivotable guard held by a spring and a catch in the same way as on the Model 1798 broadsword for light dragoons.

The regulation of 1845 introduced a uniform cavalry sabre. The blade was 864 mm long. The characteristic arch of the basket widened symmetrically from the cap down and became a wide solid guard plate, provided with a slot for a sword knot near the cap and it ended a short distance behind the

68   Prussian hussar's sabre for troopers, mid-18th century, with scabbard. The blade marked with an eagle and *POTZDAM* inscription, the hilt of iron.
Russian light-cavalry sabre. On the blade, monogram *E II* (Catherine [Ekaterina] II, 1762—96).

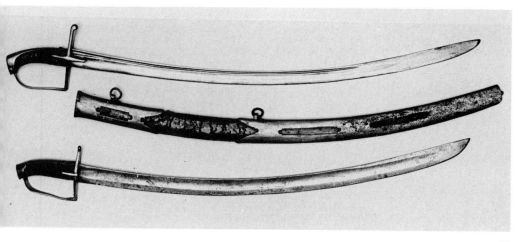

63

grip. The trooper's sabre featured a solid basket with just two rows of symmetrically positioned round openings. The basket of the officer's sabre was ornamentally pierced. It is beyond doubt that it was the British cavalry officer's sabre of the year 1834 which must have inspired the Model 1845 Austrian sabre (and its officer's version in particular), being identical not only as to the overall shape, but in the decorative pattern of the basket as well. The Austrian sabre of the year 1850 represented simply a modification which elongated the final part of the guard and introduced two slots for a sword knot at its back while closing the slot at the hood.

The modification of 1861 stipulated that the blade be thickened at the back edge and the basket pierced in geometrical patterns. The following modification of 1869 shortened the blade to 845 mm and stipulated a wide fuller on one side only. The last model of Austrian sabres was the sabre of the year 1904 with an asymmetrical basket (in contrast to Model 1869 where the basket was still symmetrical and the officer's sabre was decorated with ornamental piercing). The basket of the Model 1904 was widened on the outer side and provided with smaller circular openings on the trooper's sabre or with rich, pierced ornamentation on the officer's sabre. The statue of St George or St Barbara, sometimes pierced on the basket, were not stipulated by the regulation but were made to order individual decoration for rich cavalry or artillery officers' weapons.

Specific demand for light cavalry units in the tactical and organizational system of 18th-century armies resulted in the setting up and incorporation of hussar units in the armed forces of many countries. Along with their attractive uniforms of Hungarian origin with fur jackets and fur caps, the type of sabre used by Hungarian hussars was widespread, too. Before the mid-18th century hussars became a part of French and Prussian armies, and somewhat later, of those of Russia and some German states. Saxony, however, had only one volunteer hussar squadron in 1761, and its first hussar regiment did not originate before 1791. In Great Britain it was not until 1805 that four of the previous light dragoon regiments were transformed into hussar regiments.

In the course of the whole 18th century, sabres with slender hand-guard and langets prevailed in the equipment of hussar units in many armies. The

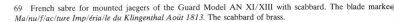

69   French sabre for mounted jaegers of the Guard Model AN XI/XIII with scabbard. The blade marked *Ma/nu/f/ac/ture Imp/éria/le du Klingenthal Août 1813*. The scabbard of brass.

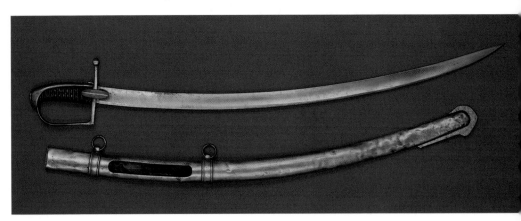

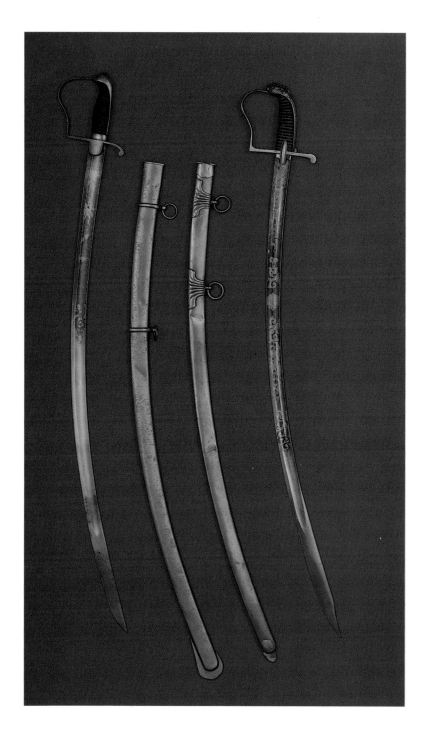

70 Prussian officer's sabre Model 1811 (*Blüchersäbel*) with scabbard. The blade blued and decorated with gilded engraving, marked *Heinrich Grath in Solingen*.
Saxon cavalry officer's sabre, first half of 19th century, with scabbard. The blade blued and decorated with gilded engraving and arms of Saxony, marked *L. Voigt Hauptzeughauschwertfeger in Dresden*. The scabbard of iron with fittings of brass.

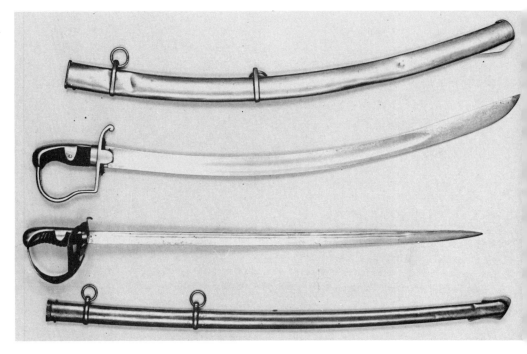

71 Prussian uhlan's sabre Model 1852 with scabbard.
Prussian uhlan's sabre Model 1873 with scabbard. The scabbard provided with acceptance marks of the 14th
uhlan regiment.

principal distinguishing features enabling attribution of a sabre to a specific
army are represented by its decoration, the sovereign's monogram or coat-
of-arms, or the maker's mark on the blade.

On Prussian hussar sabres for troopers (with hilts of iron) it is first of all

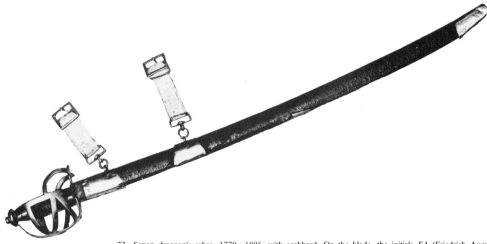

72 Saxon dragoon's sabre, 1770–1806, with scabbard. On the blade, the initials *FA* (Friedrich August,
1763–1827), the hilt of blackened iron.

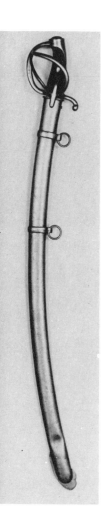

73 Russian sabre for general cavalry Model 1825 with scabbard. The blade marked on the edge *Zlatoust Maya 1826 g.* (in Cyrillic).

the tiny punched Prussian eagle, and the manufacture *POTSDAM (POTZ-DAM)* mark, or the *F II* monogram (Frederick II, 1740 – 86). Prussian sabres have scabbards with very long, simply pierced mounts with plainly shaped cutaway sections. Russian hussar sabres from the period of Catherine II's reign (1762 – 96) usually bear the *E II* monogram; the mark of the Tula manufacture can often be found on blades and sometimes the production year.

From this background of a basic type of hussar sabre even the French weapons were still being derived in the early 19th century — both for hussars and mounted *Chasseurs à cheval* of Napoleon I's Imperial Guard. The specimen of Sardinian sabre of the first half of the 19th century belongs to this type, too.

Slender hand-guards in various shapes continued to be used later. It is necessary to mention the British cavalry sabre Model 1796 with its typical concave knuckle-bow and smooth back strap with projections for the rivet. Just one langet rises from the lower edge of the cross-guard. This sabre became a pattern for Prussian cavalry sabre Model 1811, the so-called *Blüchersäbel.* The officer's sabre is derived from it with the cap fashioned as an eagle's head and the langet decorated in relief. The Prussian (German) uhlan sabre of the year 1873 reverts to this model. Basically the concave knuckle-bow was preserved as well as the cross-guard with langets. The grip, however, is profiled to facilitate grasping the weapon. The officer's sabre Model 1889 much resembles the former, but the top of the grip is ornamented with a lion's mane. On the outer langet, symbols of crossed sabres or artillery barrels can be found — sabres for cavalry officers, barrels in the case of artillery officers.

The French sabre Model 1829 falls within the category of weapons with slender hand guard, too, with its knuckle-bow situated parallel with the

74 French hussar's sabre Model AN IX (1802/03). The blade marked *M/anu/f/actu/re Imp/eria/le du Klingenthal.* The hilt of brass, the scabbard covered with leather, mounts of brass.
French sabre for general cavalry Model AN IX.

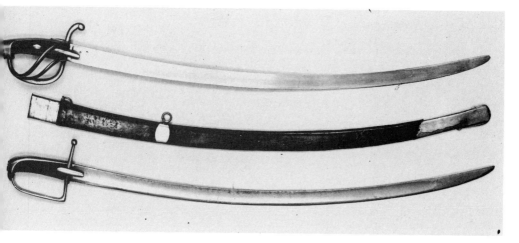

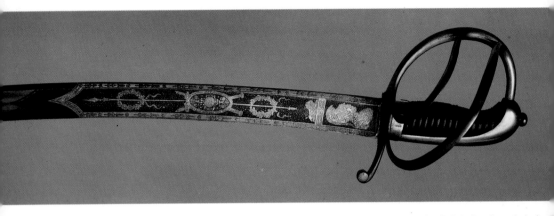

75 Russian officer's sabre Model 1809. The blade with Zlatoust engraving (*I. N. Bushuev* ?), on the back ec the inscription *Zlatoust 1823 g.* (in Cyrillic).

blade and gradually changing into the cross-guard curved down on the re; and ending with a short conical cap; the hilt is of brass. From this model t Russian dragoon sabre of 1854 was derived, which differs from the Frenc model slightly in the somewhat changed shape of the cap, somewhat wid blade, and, of course, the marks. The Russian cavalry trooper's sabre of t year 1881 bears a close resemblance, too, although the cap has been tilte forwards. Sockets to accept the bayonet are typical of these weapons' sca bards. The last variant of this sabre before World War I was provided wi

76 Belgian cavalry sabre Model 1802/1803. On the blade, the date 1888.
Dutch cavalry sabre, 1854. The blade marked *S et R H 1854*.
Swiss artillery sabre Model 1896. The blade marked *Waffenfabrik Neuhausen*.

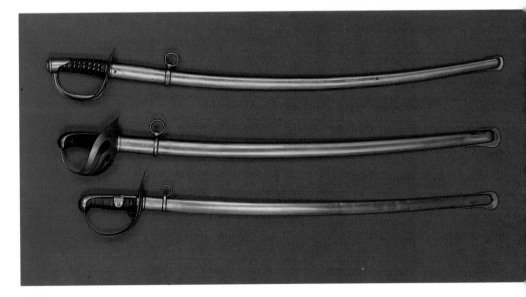

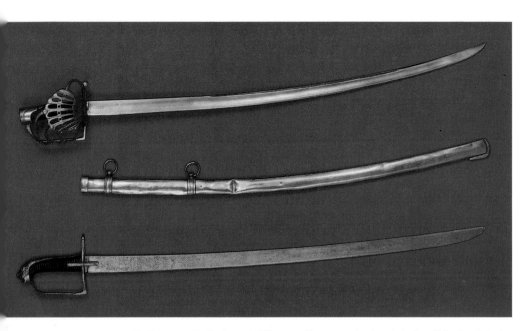

77 Portuguese officer's sabre, early 19th century. The open metalwork on the basket with fan-shaped piercing. On the blade, inscription *VIVA EL REY DE PORTUGAL*.
Sardinian officer's sabre, early 19th century. On the blade, eagle with arms of Savoy on the breast and inscription *VIVE LE ROY DE SARDAIGNE*.

◄ 78 French sabre for mounted grenadiers of the Guard, before 1815. The open metalwork on the basket showing a burning grenade, the scabbard with brass mounts.

a typical opening to accept the sword knot in the final section of the cross-guard. The blades of 19th-century Russian sabres most frequently bear the marks of the Zlatoust manufacture; in the second half of the century the mark was composed of the double-headed tsarist eagle encircled by the inscription *Zlatoust Or/uzheinaya/ Fabr/ika,* executed in the Cyrillic script. Hilts of officers' sabres were adorned in relief and on the flat of the cap with the Tsar's monogram which helps in dating the weapon.

Also weapons with a slender knuckle-bow extending into a cross-guard must

79 Belgian sabre of revolutionary period, 1791. Open metalwork on the hilt displaying a lion holding a club with Phrygian cap.

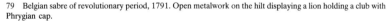

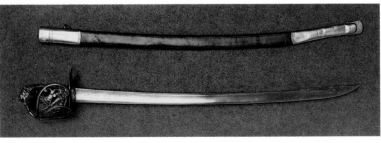

be mentioned here. A whole group of Austrian weapons falls within th[category, starting with Model 1845 as mentioned above. This particul[type, as already stated, was derived from the British sabre of the year 18[and is typical of the most of the 19th-century British cavalry sabre[Troopers' sabres feature smooth baskets. This holds true in the case of th[Model 1830 sabre whose grip is provided with back rib and side projectio[with holes for the rivets and a slightly profiled cap. It is also true of Mod[1884 with its flat cap and symmetrical plate of the guard, or in the case [Model 1899, with the asymmetrical basket extended on the outer side an[the three rivets on the grip.

Usually, the guards of officers' sabres are decorated with ornament[piercing, as in Models 1834 and 1896. The basket of the 1882 Househo[Cavalry sabre features solid plate with ornamental decoration.

A transient period is represented by the Italian cavalry sabre from th[turn of the 19th and 20th centuries which saw service in World War I. I[solid guard features two cutaway sections. A recess located behind the gr[is a feature typical of this weapon.

Cavalry sabres quite often feature hilts consisting of bars forming a cou[ter-guard, particularly on the outer side and in such a way protecting th[hand of the person wielding it. The sabre carried by the dragoons of Saxon[during 1770—1805 represents the archaic type. Its most prominent featur[is a hilt of geometrically arranged and entwining bands of iron covering th[hand on both the outer and the inner sides. The hilt of the Bavarian sabre f[light cavalry, Model 1788, is provided with two-bar outer counter-guar[The hilt of the Russian cavalry sabre Model 1809 is of a similar design. Th[sabre of French mounted jaegers Model 1790 has a slightly profiled oute[rib of a single band connected with the knuckle-bow via a profiled arm. Th[blades of these officers' weapons from the 1820s are in many cases rich[decorated. The Russian sabre Model 1809 was soon adopted by Prussia a[an officer's sabre for the guard light cavalry regiment.

The French light cavalry sabre Model AN XI (1802—03) is a classica[example of this type of cavalry weapon. The counter guard on the outer sid[is of two arms; further characteristic features are represented by the cross[guard with short langets and the oval rivet-head on the grip. This sabre wa[adopted in Russia as Model 1825 without any substantial modification. [differs only in the marks on the flat of the blade, and there is no manufactur[mark or any production date on the back edge.

The influence of this French model is evident also on some weapons o[smaller German states of the period. For example, the regulation Württem[berg cavalry sabre of the year 1817, the Baden cavalry trooper's sabre an[the Bavarian Light Cavalry sabre, both from the mid-19th century, wer[derived from this French model.

The French sabre Model 1822 for general cavalry resembles the AN X[pattern; only the langets are missing and a third lateral arm of the basket ha[been added. The Belgian cavalry sabre Model 1802/1883 was derived from[the French models. A similar type of guard, mostly with arms of rods[appeared in Great Britain, too, as seen on cavalry sabre Model 1853.

Guard of bands are typical of Prussian cavalry sabre Model 1852, whos[basket is extended on the outer side. After the modification of 1879 it staye[in service till the end of the 19th century. The Dutch artillery sabre of th[year 1854, too, features a guard fashioned from arms.

Some weapons with this type of guard feature a more complex structure[The French sabre for cavalry officers, Model 1788, has a shell-shaped[

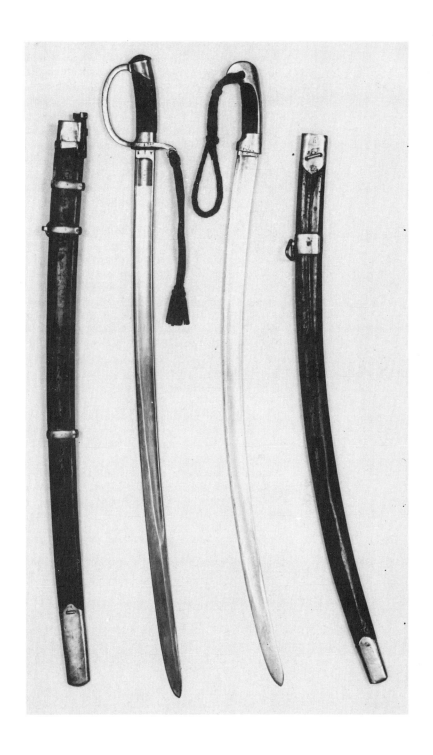

80   Russian sabre for cavalry Model 1881, with scabbard.
Russian Cossack *shashqua,* with scabbard. The blade marked *Zlatoust Iunia 1851 g* (in Cyrillic).

pierced guard inserted between the arms. The early 19th-century Portuguese sabre copied this style. On the Belgian revolutionary sabre of the year 1791 there is a relief of a lion with a Phrygian cap in between the arms as a symbol of revolution. In a similar way, the mounted grenadier's sabre of the Napoleonic Imperial Guard has a distinction between the arms — a burning grenade. The French sabre for artillery officers from the Restoration period (1815 – 30) is decorated between the arms in relief with ornaments, trophies and the royal arms under a crown.

Saxony cavalry sabre Model 1891 has modelled its hilt on the German broadsword Model 1889; however, the plate between the arms displays the arms of Saxony instead of the Prussian eagle. The hilt of the Serbian sabre from the turn of the 19th and 20th century is fashioned in a similar way, showing the King of Serbia's arms. The Swiss artillery sabre of the year 1895 also comes into this category with the Helvetian cross on the basket.

Before the final word on cavalry sabres, a special Russian Cossack *shashqua* sabre must be mentioned. The weapon is of entirely open type without any hand-guard or cross-guard and was derived from Caucasian-type sabres. The first weapon was introduced in the Russian army in 1836; this model is uncommon outside Russia. The mid-19th century weapons are more likely to be encountered with the grip still provided with a brass back strap. *Shashqua* Model 1881 is more common; there is no back strap and the scabbard is provided with sockets to take the bayonet.

The Infantry Sabre

The introduction of the bayonet in the 17th century resulted in the disbanding of pikemen. The relatively heavy and long flintlock musket with a bayonet became the principal infantry weapon. However, the bayonet was not considered a side-arm. It was a part of the gun and attached to it. In a number of armies the infantrymen, in the same manner as the former musketeers, were equipped with a side weapon necessary in hand-to-hand combat. The hanger was the prevailing side weapon in the 17th century; in the

81 Prussian grenadier's sabre Model 1715. On the blade, engraved monogram *FWR* (Friedrich Wilhelm I, 1713 – 40) and a burning grenade, the blade marked *POTZDAM*. Hilt with two kidney-shaped shells.

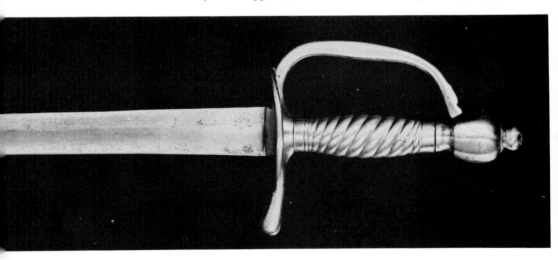

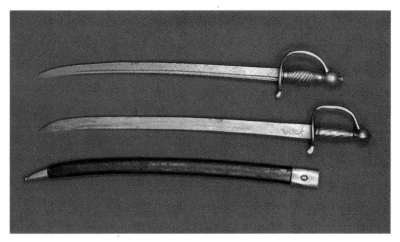

82 Prussian grenadier's sabre *c.* 1750. *FR* monogram on the blade (Friedrich II, 1740 – 81). Heart-shaped shell guard.
Russian grenadier's sabre, 1783, with scabbard. On the blade, *EA* monogram (Ekaterina Aleksandrovna II), engraved crown and *Tula 1783 g* mark (in Cyrillic).

first decades of the 18th century it was rather the sabre with a shorter yet wider curved blade that was preferred.

The Prussian grenadier sabre introduced during Frederick William's reign (1713 – 40) in the year 1715 was probably the very first regulated infantry side weapon. It has a slightly curved blade with a fuller on each side. The grip is of brass with a prominent pommel and a pommel finial. The knuckle-bow is of a single bar and the shell takes the shape of the kidneys. The following evolutional type, introduced after 1740 during the reign of Frederick II, has the shell fashioned in the shape of a heart. This type stayed in the Prussian army till 1816.

Similar sabres with a heart-shaped shell were also part of the equipment of British infantry from the 1740s – Model 1742. In the Russian army this type of side weapon, called a 'half-sabre', appeared between the 1740s and 1760s until 1762 and again as a grenadier's sabre from 1783 on. It was still in use during the Napoleonic Wars in the early 19th century.

The earlier types of Saxony infantry sabres usually have a more developed protection for the hand, either with a lateral shell or with two symmetrical arms ending in the edge of the heart-shaped shell. Most of these weapons feature a grip cast of brass in one piece, often with oblique fluting and back strap. In the second half of the 18th century, hand-protecting elements were disappearing from Saxony weapons and only a slender knuckle-bow remained.

The French grenadier sabre from the mid-18th century was provided with a shell on one side only, which, however, was omitted on Model 1770, so that only a slender knuckle-bow remained. The same goes for grenadier's sabre Model 1786 for which langets on the upper surface of the cross-guard only are typical.

Sabre Model AN IX (1800 – 01), commonly called a briquet, is of a simple design. The grip and the knuckle-bow passing into the cross-guard are of brass, cast in one piece. This infantry sabre was then used, with minor modifications of the scabbard, as Model 1816 even after the Napoleonic

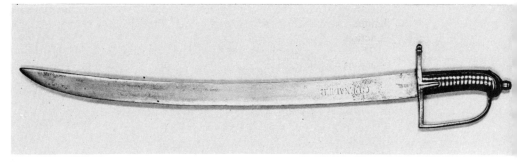

83 French grenadier's sabre Model 1786. On the blade, double *L* in mirror image (Louis XVI, 1774—92) an inscription *GRENADIER*. Marked *M/anufac/ture R/oya/le D'Alsace.*

Wars when, as a war prize, these weapons were taken over by the armies of a number of countries. This was true for Prussia in particular where it became Infantry Sabre Model 1818, and also for the Netherlands and Belgium. Consequently we come across weapons with complete French marks on the back edge of the blade, but provided with Prussian marks indicating the regiment, the company and the number of the weapon on the cross-guard. After the stock of prize weapons had been exhausted, weapons of this type were being produced in Prussia, for the navy in 1848—52, among other instances. Some police units were equipped with this sabre as late as the early 20th century.

Austria, too, introduced this weapon after 1815. It was used by some naval units and later on in the Austrian gendarmerie where it stayed in use until 1918.

Until 1765, sergeants and grenadiers only carried side weapons in the army of the Central European Hapsburgs; infantrymen were equipped with gun and bayonet. The grenadier's sabre featured a relatively long blade and hilt of brass; the scabbard was of leather. The sergeant's sabre of the Hungarian infantry had a thumb ring on the inner side, a slender knuckle-bow and the pommel fashioned as a lion's head. The trooper's sabre had a smooth pommel finial.

'Ordinary fusilier's sabre' Model 1765 was introduced into the so-called German infantry and the frontiersmen units. It was provided with a short (53 cm) blade of flat cross-section without fullers. The grip was provided with a brass knuckle-bow, the cross-guard was short, slightly S-shaped at first and subsequently straight. It was an open-type sabre with no knuckle-bow. After it was set aside in 1798, infantry troopers were equipped only with a gun and a bayonet. From 1765, grenadier sergeants carried a sabre with slender knuckle-bow, rhomboid langets and a smooth back strap ending with a finial shaped as a lion's head.

The regulation of 1802 stipulated a new grenadier sabre with hilt of iron for grenadiers, musicians, artillery drivers and other specialists. Minor modifications made in the years 1809 and 1824—28 were not of any consequence. Along with Model 1802, the previous brass mounts of the scabbard were replaced by iron ones and in 1828 a scabbard of iron sheet covered with leather was introduced. In 1837 the knuckle-bow was provided with the then fashionable convex outline, replaced in 1862 with a knuckle-bow

74

slightly concave in the middle. From 1867 onwards the use of this sabre was limited to musicians, NCOs, and to accountants and other non-combat functions.

The jaeger units created in 1758 carried a falchion or a curved sabre with a slender knuckle-bow. In 1767—89 they were equipped with the so-called ordinary fusilier sabre Model 1765, which was then set aside after 1789 and replaced with a bayonet.

The artillerymen of the Austrian army carried falchions from the end of the 17th century; from 1758 on they were equipped with a grenadier's sabre. The regulation of 1774 specified a sabre for artillerymen and miners; it resembled the grenadier's sabre, but the blade was more robust and there were minor differentiations on the hilt. The artillery sabre kept its hilt of brass even after 1802 along with the short langets. The regulation of 1828 somewhat modified the artillerymen's and miners' sabre. The regulation of 1851 stipulated an infantry sabre for artillerymen and a cavalry sabre for their drivers.

Technical units, which had originally been divided into several categories before merging as pioneer and sapper units later on, used the grenadier's sabre till 1765. Only the 'tchaikisten' — special boat units on the Danube — were from 1764 (1773) equipped with a different side weapon with a slightly curved blade and a saw-toothed back edge. The hilt of brass was provided with wooden scales and the slightly S-shaped cross-guard was thickened in the middle. The other technical units carried a sabre which was similar to the grenadier's weapon but the blade was given a saw-toothed back edge and the hilt was more massive.

Up till 1798 there had been no regulation stipulating specific side weapons for infantry officers. In Maria Theresa's time just 'a good military blade and gilded hilt' were required. Officers of the Hungarian Pandurs carried sabres similar to hussars' ones. Such a mid-18th-century sabre differs only in the engraved depiction on the blade of a foot warrior with drawn sabre.

The regulation of 1811 introduced a pattern for the rapier for officers of the so-called German infantry (e.g. for the non-Hungarian lands). In the

84   Austrian ordinary fusilier's sabre Model 1765.
Austrian sabre of sergeants and grenadiers Model 1765.

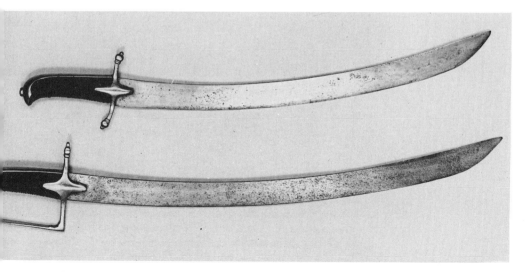

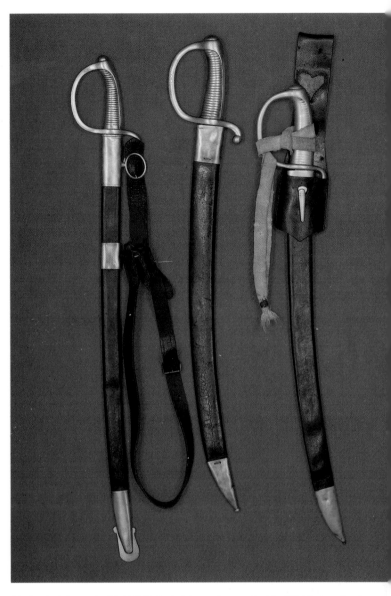

85 Prussian infantry sabre Model 1818. On the hilt, acceptance marks of the 49th infantry regiment.
French infantry sabre Model AN IX/XI (*briquet*) with scabbard. The blade marked *Manuf/actu/re du Klinger*
thal. Austrian gendarmerie and naval sabre, after 1824, with scabbard, sword knot and frog.

same year a sabre for officers of Hungarian infantry was introduced in two
variants using one blade type (74—84 cm long). The first variant featured
just a simple decoration, engraved lines parallel with the edges of the slender
knuckle-bow and the back strap; the other one had the hilt decorated with
a relatively rich relief. It gradually became a custom that the former type was
carried by grenadier and jaeger officers, the latter by officers of Hungarian

and border infantry. This custom was confirmed in the regulation of 1827.

The regulation of 1837 introduced a new sabre for officers and generals. The blade was rather deeply curved, the slender hand-guard was of polished iron and featured a convex knuckle-bow; the cross-guard was provided with shield-shaped langets protruding downwards. The scabbard of iron had two mounts provided with round bulging swellings. This simpler variant remained in use in grenadier and jaeger units. Blades of these sabres often bear reminders of the revolutionary year of 1848, since the weapons were also used by the National Guards.

On the other officers' and generals' sabres, two kinds of modifications were permitted — although not stipulated. Both of them were targeted at increasing protection of the hand. The first one consisted of adding a horizontal, almost circular and slightly convex shell to the cross-guard and fixing it there with two screws from beneath. This type is represented by a general's sabre with a richly decorated blade dated 1844 produced in the workshop of P. D. Lüneschloss in Solingen. The other modification called for adding a pivotable hand-guard held by a spring and a catch in the same manner as on some weapons already mentioned above. While the first variant disappeared later on, the second one was universally stipulated for staff- and high-ranking officers in the regulations of 1850.

Finally, in 1861 the best-known type of Austrian infantry officer's sabre was introduced with slender knuckle-bow slightly S-shaped, and a scabbard on which the upper ring was replaced with a firmly fixed rectangular attachment on the inner side. This side weapon stayed in use till the end of the Austro-Hungarian Empire. A short version of this model was used by mountain jaegers for easier freedom of movement.

With regard to infantry officers' sabres, what has been said about Austrian weapons generally holds true for them, too. Up till the early 19th century, if side weapons for officers were standardized at all, the rapier was mostly carried by infantry officers. Only in the 19th century did the sabre

86 Austrian artillery sergeant's sabre, after mid-18th century. On the blade, engraved crossed barrels and inscriptions *VIVAT MARIA THERESIA ./. VIVAT FRANCISCUS I^{mus}*.
Austrian sabre Model 1828 for artillerymen and sappers. The blade marked *Fischer 1831*.

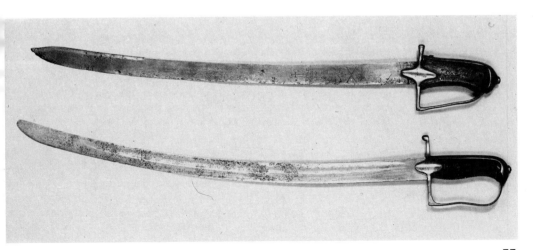

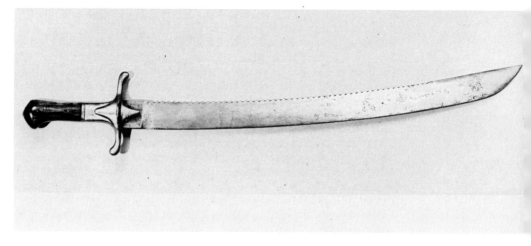

87 Austrian *tchaikisten* sabre Model 1764. The back edge serrated.

begin being incorporated into their equipment more frequently. In some armies there was either no difference in officers' sabres according to different army specialization, or else the difference consisted of symbols on the visible part of the hilt as in Austria.

On early 19th-century officers' sabres the aesthetic views of the Empire style were reflected in design and decoration of swords. French officers' sabres were based on the Empire style throughout the whole of the 19th century (although modified during the course of time). The French sabre Model 1821 for infantry officers shows Empire influence, too. The Baden sabre for infantry was derived from it. The hilt is of brass with back-strap (and finial) of French type. Model 1816 of Saxony also features a hilt of brass with a lion-shaped pommel and a slightly convex knuckle-bow with the arms of Saxony. The 1855 Model of Hessen-Darmstadt with basket of brass pierced in an ornamental pattern is provided with a leather strap at the base of the grip. The Bavarian sabre of the same year is much simpler. The smooth hilt resembles that of the Austrian sabre Model 1861; however, the material differs, as the Bavarian hilt is of brass. The Prussian sabre for fusilier and jaeger officers with a convex knuckle-bow of brass and rectangular langets is provided with a smooth back-strap featuring side projections. It is the archetype of the German sabre of the year 1889.

The French sabre Model 1845 for lower-ranking cavalry officers remained in use till World War I. British sabres of this type are represented by sabre Model 1882 from mid-19th century with the initials *VR* under the crown (Victoria Regina, 1837–1901), on the blade and once again, this time pierced, on the asymmetrical hilt of brass.

78

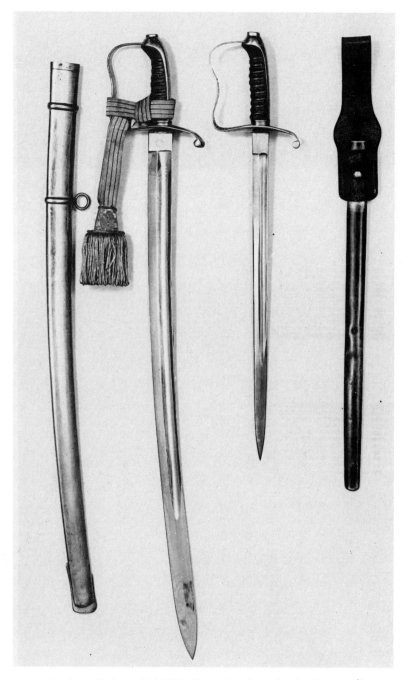

88 Austrian infantry officer's sabre Model 1861 with sword-knot. Shortened version of the weapon for mountain-jaeger officers.

89 Sabre for generals and infantry officers Model 1837 with 1838 modification. The blade decorated with blueing, gilding and silvering and marked *P. D. Lüneschloss Solingen 1844.*

90 French sabre for non-commissioned officers Model 1845 E.
The blade marked *Manufacture Nationale d'Armes Chatellerault Juillet 1916. Adj¹ Inf^(rie) M^(le) 1845 E.*

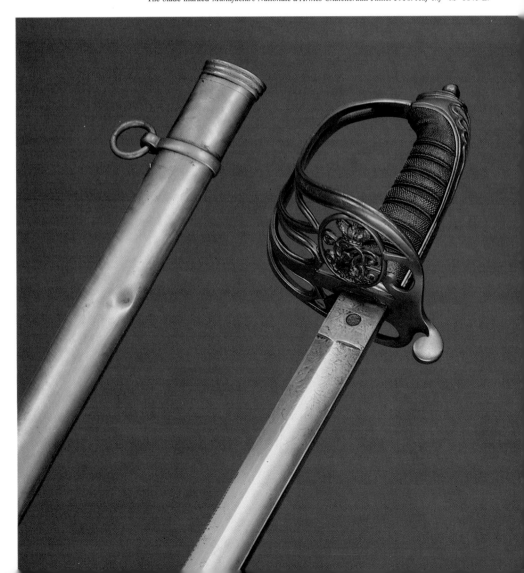

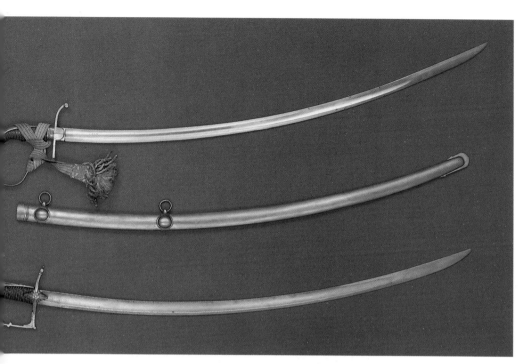

91 Austrian sabre for jaeger and grenadier officers Model 1837.
The hilt of iron, jaeger sword-knot, the blade marked *NIXDORF*.
Hungarian infantry officer's sabre Model 1811. The hilt of brass, with relief.

The Naval Sabre

Navies, too, used sabre-type weapons. They were intended for rank-and-file
seamen in hand-to-hand combat on board either the defending or attacking
ship. Generally they featured a shorter, stronger blade and usually a good
protection for the hand.

French naval sabre Model AN IX (1800 − 01) and its later modification,
Model 1823, was provided with a wide, slightly curved blade, a straight grip
with a finial and a solid guard on the outer side. The British navy weapon
(the cutlass) of the years 1810 − 20 differed from the former in its straight
blade. Moreover, the knuckle-bow was widened at the front and provided
with a slit for the sword knot at the top. The cross-guard was developing into
an almost round-shaped shell.

The sabre introduced into the Austrian navy in 1849 was based on the
French model. It, too, featured a grip of iron and a solid guard plate on the
outer side. The regulation of 1862 stipulated a new naval sabre whose blade
was almost straight and was provided with a back rib. The knuckle-bow was
an iron band and the hilt was complemented with a strong solid guard plate
on one side. In contrast to the above mentioned weapons this sabre was

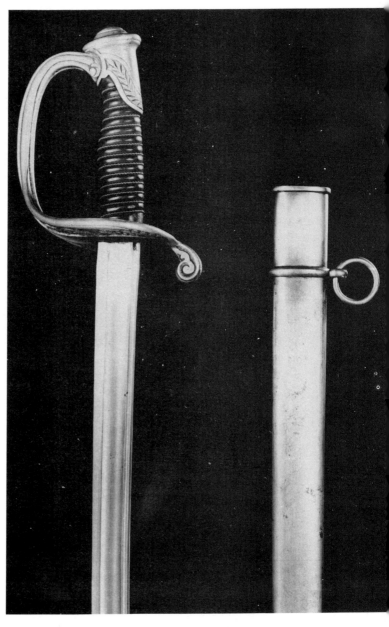

92   British officer's sword, *c.* 1840. On blade and basket, *VR* monogram (Victoria Regina, 1837–1901).

provided with an iron scabbard covered with leather. It was abandoned in 1871. The Prussian naval weapon was modified to a great extent — following the French pattern — in the mid-19th century, at least as to the shape of the iron grip and hilt. The blade, however, is of a slightly machete form

The Dutch sabre of this category, datable after the mid-19th century, is provided with a slender hand-guard and a scabbard of iron.

The Russian naval sabre of the year 1857 was of a different type. The blade was provided with back rib and an asymmetrical solid plate guard.

In addition to the already mentioned naval weapons the Austrian navy was also equipped with a sabre derived from the French infantry briquet. It was used by the marines (from 1818), seamen (from 1820) and navy gunners (from 1824) and was confirmed in the 1828 regulation. A sabre of similar type was also part of the equipment of marines of the Imperial German Fleet (*Seesoldaten*) between 1848 and 1852.

Naval officers' sabres were mostly just off-duty weapons. The British naval officer's sabre of the year 1827 provided a model for some of them. Its back strap ended with a pommel fashioned as a lion's head and the asymmetrical hilt is decorated with the symbol of a fouled anchor under the royal crown in relief. The 1848—52 sabre for officers of the Imperial German Fleet is almost identical; the relief on the hilt, however, consists simply of an anchor and cable. In 1877, Spain introduced a very similar weapon for its naval officers. French weapons of this category had hilts of gilded brass decorated in ornamental relief in which the anchor motif dominated, also being shown on the scabbard mounts.

The Austrian naval officer's sabre Model 1827 used a strongly curved blade and the hilt resembled the Model 1827 sabre for jaeger and grenadier officers. However, its grip is of horn and the hilt of brass. The langets are decorated with an anchor motif executed in relief and there is the double-headed Imperial eagle on the round part of the knuckle-bow. This sabre was replaced with another model in 1847 whose widened hilt of brass was decorated with pierced relief ornament dominated by the anchor motif. The last model of 1850, confirmed by the regulation of 1854, had its pommel shaped as Neptune's head (Hercules' head according to Dolleczek, 1896); the hilt resembled the preceding model, but the relief was enriched by the addition of two mermaids and the imperial eagle.

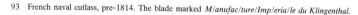

93 French naval cutlass, pre-1814. The blade marked *M/anufac/ture/Imp/eria/le du Klingenthal.*

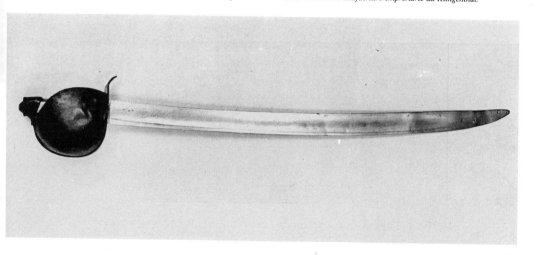

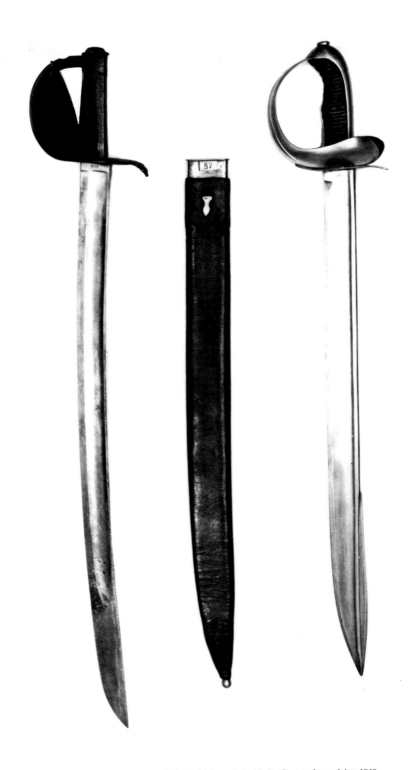

94 Austrian naval cutlass, 1849. The blade marked with *S et R*, an anchor and date 1849.
Austrian naval cutlass Model 1862 with scabbard. The blade is marked *F. S. Jung 1862*.

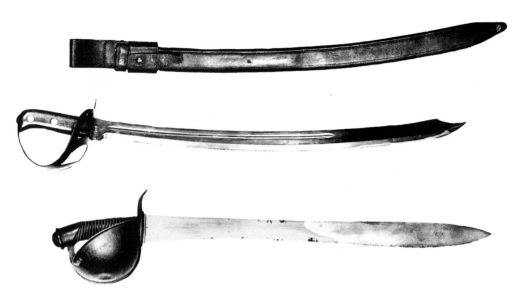

95 Dutch naval cutlass, after 1850. The blade marked *HEMBRUG*.
Prussian naval cutlass, *c.* 1850. On the blade, *FW* and a crown (Friedrich Wilhelm IV, 1840−61). It remained in use in the Imperial navy till 1874.

Finally, it is necessary to point out that the sabre also became part of the equipment of various civil dignitaries as the clerk's sabre. There appeared sabres for state officials, but also for officials of the mining industry and other dignitaries.

Fencing using the sabre, which originated in the second half of the 19th century, was gradually evolving into a sport and gave rise to a special sabre type with a very narrow curved blade and a solid basket covering the hand. In collections we also come across similar sabres with a narrow blade, which, however, is sharpened towards the end, the complex basket of entwined metal rods being inlaid with coloured cloth. These sabres were used by nationalistically minded German students organized in so-called *Burschenschaften* in their attempts to present a tough masculine appearance by displaying duel scars on their faces.

Among sabres, too, even in the 19th century (especially in the early part) status-symbol examples appeared. These were often executed with high art and craft standards featuring rich decoration in Neo-Classical and Empire styles and later also in the Romantic styles quite popular in the 19th century.

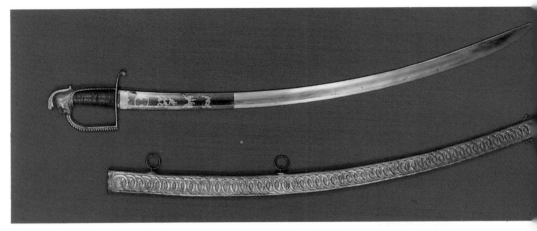

96 Neo-Classical sabre, early 19th century. The blade blued with gilded engravings, the scabbard of brass decorated with engravings.

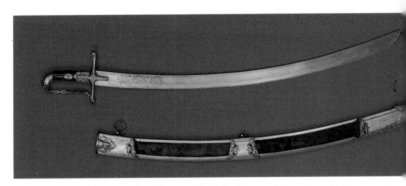

97 Hungarian magnate's sabre, 18th – 19th century. The blade with engraved decoration marks *FRINGIA*. The grip of horn, chain instead of knuckle-bow.

98 Austrian naval officer's sabre Model 1827. The blade with etched decoration, on the knuckle-bow a double-headed eagle and an anchor on the langets.
Austrian naval officer's sabre, Model 1850/1854. On the blade the arms and a crowned anchor. The basket with mermaids and a double-headed eagle.

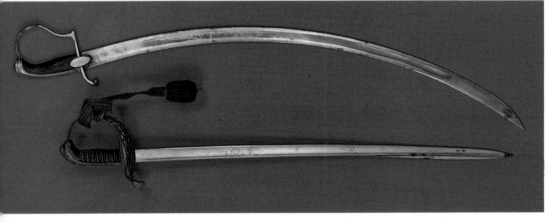

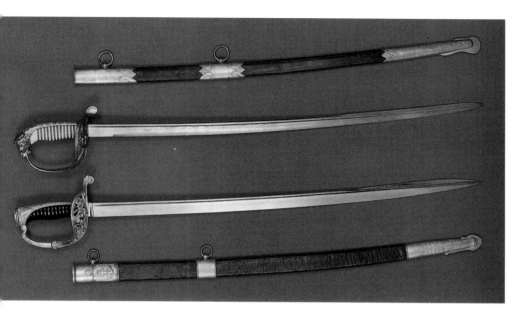

99 German naval officer's sabre, second half of 19th century. The blade etched with ships and marked *Herrmann Holsten, Kiel.*
French naval officer's sabre, second half of 19th century. The hilt gilded and featuring an anchor in relief.

SHORT-BLADED CUTTING WEAPONS

This category of side weapons includes those with a shorter blade (40–60 cm) which is single-edged and mostly wedge-shaped in cross-section. In addition to weapons with a straight blade weapons with a curved blade and with the blade widened in its lower part are included.

The simplest type of short-bladed weapon is found in the period of High Middle Ages and is represented by the falchion. The blade is usually straight or, just exceptionally, slightly curved, of wedge-shape cross-section. The grip is simple. Usually, on the surviving specimens the tang of the flat cross-section is preserved with a few openings to accept the rivets fixing the grips, mostly of wood, to it. The grip terminates with a pommel fashioned as a roof- or slightly beak-shaped hood, sometimes of solid iron, in other cases formed of forged lamellas. This side-weapon type has no cross-guard, but sometimes a ridge appeared at the junction of the blade and the tang. Falchions of this type appeared in the 14th century throughout Central Europe and were still in vogue in the first half of the 16th century. The later examples sometimes feature a short lateral projection at the junction of the blade and the tang. It is the case of a typically rustic peasant weapon of the Late Middle Ages. This is attested to not only in the German nomenclature of the period (*Hauswehr, Bauernwehr*), but also in the evidence, particularly in that of the first quarter of the 16th century, when peasants carried weapons of this type at their belts.

100 Section of falchion, the pommel composed of small plates, the blade of wedge cross-section, 15th century. Short falchion with solid-iron pommel, the blade of rhombic cross-section, 15th century.

Another type of medieval short cutting weapon is represented by a single-edge blade widened near the point. In the 14th century these weapons were known under the French name of *fauchon* even in England. Later on, the name of falchion became attributed to them. In the Germany of the High and Late Middle Ages the term *malchus* was used to describe them. Today two typological groups are recognized: the first is exemplified by its straight back edge while the convex sharp edge is widest in the lowest third. It is a

relatively scarce type used mostly in the British Isles and in North-West Europe.

The other type, appearing in pictorial evidence from the end of the 13th century, is characterized by its curved blade extended in its lower third into a more or less outstanding lateral point forming an obtuse angle. The illuminators of medieval manuscripts as well as artists depicting battle scenes from the Bible generally showed these weapons wielded by heathens, suggesting in such a way their apparently non-European, oriental origin. Pictorial evidence attests to the widespread use of the falchion over a considerable part of Europe: at the end of the 13th century in Norway, in the 14th century in France, England and Italy, and in the 14th and 15th centuries in Germany and Bohemia. The Renaissance period recorded another upsurge in the use

Malchus, 14th century

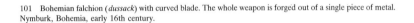

101 Bohemian falchion (*dussack*) with curved blade. The whole weapon is forged out of a single piece of metal. Nymburk, Bohemia, early 16th century.

of these weapons mostly originating in Italy — whence the term *storta*.

Another type of cutting weapon with a curved blade is the so-called *dussack* (*dusseghe*). The etymology of this word, rather strange-sounding in German records, is explained in Saxon archives of the late 16th century describing the weapon as *der behemische Dussack* (from the Czech *tesák*). Pictorial evidence shows this falchion as a very simple weapon without a hilt, forged out of a single piece of iron. The short curved blade rises from a flat block rounded off at its upper end; the block is provided with a cutaway section enabling the weapon to be gripped. Examples of the earliest type have not survived and preserved examples feature an advanced variant. Although it is fashioned out of a single piece of iron, its grip is extended to form a rod shaped as a knuckle-bow.

Curved blades were still to be found in this category of weapon. One type of curved-blade hunting weapon, the so-called *Jagdplaute*, appeared quite frequently as late as the 18th century.

However, hunting equipment in the course of the Late Gothic and the Renaissance period was dominated by straight-edge falchions. Some of them, due to their length, could be classified as hunting swords (*Jagdschwert*). The ostentatious weapon of Maximilian I, dated 1496, by Hans Summersperger from the Tyrolean Hall, ranks among the best known examples. The weapon, datable to *c.* 150 years later and yet similar to the former, with the hilt decorated by Caspar Späth of Munich (*c.* 1650), indicates that even as late as this period weapons of this type were still in vogue.

Italian falchion (*falcione, storta*), first half of 16th century

Späth's design, including the slender knuckle-bow and the cross-guard

89

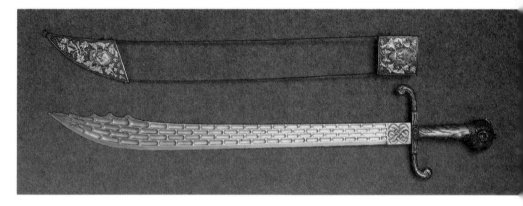

102 Falchion, Brescia, Italy, first half of 16th century. The blade surface with ridged network, the ricasso marked *FAUSTINO GELPHO BRESCIANO*, the hilt carved in relief and with residual gilding. The frame of the scabbard with gilded reliefs both on the locket and the chape.

Bohemian falchion (*Duss-ege*), 16th century

with bent-down shell on the outer side, represents a type quite popular throughout the 17th century. Ordinary examples of these hunting falchions (*Hirschfänger*) were provided with smooth hilts sometimes featuring simple linear decoration. The grips were often of wood or staghorn. However, there also appeared falchions with open hilt without any knuckle-bow and with grips or other parts of bone or ivory. Decorative carvings depict figural or hunting motifs as well as ornamental ones.

Falchions display more diversified shapes in the course of the 18th century. As well as examples with a knuckle-bow there often appeared pieces with open hilt design. Both the types, however, featured hilts of gilded brass or bronze. Hilts of silver are less frequent. Decoration was represented by rich relief featuring hunting motifs as well as ornamental elements of Late

103 Long hunting sword, Caspar Späth, Munich, *c.* 1650. The blade marked with king's head (Peter Koel[?]) and inscription *FIDE SED CVI VIDE — ME FECIT SOLINGEN*. The iron hilt carved in relief on gilded background, plant ornaments, hunting motifs, on the reverse side scaled ornament of gold nails.

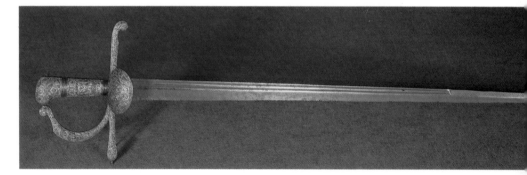

Jagdplaute, 18th century

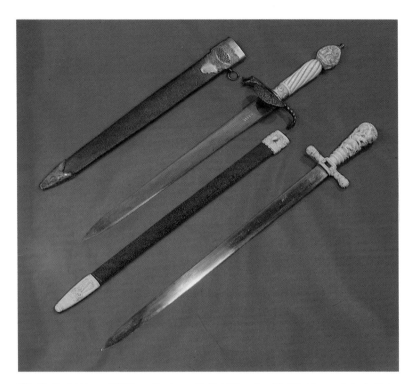

104   Hunting falchion, *c.* 1700, the scabbard second half of 18th century. The hilt and pommel of carved bone or ivory with relief scenes.
Hunting falchion, early 18th century. The hilt and scabbard mounts of bone with carved animal motifs.

Baroque or Rococo character. Tangs were overlaid with horn or bone, the latter dyed, most often in shades of green. Around the mid-18th century, grips of porcelain appeared, painted under the glaze.

The hunting falchion did not disappear from the hunting equipment of the 19th century, and its stylistic modifications fully reflect the aesthetic view of the period and various modifications. The aesthetic concepts of Neo-Classicism and the Empire fully asserted themselves and later on Romantic elements also appeared, most often those of Neo-Renaissance and Second Rococo. Not only marks, but also blade-decorating techniques are significant for precise dating. While engraving is typical of decorations of 17th- and 18th-century weapons as well as of those datable to the first third of the 19th century, flat etching on nickelled or chromium background is typical of later weapons.

Rich noblemen and princes, and the proprietors of large estates which included woods were often in the habit of providing their woodkeepers with livery and uniform falchions as well. Weapons of this type then frequently feature the coat-of-arms of the magnate.

The equipment of noble sportsmen also included special carving and table sets designed for outdoor use and called *Weidmesser* or *Weidbesteck.* Occasionally they appear as early as at the turn of the 15th and the 16th century but they occur more frequently between the 16th and the 18th century. A wide short blade, often rounded off or cut off obliquely at the

Hunting falchion, 18th
century

Hunting falchion, second half
of 17th century

lower end, is typical of this hunting equipment. There also appeared bla
widened at the end section. The cross-guard is mostly missing and the g
of a simple outline on early examples, often features a covering richly in
with coloured wood, metal or mother-of-pearl. The Baroque and Roc
pieces have hilts of gilded brass decorated with rich relief motifs, most of
of hunting scenes. Scabbards with metalwork frames, most commonly
iron in the 17th century, were quite frequently fully covered with brass in
Late Baroque and Rococo period, with rich ornamental and figural deco
tion in relief. The scabbard usually featured a receptacle to hold a knife
fork in its upper section.

Large folding knives with a spring safety catch come into the category
short weapons with a cutting function. The *navaja* was the most comm
and was widespread in Spain where, in the 18th and 19th centuries, it ser
as a popular personal weapon, particularly among the poor of so
ety. It seems, however, that it may have only rarely spread as far as Cen
Europe.

The falchion (*Faschinenmesser*) also represents a part of army equ
ment. Naturally it is a weapon, but it can also be utilized as a tool. In
equipment of special technical units such as sappers or pioneers the t
function was of decisive importance and consequently also influenced so
typological features of the falchion.

For the first time a weapon of falchion-type appeared in the weapons
an infantry unit created in the first third of the 18th century by August
Strong, King of Poland and Elector of Saxony. This unit, a part of his gua
was equipped after the pattern of Turkish elite infantry units.

In general army equipment the falchion was gaining in favour slowly a
gradually. According to Dolleczek's data (1896), the previous sword of
Hapsburg Imperial army artillery was replaced by a shorter falchion as ea
as 1666. It was by no means a question of a weapon strictly and precis
stipulated by a regulation; evidently it was just an indication of a weap
type. Moreover, as already mentioned above, artillerymen later carrie
grenadier's sabre. The situation was similar also in the then early jae
units. The jaegers, first appearing in the year 1758, at first carried sabre
falchions whose exact specification was not described. We can apparer
imagine it as a normal hunting falchion. Later on, the ordinary fusili
sabre served as their side weapon (1767–89). Only for the Model 1789
a falchion (*Hirschfänger*) introduced which could be attached to the gur
a bayonet. In six years it was replaced with a real bayonet attachable to
barrel of the gun. Pioneer and technical units of the Austrian army u
sabres, which, however, in the case of the Tchaikisten units, were rather
curved-falchion character with saw-backs, no matter that the regulat
called them sabres. As a matter of fact the first real falchion, also cal
Faschinenmesser in Austria, was Model 1850/53, intended for pionee
artillery gunners and mounted artillery. A wide blade, a hafted grip of h
and a scabbard of horse leather were its principal features. The mo
fications of 1862 were insignificant although Model 1862 is mentio
quite frequently. From 1889 on, grips of wood were gradually introduc

Prussia introduced a fusilier's falchion in 1787 featuring a straight bla
somewhat widened in its lower part, a grip of brass and a simple straig
cross-guard. A similar grip and cross-guard can also be met in the pionee
alchion Model 1812; the back edge of the blade, however, is fashioned
a saw-blade. The artillery falchion of the mid-19th century featured a slig
ly curved blade, S-shaped cross-guard and a grip with a beak-shaped t

Swedish artillery falchion,
end of 17th century

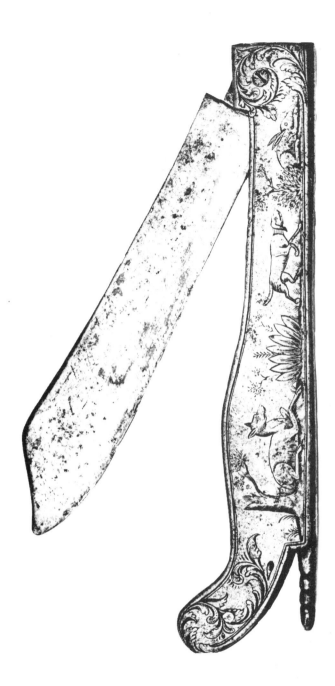

105 Large folding knife of the Spanish *navaja* type, Spain; modification Central European, first half of 18th century. The blade with spring mechanism. On the handle, engraved acanthus ornaments and hunting motifs.

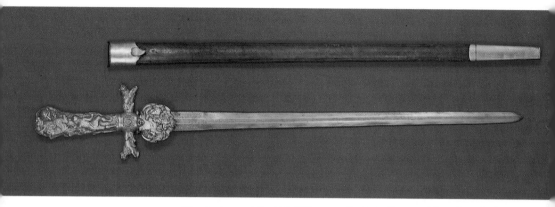

106 Hunting sword, first third of 18th century. The blade with engraved decoration and residual gilding, the
of gilded brass with scenes in relief.

Jaeger's falchion Model 1857 has a straight blade and a grip with a flatten
pommel. Saxony jaeger's falchion Model 1813 preserved the appearance
the original hunting falchion with a grip of staghorn. Bavarian falchio
from the first half of the 19th century feature grips with pommels fashion
as a lion's head.

The French artillery falchion (called, however, *sabre d'artillerie*) of t
years 1771–90 can be identified according to its tongue-shaped blade a
grip shaped as a relief representation of an eagle's neck and head. Eag
head shaped pommels appeared also on French falchions for sappers of t
general infantry from the years 1810–12, but the blade has a saw back. T
falchion intended for pioneers of the Guard resembled the aforemention
weapons, being of the same date; its pommel is shaped as a Gallic coc
head.

French artillery falchion Model 1816 is significant for its further evol
tion. Its blade is tongue-shaped, the cross-guard ends in smooth discs and

107 Hunting carving knife (*praxe*) once belonging to Julius, Duke of Brunswick (born 1528, duke between 15
and 1589), Germany, second third of 16th century. On the blade, engraved and gilded ornaments and coat of a
enclosed in inscription *JVLIVS DVX BRVNSVICENSIS ET LINEBURG...* The grip encrusted with b
and coloured wood.

108   Hunter's trousse (*Waidbesteck*) once belonging to Lobkowicz family, Prague (?), first third of 18th century. The blade is single-edged, the hilt gilded brass with hunting motifs in relief. The scabbard of wood, covered with velvet and provided on the front side with mount of gilded brass with Diana, coat of arms of counts of Lobkowicz and hunting motifs in relief. Small sheaths on the scabbard hold knife and fork.

109   Falchion of a guard of Augustus the Strong, Saxony, first third of 18th century. On the blade, engraved *AR* monogram under a crown, the same monogram in relief on the cross-guard.

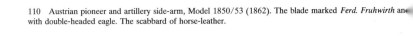

110   Austrian pioneer and artillery side-arm, Model 1850/53 (1862). The blade marked *Ferd. Fruhwirth* and with double-headed eagle. The scabbard of horse-leather.

Austrian sapper's falchion
Model 1769 (*Tschaikisten-säbel*)

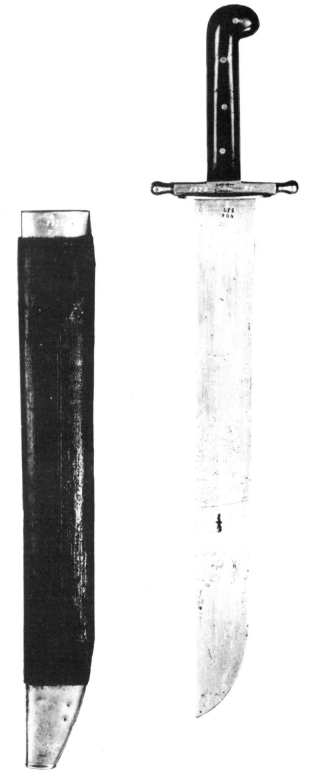

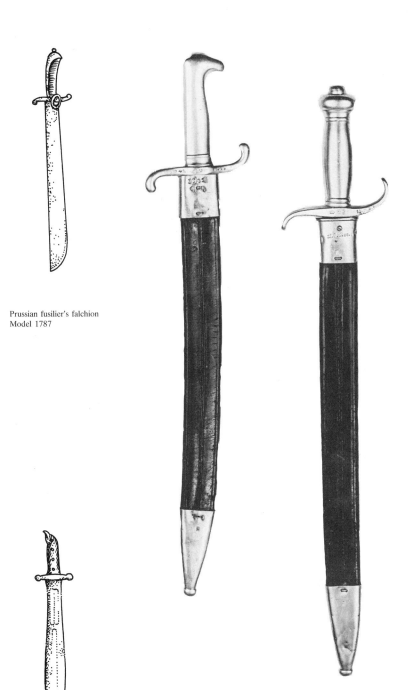

Prussian fusilier's falchion
Model 1787

French artillery falchion,
1771—90

111   Prussian artillery side-arm, *c.* 1850. The blade slightly curved, the hilt of brass.
Prussian jaeger's side-arm Model 1857. The blade marked *A. Werth, FW 66* punched on the hilt.

French artillery falchion
Model 1816

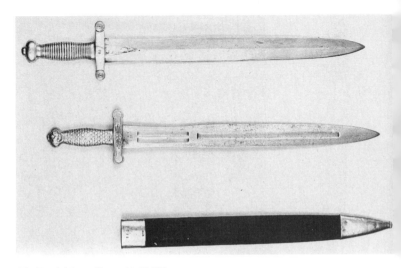

112 French infantry side-arm Model 1831.
French artillery side-arm Model 1816 with scabbard.

grip has a scaled surface with a flattened pommel. French artillery falchion Model 1831 was derived from it, too, with a blade of rhomboid cross-section and discs profiled with concentric circles. The Russian falchion for artillerymen and sappers of the years 1833—80 was derived from Model 1831. The blade, however, was provided with a saw-back. A similar Hanover pioneer and artillery falchion of 1840—67 is provided with a tongue-shaped blade and a grip covered with leather. The Swiss pioneer's falchion of the mid-19th century, too, followed the Model 1831 French pattern. Its blade features a saw-back and a Helvetian cross on the cross-guard.

Nordic weapons of this category are of quite a different type. Swedish falchion Model 1849 has a simple hafted grip, the blade is straight at the back edge but prominently waved at the sharp edge. A separate group is formed by falchions with a closed hilt resembling that of the sabre, including e.g. Swedish falchion Model 1788 with its pommel shaped as lion's head and with arched knuckle-bow, or Danish falchion Model 1840 provided with a convex knuckle-bow. British pioneer units, too, were using falchions with saw-back and a convex knuckle-bow between 1856 and 1903.

113 French side-arm for pioneers of the Guard, 1810—12.

98

Swedish infantry falchion
Model 1848

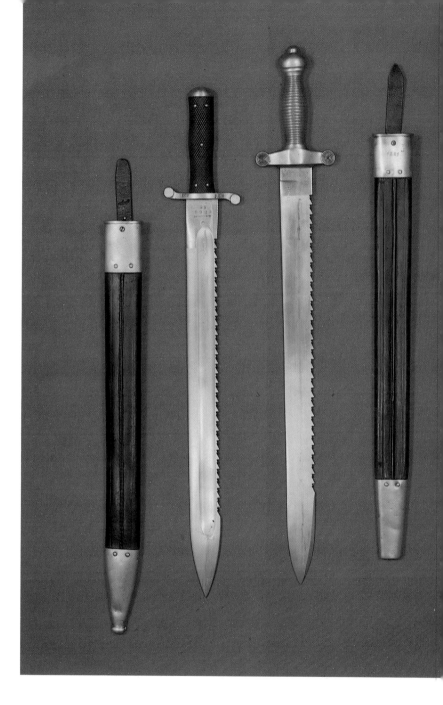

114 Swiss side-arm Model 1875.
Swiss pioneer's side-arm, c. 1850.

Spanish pioneer's
falchion Model 1877

99

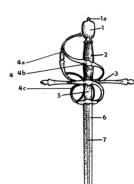

THRUSTING SIDE WEAPONS

The 'thrusting' attribute is applied to weapons with blades, usually quite narrow and tapering into a sharp point and consequently used for thrusting in combat. Rapiers, small-swords, poignards and their varieties with long blade and daggers with a short blade fall into this category.

The Rapier and the Smallsword

The rapier is a weapon with a blade of considerable length which is rather narrow and mostly double-edged. Thrusting represents the principal application although cutting is possible as well.

The nomenclature presents considerable problems. German, using the expression *Degen*, clearly distinguishes this category from the sword, while in most European languages the nomenclature includes both thrust and cut varieties of side-arms, e.g. *épée* in French or *spada* in Italian. English, too, commonly uses the general term of sword, although the limiting expression of smallsword exists, too. It is interesting to note that in some Nordic languages (Danish, Norwegian) this weapon is known as *karde* or *korde* (Seitz 1965) which evidently came from the same origin as the Central European expressions (*kárd* in Hungarian and *kord* in Czech). The rapier's origin should be looked for in the cutting sword which first appeared towards the end of the 13th century. Its importance grew in the decades to follow to such an extent that cutting swords represent about one-third of all extant swords surviving from the turn of the 14th and 15th centuries.

However, it is the Renaissance which is the main period for the weapon which is inseparably connected with the evolution of fencing and vice-versa. The Renaissance brought about an upsurge of fencing and of fencing schools. Their influence soon spread from Italy into Western and transalpine Europe and stimulated the spread of thrusting side-weapons. However, the rapier not only won through as a duelling or noblemen's weapon, but became a military weapon as well. It is impossible to imagine an infantryman — be he a musketeer or a pikeman — without a rapier necessary for hand-to-hand combat in the course of the 16th and most of the 17th century.

Rapier
1 Pommel
  1a) Finial
2 Grip
3 Cross-guard
4 Hilt
  4a) Knuckle-bow
  4b) Arms
  4c) Lower arms
5 Bridge (ricasso)
6 Blade
7 Groove (channel)
8 Point

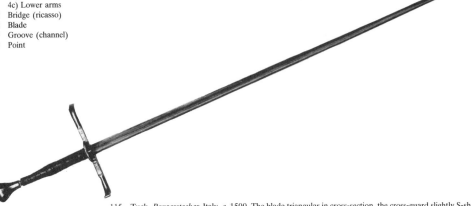

115 Tuck, *Panzerstecher*, Italy, *c.* 1500. The blade triangular in cross-section, the cross-guard slightly S-shaped

Four-sided blade with flat sides

Four-sided blade with con-cave sides

Three-sided blade with flat sides

Three-sided blade with con-cave sides

Thrust blade (rapier, dagger) — cross-sections (above)

From the typology point of view, the evolution of hand-protecting elements represents the principal feature. In this sense the evolution of the rapier is to a considerable extent identical with that of the Renaissance sword. The individual elements found application first of all on and below the cross-guard. Rapiers with a protection system below the cross-guard, too, emerged in the early 16th century, on a larger scale from the middle years onwards and were more or less in favour during the whole century.

Another type is represented by weapons with a protection system below the cross-guard featuring a prominent vertically S-shaped cross-guard whose front section reaches as far as the middle of the grip height, thus

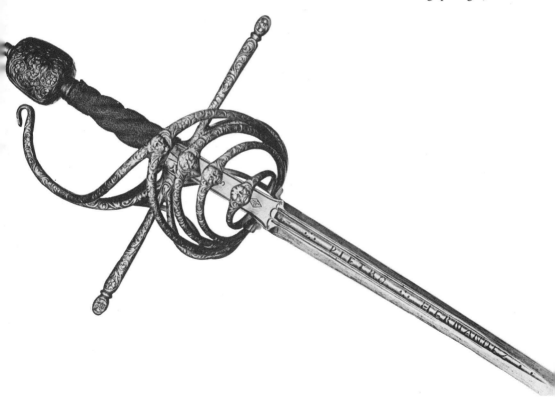

116   Rapier, Italian blade (?), hilt Central European (?), c. 1600. The blade marked *OT* in rhomboid, inscription *PIETRO HERNANDEZ* in the groove (Italian imitation of probably Spanish mark). The iron hilt with ornaments and masks carved in relief.

101

forming a precursor of the knuckle-bow. The occurrence of this type can b
dated to the second half of the 16th century.

As early as the first half of the 16th century, in southern Europe i
particular, there appeared weapons with the knuckle-bow coming out of th
cross-guard and connected with the pommel. This type spread until it wa
general towards the end of the 16th century. In the last decades protectio
of the hand reached its peak of complexity. Inner and outer arms starte
splitting from the knuckle-bow (the ribs sometimes forming forks with mor

117 Rapier, Toledo blade, North Italian hilt. On the ricasso, lion-shaped mark, probably Pedro de Toledo, an
moon with human face (Expadero del Rey). The hilt encrusted with silver, decoration of floral scrolls an
medallions.

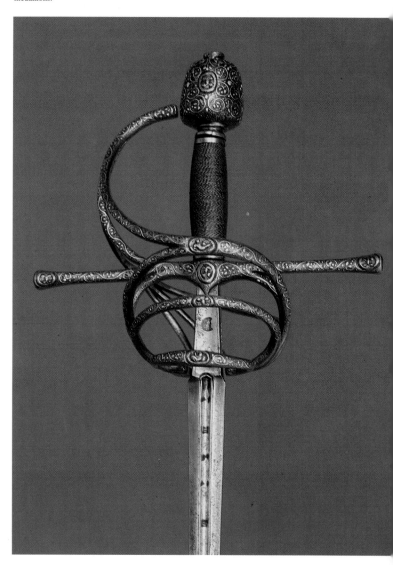

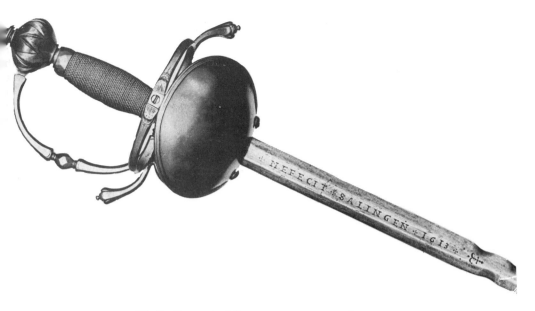

118 Flemish-type rapier, Solingen, 1613. The wavy blade marked *Weilm ROD BRAS ME FECIT SOLINGEN 1613*. The hilt fitted with shells.

arms) and were connected with rings and arms of the lower guard to create a system of arched lines both below and above the cross-guard. The pommel may be barrel-shaped, flattened pear-shaped, egg-shaped or show other variants. Plain military-weapon types show these elements either smooth or simply decorated with punched or linearly engraved ornaments. Ostentatious noblemen's weapons feature both ribs, rings and facettes of the individual parts decorated with the most varied art and craft techniques.

At the turn of the 16th and 17th centuries there originated another element further improving protection of the hand. The existing system of the complex basket was complemented with shells which sometimes replaced arms, particularly those below the cross-guard.

119 Smallsword, Germany, 1635, the hilt second half of 17th century. The blade marked *JOHANNES TESCHE 1635 ME FECIT SOLINGEN*, engraved inscriptions *FIDE SED CVI VIDE ./. SOLI DEO GLORIA, VINCERE AUT MORI*. The cross-guard with hooked bars, the shell of double-kidney shape pierced in relief (acanthuses, flowers, a woman's head). The grip bound with an intricate system of copper wires.

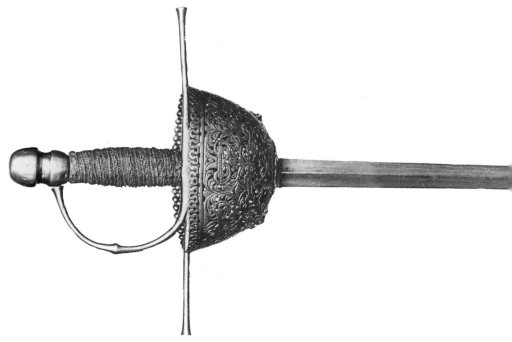

120 Cup-hilted rapier, first half of 17th century. The Spanish-type blade of rhombic cross-sèction, the cup of pierced iron.

121 Baroque sword, mid-17th century. The blade engraved with ornaments and the statue of Justice. Kidney-shaped shells with battle scenes executed in relief.

This variety of hand protection is often used on the so-called cup-hilted rapier. Generally it can be said that the cup-hilted rapier first of all features a blade considerably longer than that of the ordinary rapier. In all cases, however, the blade is very narrow, often of diamond section and designed for thrusting only. The best known cup-hilted rapier type originated in Spain, then spread to Italy, but also won favour further north. Its characteristic features are a simple knuckle-bow and a long cross-guard and below them is a round bowl often scalloped or turned around the edge. Cups are often decorated with engraving, although the technique of chiselling and pierced ornamentation in iron is most frequently encountered. The same style is sometimes used also for decoration of the grip and the pommel. Early examples from the first half of the 17th century used to have simple cups; later ones featured a turned edge, which apparently was to increase the chance of catching the opponent's blade. These cup-hilted rapiers are often associated with similarly decorated left-hand daggers used for fencing with rapier and dagger. These made their presence felt mainly in the 17th century, but can be found even in the 18th century.

Simplification of the hilt became the characteristic evolutionary feature of the 17th century. A simple knuckle-bow and a horizontal shell became the principal characteristics; the complex basket disappeared. A simple guard shell is typical of the Netherlands type of the weapon from the first half of the 18th century where it is situated on the outer side only. Otherwise round- and oval-shaped shells were common, the panelling of which was pierced in a net-like pattern or decorated with wrought ornaments or battle-scenes in relief. In the last quarter of the 17th century we meet shells fashioned in the shape of two opposite-lying kidneys.

In the course of the 16th and 17th centuries the rapier completely usurped the sword as a symbol of social superiority. As to blades, the most favoured ones came from the Spanish town of Toledo, but blades by makers in Milan were also sought after. Side by side with them products by blademakers from the German town of Solingen were becoming sought after in the late 16th and early 17th centuries.

Along with the evolution of the French fencing school, a new weapon

122 Hungarian tuck, with scabbard, early 18th century.
The blade triangular, the hilt with long langets, the scabbard with frame-type metalwork.

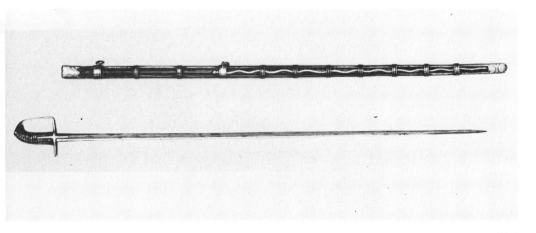

originated some time in the early 17th century, the pillow sword. Its basic feature is a horizontal shell, sometimes flat, at other times bowl-shaped, and with two curved bars springing from the bottom surface of the cross-guard, curving, allowing the weapon to be gripped with two fingers inserted through them. The hilt is of open type; there is no knuckle-bow.

Towards the end of the 17th century, another weapon with a long blade gained popularity, the tuck. Its forerunner, too, is to be sought back in the Middle Ages. Possibly as early as the end of the 14th century, but certainly in the course of the 15th century, there arose a demand for a weapon capable of penetrating between the individual armour plates or rings of the coat-of-mail better than the thrusting sword. In such a way the so-called *Bohrschwert* originated — called *estoque* in Spanish, *estoc* in French and

123 Sword worn with the uniform of the Bohemian nobility, the hilt of silver, Jan Piskáček, goldsmith, Prague 1813.

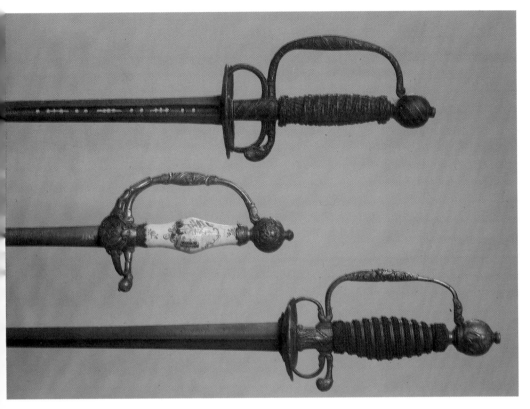

124 Smallsword, Central Europe, first half of 18th century. The blade pierced, the hilt with hooked bars, knuckle-bow and bottom shells.
Rococo smallsword. The grip of porcelain painted under the glaze. Saxony (?), second third of 18th century.
Court smallsword, France (?), second quarter of 18th century. Remnants of engraving on the blade, the hilt of iron carved with ornamental and figural relief on gilded background.

125 Late-Empire smallsword, Central Europe, c. 1820. The hilt of iron decorated with faceted studs and pendants.
Neo-Classical smallsword with heart-shaped shell. France (?), end of 18th century.

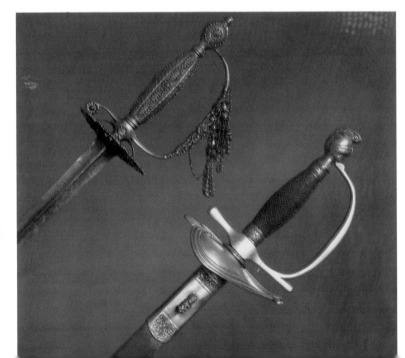

tuck in English. The blade was very long and narrow, and three- or four-edged. The estoc in the proper sense of the word could be found practically all over Europe as late as the mid-16th century. Later it disappeared in the West and in the South, but the Turkish invasion of Central Europe in the course of the 16th and 17th centuries caused this weapon to remain in use, particularly in the Polish and Hungarian regions, but also in the army of the Central European Hapsburgs. It was a horseman's weapon which, due to its extraordinary length (up to 150 cm), was carried on the saddle and was suitable for fighting the Turkish enemies who still wore coat-of-mail armour. The early examples usually have an open hilt, sometimes with lower protective elements, just exceptionally with a rectangular open knuckle-bow. Later estocs, datable to *c.* 1700 and later, were provided with sabre-type hilt, i.e. they had a hooded grip, arched knuckle-bow and cross-guard, sometimes with long cross-guard catches.

Conspicuous refinements can be traced in the evolution of noblemen's and court smallswords from the end of the 17th century and particularly in the 18th century. This variety was gradually losing its characteristics as a weapon and becoming a male fashion accessory.

The blades got shorter; their cross-section is either rhomboid, or lenticular, or three-faced. Some of them, especially those from Toledo, are pierced in the central groove. The prevailing style of hilt is simple in the outline yet richly decorated. The pommel is oval-, round- or onion-shaped. The shell is placed under the cross-guard, initially of double type, later simple and heart-shaped. The grip is wound with intricately woven wires of non-ferrous metal often combined with bands of brass. Grips cast of brass or other alloys may also be found. Brass is the most frequent material for hilts (sometimes with a high proportion of copper), or bronze. The hilts are often richly gilded. Silver hilts are also quite common. Figural and ornamental elements based on Baroque and, later, Rococo pattern books appear in decoration.

After the mid-18th century, the grip, particularly in Germany, was shaped of porcelain and painted under glaze. The counter-guard shells in particular provided suitable space for decoration. The blades were engraved and gilded in the second half of the 18th century often blued and complemented with gilded engraving. Neo-Classicism with its antique elements was becoming dominant in the fashioning and decoration of hilts in the last quarter of the 18th century. The pommel often assumed the shape of an antique helmet or of a helmeted head. Neo-Classical and, later on, Empire elements made themselves felt in the fashioning of the hilt and on the tilted shell.

The first part of the 19th century when even the accessory role of the rapier as well as that of a status symbol had come to an end, was at the same time the period of advancement in iron metallurgy. This enabled not only the production of decorative objects, but the creation of fine jewellery items as well and also resulted in the fact that cast iron became a fashionable material in the decoration of the rapier of the period, too. As to the shape, elements of the Late Empire were involved and with regard to decoration two basic trends can be traced. One is characterized by the smooth surface of the individual parts of the hilt, frequently faceted, polished to mirror-effect and blued or blackened. The other trend employed articulation of the surface achieved through lines, rosettes or other shapes composed of tiny, intricately faceted imitations of diamond cutting. They were complemented with delicate chains or linked pendants composed of faceted beads. This

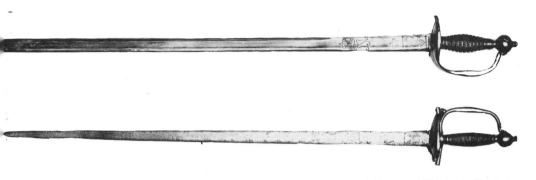

126 Officer's sword, *c.* 1750. On the blade, monograms *MT* (Maria Theresa) and *FC* (Franciscus Caesar), the hilt of bronze.
Officer's sword, 1780—90. *J II* monogram on the blade (Joseph II), the hilt of brass.

fashion, however, did not last long. In the late 1820s the smallsword disappeared as a civilian dress accessory.

It continued, though, as an accessory to the uniforms of civil servants. The officials of government bodies and diplomats in most European countries carried smallswords often imitating patterns of the past. Gilded hilts and scabbard-mounts, mother-of-pearl and arms of countries or of sovereigns are features typical of them. In addition further types of smallswords can be encountered, e.g. those designed for officials of the postal service or railways or for high-ranking dignitaries of the mining industry — provided with the appropriate emblems of the relevant function.

The sword, however, was a part of the officer's equipment in the 18th century; in the infantry primarily, where it was a side weapon, whereas the spontoon served as a status symbol. In the army of the Austrian Hapsburgs it was carried by officers of the so-called German infantry, while in Hungary even infantry officers were equipped with a sabre. Officers' swords had not been regulated in any way until the end of the 18th century. As shown in the records datable to the time of Maria Theresa's reign, just a 'good, military-type blade' was required. It is therefore possible to make the assessment that officers' equipment included weapons provided with a more massive blade than that used on court smallswords of the period, the former moreover provided with the sovereign's monogram. Fashioning the hilts was entirely left to the user's discretion, and this must have resulted in decrees targeted at eccentricities appearing on officers' weapons (Dolleczek, 1896).

Officers' swords were first regulated in 1788 in their appearance, which, slightly modified, was then confirmed as Model 1811. From 1802 on it was also stipulated as the side weapon for army officers and doctors. The hilt was gilded with a heart-shaped shell, the scabbard was of leather. The sword was then modified by the regulation of 1837. It was similar to its forerunner, but the blade was single-edged. The shell was symmetrical, composed of two oval parts, the inner one being tilted. After the introduction of the sabre for the infantry officers, this sword remained the officers' army weapon until 1918.

The 18th-century position was similar in other countries as well. Not even in Prussia was the officer's sword regulated. However, the weapons used by officers can often be easily distinguished from the court varieties. The more massive and longer blades indicate that these are weapons designated for combat, and the hilts are of a more robust design and less decorated. The

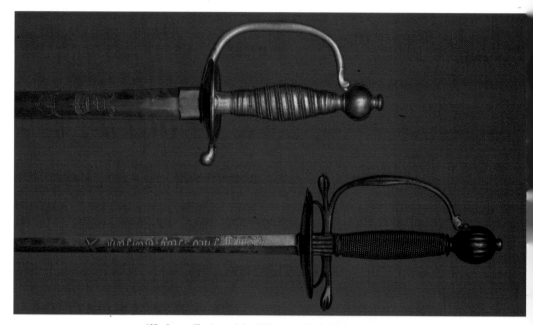

127 Saxon officer's sword, late 18th century. On the blade, engravings and *FAR* monogram (Friedrich August III, 1763–1806). Saxonian-Polish officer's sword, 1st third of 18th century. The blade or rhomboid cross-section, engraved and with gilded arms of Saxony plus inscription *FRIED. AUG. CHURFURST*. On the other side the arms of Poland/Lithuania and inscription *UND KONIG IN POHLEN.*

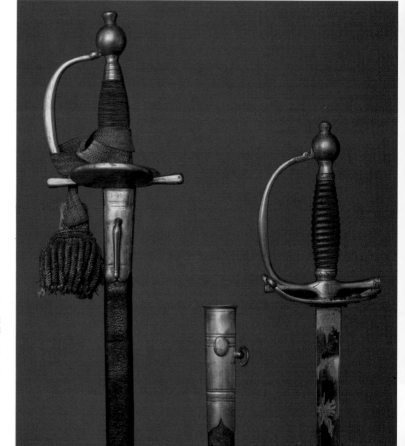

128 Austrian infantry officer's sword Model 1827 (later on also carried by army officials and clerks) with scabbard and sword knot.
Austrian officer's sword Model 1798/1811 with scabbard.
The blade blued and decorated with gilded ornaments.

110

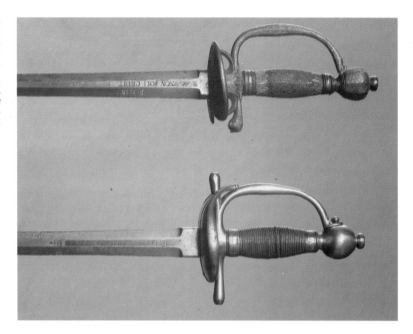

129 Prussian officer's sword, the blade 1724, the hilt after mid-18th century. On the blade, inscription *ME FECIT SOLINGEN 1724* on grip of brass, the hilt of brass with heart-shaped shell.

Prussian officer's sword, 1740. On the blade, *ME FECIT SOLINGEN* on the one side and *NON POLI CEDIT* on the other. All-brass hilt with kidney-shaped shells.

130 Russian officer's sword, Zlatoust 1823. The blade with Zlatoust-type engravings depicting classical motifs, marked *Zlatoust 1823 goda* (in Cyrillic) on the back edge, the hilt of gilded brass.

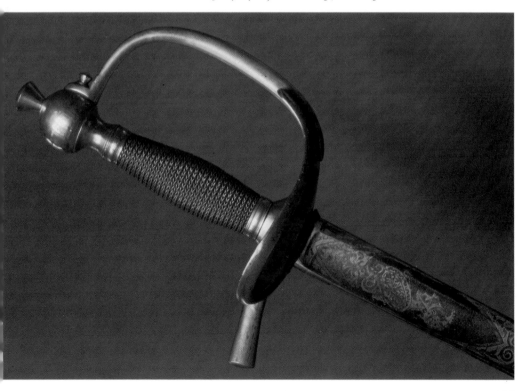

already mentioned evolutionary features hold true for officers' swords as well. The shell shaped as two opposite-positioned kidneys is typical of earlier weapons, whereas the heart-shaped variety appears on the later examples.

In France, too, infantry officers carried a spontoon and a sword. Whereas the spontoon was regulated in 1690 and 1710, the earliest sword regulation is dated to as late as 1767. The sword was to have the blade 703 mm long (somewhat longer for staff officers). The hilt of gilded brass was to be adjusted *à la mousquetaire*. This represented the hilt comprising the grip ending in pommel and cap, a simple knuckle-bow merging into cross-guard with guard bars and the oval-shaped shell. The sword regulated in 1779 and 1786 featured a grip wound with twisted wire and the shell shaped as two opposite-positioned kidneys. According to the 1812 regulation, the officer's sword was to have the blade 76 cm long, with a 200 mm blued section bearing the gilded inscription of *Vive l'Empereur*; the hilts were of brass gilded or silver-plated. The sword of 1818 for higher-ranking officers emphasized the symbols of the restored Bourbon monarchy. From 1821 on, the French army specified sabres instead of swords for infantry officers.

In the Russian army, Peter the Great stipulated swords for the whole army in 1708; after the introduction of the infantry sabre for troopers in 1741 the sword became an officer's weapon. The swords also featured the 'musketeer's' execution. In the first half of the 18th century their shells were mostly of the two opposite-situated kidneys shape; later on they assumed the heart-shaped outline. Russian officers' swords, too, included examples of ostentatious character, frequently with rich decoration of the blade.

The Dagger

The dagger is a short thrusting weapon suitable only for hand-to-hand combat. It is essentially a single-purpose weapon since its hunting application could be only incidental and its sporting application is virtually non-existent. Rapier- and dagger-fencing, flourishing in the 16th and the 17th centuries, was rather a kind of purpose-oriented training than a sport in today's sense. Yet the dagger was often a treacherous weapon, since it was easy to conceal.

As already mentioned, the dagger represents one of the earliest types of weapon intended for hand-to-hand combat. It appeared as early as in the Neolithic Age and in the Early Bronze Age. The not too numerous flint daggers seem to be imitations of metal daggers executed in stone. In the periods to follow, however, the occurrence of dagger-type weapons was sporadic. Other implements such as knives apparently found favour as thrusting weapons. A prominent weapon type which could be defined as a dagger did not appear till the late Middle Ages and it spread during the second half of the 13th century.

Basilard, 14th—15th century

131 Rondel dagger with disc-shaped pommel and cross-guard, 14th century. The blade is single-edged, the grip of horn provided with six rows of iron studs or nails. The pommel and the cross-guard of wood, covered with iron plate.

The dagger blade had to be adapted to the purpose of thrusting. That is why it is generally short and tapers abruptly. The blade cross-section is very varied. A rhombic cross-section is quite frequent but blades also exist which feature an asymmetrical rhomboid cross-section or a flattened hexagonal section. Blades with a single sharp edge becoming double-edged near the point are relatively frequent. The requirement of adequate thrusting penetration is also fulfilled with triangular and diamond section.

Dagger with disc-shaped finial and cross-guard, 15th century

132 Dagger with arched pommel, 14th century. Double-edged blade, the cross-guard and the pommel arched. In the cross-guard, a slot for the grip. In the pommel, two openings for nails.

113

133 Dagger of basilard type, Italy(?), second half of 14th century. Double-edged blade with two grooves. The tang grows into arched pommel of double band with an opening at each end.

One of the most frequent types of dagger of the late Middle Ages is the rondel dagger (*Scheibendolch*). This type appeared *c.* 1300 and was known throughout the Middle Ages and sometimes in the Renaissance period. The grip was barrel-shaped on the early examples, at other times shaped for the hand or even polygonal; it was made out of wood, horn, iron or brass plate. The pommel and the cross-guard are round discs, sometimes shaped around their circumference.

Daggers with a voluted pommel were less frequent. The band of metal forming the pommel is arched in such a way that it creates a part of an open circle. In the pictorial records of the period they are mentioned as early as about the mid-13th century; they occurred rarely in Central and Western Europe till the end of the 14th century. Daggers of the Ringknauf type (with a ringlet-shaped pommel) may be related to the previous kind; they originated about the mid-14th century, but went out of fashion about 1400.

The basilard-type daggers with the blade quite wide at the base but steeply narrowing towards the point ranked among Europe's most widespread kinds for about a hundred years from the mid-14th century till the mid-15th century. The pommel and the cross-guard of metal band are mostly straight, sometimes bent, and the pommel is sometimes provided with a narrow opening at the top. The grip is fitted with plates.

Another medieval dagger, named, after the shape of the cross-guard, the kidney or ballock dagger, the *Nierendolch*, was widespread all over Europe. In pictorial evidence it is attested to as early as *c.* 1300, in archaeological finds somewhat later, and it kept appearing as late as in the 16th century. The hilt is composed of the grip extending upwards, which grows up from

Nierendolch, 15th century

134 Ear dagger, Italy, 15th century. Double-edged blade, the grip of black horn, the circle of the pommel bone with metal plates beneath; bronze buttons in the middle.

Dagger with bronze grip,
14th century

135　Ballock dagger, Prague, turn of 15th and 16th century. Double-edged blade, the grip with flat cap and recognizable 'kidneys'.

136　*Cinquedea* dagger with scabbard, north Italy, *c.* 1500.
On the blade, spetum-shaped mark, grip covered with ivory (?) pierced rivet-heads. The cross-guard with etched and engraved decoration. The scabbard of leather with incised and impressed ornament.

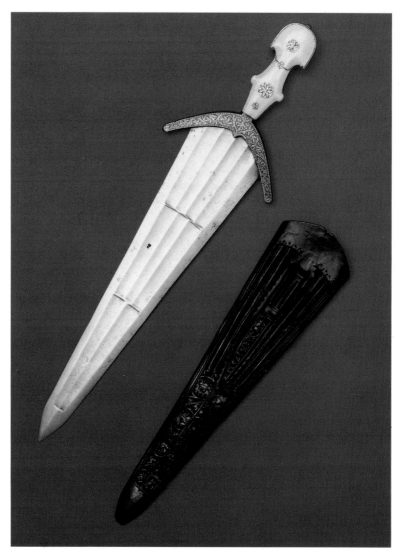

Cinquedea (*Ochsenzunge*),
Italy, *c.* 1500

Ear dagger (*Ohrendolch*),
15th century

the base consisting of two kidney-shaped objects. The blades are mostly single-edged, sometimes of the very narrow misericordia type. Grips are of wood or of horn but also of metal sheet, with the hollow kidney-shaped forms mentioned above.

However, the variation of dagger types is remarkable. Styling often copies the pommel and cross-guard design from swords of the period and the resulting execution on a smaller scale is relatively frequent. A globose pommel is the most usual type, but there also appeared other pommel shapes known from the various periods. This dagger-type appeared as early as *c.* 1300, but more frequently in the 15th and 16th centuries.

Ear-daggers rank among particular types of medieval daggers. The weapon is of Middle Eastern origin and reached Europe via Spain and Italy. The first traces can be recorded in Spain as early as the 14th century and somewhat later in Italy. The split pommel, growing out of the grip in the form of two round, obliquely positioned discs, is typical of it. The blades were originally double-edged, sometimes with an asymmetrical ricasso at the base. Grips and pommels were richly decorated. In Italy, the term of *pugnale alla stradiota* was used to describe these weapons, derived from the name *stradiots* — Albanian and Dalmatian horsemen in the service of the Venetian republic who favoured this dagger-type. This particular weapon remained in use in Italy during the whole 16th century.

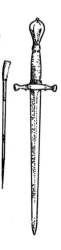

Another particular dagger-type, the origin of which is datable to the second half of the 15th century, is the so-called cinquedea, suitable for both cutting and thrusting. The blade is relatively broad at the base and quite long, and some experts rank the weapon among short swords. The name in a number of languages (*Ochsenzunge* in German, *langue de boeuf* in French, and the Italian expression *cinque dita* [five fingers]) apparently emphasized the blade width at the base. The blade is distinctly channelled: most frequently there are four channels. The short cross-guard is arched, the hafted grip is mostly fashioned so as to resemble a violin and provided with a semicircular-shaped pommel. The grips are mostly of rare wood, but there

Landsknecht dagger with
scabbard and furniture,
mid-16th century

116

also exist examples with hafts of ivory or gilded silver. The rivets originally
had heads fashioned in Gothic style and the sides were overlaid with bands
of brass or silver, often with niello-executed inscriptions. This variety was
common in Italy, but was also known in Spain, France and in Burgundy in
particular. It appeared about 1460 and stayed in vogue for about 60 years,
till the first quarter of the 16th century. Even prominent artists took part in
the rich decoration of some examples, e.g. Ercole dei Fideli from Ferrara.

The Swiss dagger also originated in the 15th century. Its rather wide
double-edged blade is provided with a grip which has a bow-shaped pommel
on one side and a cross-guard on the other end which is the reverse curve of
the pommel. This weapon became popular in the 16th century and the
scabbards decorated in rich pierced ornamental and figural reliefs are especially renowned, having been executed after designs by the foremost artists
of the period (Hans Holbein the Younger, Lucas van Leyden, and H. Ale-
degrever). Landsknecht daggers, too, were used as early as the 15th century,
but became common later, in the following century. The grip, extending
upwards, sometimes profiled, and robust scabbards, mostly balluster-struc-
tured, are characteristic.

Late Gothic sword-type daggers are a forerunner of the Renaissance
daggers. The prevailing Renaissance dagger-type is represented by a weapon with a straight or down-turned cross-guard. Quite often the cross-guards
were balluster-profiled. Dagger-pommel evolution followed the same path
as that of the Renaissance sword pommels. Cross-guards were reinforced
with a guard ring in the middle.

Fencing with the rapier and dagger, a significant novelty of the period,
influenced the evolution of the cross-guard in particular. Left-hand daggers
with arched cross-guard, the ends often bent forwards, were especially
suitable for this purpose, since the shape of the cross-guard ends made it
possible to catch the opponent's blade. Another left-hand dagger type of the

138 Left-hand dagger of Spanish type, Southern Europe, first half of 17th century. The blade double-edged in
its lower part, the ricasso profiled, with symmetrical openings. Straight cross-guard, the shell and the pommel
pierced in rich ornament.

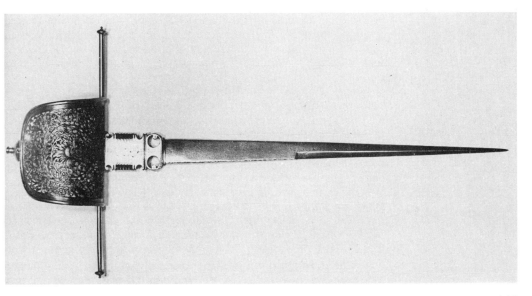

117

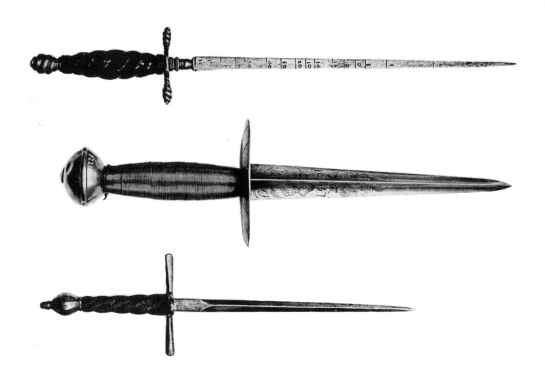

139 Tiny stiletto, first third of 17th century. Double-edged blade, the cross-guard with a little side ring.
Dagger, Germany (?), *c.* 1600. The blade cross-shaped in section, round cross-guard.
Gunner's stiletto, Central Europe, second half of 17th century. The blade three-faced with an engraved scale, the grip decorated with small nails.

17th century is the Spanish dagger. This weapon has a straight and long cross-guard with a triangular guard arching up to the pommel. The blade is often of asymmetrical type, one-edged down to half of its length (sometimes even more); the ricasso is profiled at the edges, sometimes with pierced openings. The guard, triangular in the first half of the 17th century, later on oval or almost round, was often pierced in the same way as the grip and sometimes the pommel. Many were decorated *en suite* with a matching rapier.

In the early 16th century, there appeared in Italy a tiny dagger with a straight, short, cross-guard called the *stiletto*. It was a dangerous weapon, since it was easy to conceal. It was widespread until the end of the 16th century. Another type linked with it was the so-called gunners' stiletto with a triangular blade showing the numerical data necessary for artillery calculations. Usually simple with a short cross-guard and the grip most often of horn, it appeared as late as the end of the 17th century.

In the same manner as the stiletto, another weapon, a multi-bladed dagger (*Springklingendolch*) was dangerous as well. Its double-edged blade was formed of arms which, using a spring mechanism, could be opened to an angle of 50−70°. Mostly it was a left-handed dagger with the cross-guard arching down prominently. In Italy these daggers appeared in the second half of the 16th century to spread more generally at the turn of the 16th and 17th centuries. After the mid-17th century their occurrence was rare.

Left-handed dagger, first half of 17th century

Dagger with dividers,
first half of 17th century

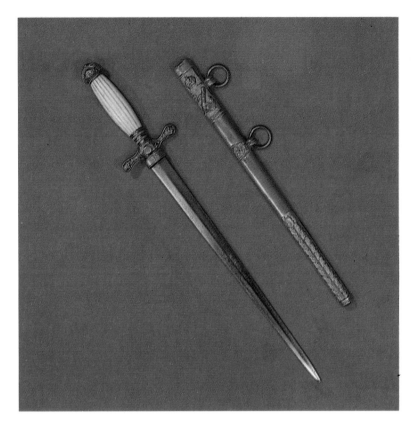

140 Austrian naval officer's dagger Model 1854 with scabbard. Etched ornament on the blade plus imperial arms and an anchor under a crown. The pommel shaped as Hungarian crown.

Dagger, 17th century

The Scottish dagger, called the dirk, can be ranked among typically national weapons such as the Swiss dagger. Its forerunners were represented by Scottish specimens derived from the ballock dagger which appeared about 1600. The dirk itself developed in the course of the 17th century. It is characterized by a strong single-edged blade and a prominently profiled hilt of barrel cross-section with a flattened pommel. In the course of time, the dirk became a symbol of honour and in the 18th century it was even sworn on. It also formed part of the weaponry of Scottish infantry. Even today, in the style that originated in the 18th century, it is a part of the dress uniform of Highland Light Infantry officers.

Dagger types did not change much in the 17th century compared with the preceding period, merely in the details of fashioning their individual parts which were influenced by the aesthetic view of the period. The significance of the dagger decreased from the 18th century on. In the 19th century it was still possible to encounter the masonic daggers, mostly in the stiletto fashion, whose cross-guard was usually shaped as crossbones and the pommel sometimes shaped as a human skull. The fact that in the course of the 19th century there appeared hidden daggers, concealed in a walking stick, is worth mentioning.

119

Naval daggers belong to this chapter, too. The Austrian naval dagger (*Borddolch*) Model 1827 featured a grip covered with ebony, the profiled cross-guard, and the pommel as well as the scabbard mounts adorned with a formalized anchor. Model 1854 used bone on the grip; the pommel was fashioned in the shape of the Hungarian crown and the metal parts were decorated in more ornate relief.

Daggers for naval officers were, in the course of the 19th century, introduced into the navies of most European nations, since the cramped space on ships prohibited the free movement of officers with a sabre hanging down from the belt.

In the 20th century the officer's dagger became an accessory to off-duty dress or gala uniform not only in the navy, but also in the airforce and often in the army. On special occasions it is even worn today.

STAFF WEAPONS

We attribute this term to edged weapons which require a shorter or a longer haft to be wielded and used. Both cutting and thrusting weapons fall within this category as well as weapons combining both functions and, finally, percussive weapons.

An attempt to differentiate these weapons according to the length of the staff would be unsatisfactory. It is true that the mace and its related varieties are exclusively weapons with a short haft. However, the length of the axe haft varies, for side by side with horsemen's axes with short handles there exist weapons for foot combat with long hafts. Consequently it seems advantageous not to classify these weapons according to the manner of wielding them, but according to their function, whether cutting or thrusting, and only within these categories would the manner of wielding be considered.

141   Axe with rear projections, 11th—12th century.
Slavonic axe with projections, 9th—10th century.

CUTTING STAFF WEAPONS

First of all the axe, some halberd types originating from the axe and finally
the couse fall within this group. A subgroup is represented by halberds with
primarily a cutting function but effective thrusting weapons as well.

The Axe, the Scythe and the Couse

The hatchet known as the *francisca* is generally ascribed to the early centuries A.D. It was an axe with an arched head and extended blade section
the cutting edge being oblique or arched. The handle formed an obtuse
angle with the axis of the axe. This weapon was used from the 5th century
onwards, particularly by the Franks, whence comes their name, but also by
other Germanic tribes, as a throwing weapon.

The axe also represented an important weapon for the Nordic nations, the
Vikings in particular, between the 8th and the 11th centuries. The broad axe
(*Bartaxt* — bearded axe) ranked among the basic types. It originated in the
7th century and was still in use in the Viking period. Its blade section is exten
ded downwards in the way that gave birth to its name; the cutting blade i
arched, but the upper side remains basically straight. Another type is represented by a relatively narrow axe with the blade section extending
symmetrically to both sides; small projections appeared on both sides of the
opening to take the handle. It was one of the weapons characteristic of the
Vikings from the 8th till the 10th century. Out of it, there apparently developed the axe with prominently convex cutting edge, whose blade part was
narrowed concavely into the neck, the opening for the handle featuring small

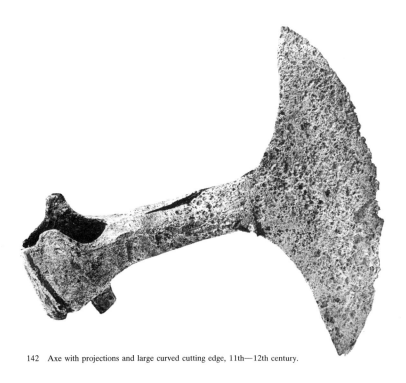

142   Axe with projections and large curved cutting edge, 11th—12th century.

122

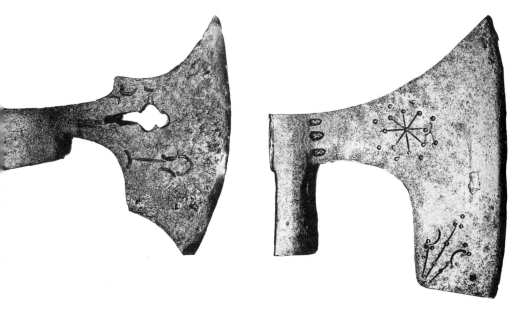

143 Axe with profiled head and curved cutting edge, Bohemia, 14th century. On the neck, punched mark in elongated recess representing upper part of a sword with circular pommel and short cross-guard. Remnants of engraved decoration on the blade.

144 Broad-axe with engraved decoration on the blade, 15th century. On the neck, three punched marks.

145 Throwing axe with a socket (the handle reconstructed), Bohemia, mid-15th century.

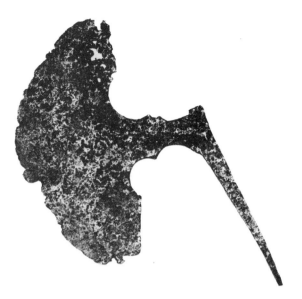

146 Throwing axe with a tang to be inserted into the handle. Bohemia, early 16th century.

projections. This type of broadaxe (*Breitaxt*) was used in great number well up till the 11th century, and even later in Scandinavia. Both the above-mentioned types were among equipment favoured by the Vikings and were decorated with inlay and overlaying with precious metals. The famous Bayeux tapestry, depicting the conquest of England by the Normans in the 11th century, attests to the fact that broadaxes of this type were not only part of Norman weaponry, but that they were used in England as well.

The other area where the axe played an important role in the warrior's equipment was the Slavonic territory in Central and Eastern Europe. At least from the 8th century onwards, the axe, together with the lance and the bow, ranked among the basic armoury of Slavonic warriors. However, it appears also in the graves of the equestrians, members of the privileged body of retainers, side by side with the sword which was their principal weapon. It is either an axe with straight or slightly curved narrow head with oblique or curved cutting edge, or the type where the blade part reaches downward into a prominent extension (*Bartaxt* — the bearded axe). Both types feature triangular extensions on both sides of the opening to take the haft (probably for better stabilization of the setting), and a blunt, flat rear part. Numerous finds attest to the occurrence of both types in the 9th and 10th centuries and even later.

Extensions remained an attribute of a battleaxe, particularly in Central Europe, for a long time. In the 11th — 12th centuries there also appeared an axe similar to the Viking broadaxe with arched cutting edge symmetrically extended, and, of course, with prominent extensions. Another type from approximately the same period is an axe with a narrow head extending (widening) forwards and the cutting edge slightly arched. By the opening to take the handle lobes appeared again but this time on the rear part.

From the 12th — 13th centuries onwards, the opening to take the handle was transformed into a shorter and subsequently a longer socket facilitating strengthening of the staff. On the later axes, of a lighter, probably equestrian type, there appeared, in the 14th century, an aesthetic influence in the cutting out of the rear part of the head and in decorating it with grooves or sometimes with piercing, most often shaped as an elongated trilobe.

More frequent, however, particularly in the equipment of the warriors on foot, were broadaxes as recorded by the pictorial records of the 14th century. These axes have — as attested by the surviving 14th- and 15th-centuries specimens — usually a short handle set into the socket, a short neck and a sizeable blade-part, generally straight in the upper outline and considerably extended downwards, with a curved cutting-edge. From the evolutionary point of view it should be mentioned that these axes of the 15th century had the socket closed at the top and the blade section extended upwards somewhat including the cutting edge.

Weapons of this kind are also included, because of the short handle, as throwing axes (*Wurfaxt, Wurfbeil*). This sort of hatchet used to be considered in earlier literature to be a typically Czech weapon of the late Middle Ages. This may be doubted, since so far only five specimens have been discovered in Czech and Slovak collections, whereas in German and Hungarian museum collections several dozen are included. Two basic types can be recognized; the first has no socket and a pointed tang is used to attach it to the handle and it occurs from as early the turn of the 14th and the 15th centuries until as late as the early 16th century. The second type features a normal staff inserted into the socket. The earlier axes have the head of an almost almond shape with a spike at the back; the later ones are commonly of the broadaxe (bearded) type, sometimes with the upper front end extended into a pointed shape. The later *Wurfbeil* modifications with an almost S-shaped narrow head are datable to the end of the 15th and to the 16th century, and are known mostly from Bavarian collections.

However, axes provided with short handles did not disappear in the period to follow. Their combat function was to a certain degree limited to Eastern Europe, to Poland, Hungary and Russia. From the 16th and the 17th century a number of axes of the type of the Hungarian *fokosh* or the Polish *topor* were preserved. Often they were combined with pistols. Many of them, however, became simply ceremonial in the 17th century, with the

147 Axe of a mining dignitary, Saxony, 1718. On the bone covering the haft engraved scenes from a miner's life.

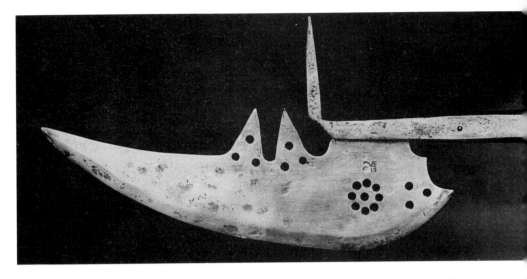

148 Axe for combat on foot with a hook and teeth. Germany, *c.* 1500. On the perforated blade, a punched mar

Bardiche, 17th century

cutting edge, usually decorated and pierced, mostly blunted instead o
sharp-edged.

However, in discussing the axe we must not forget to mention the rusti
varieties from Moravia and Slovakia, the shepherd's hatchet-stick. A hatch
et was a tool as well as a weapon, and also a part of folk costume. Up till th
19th century, there also appeared miners' hatchets. Outstanding specimen:
particularly dating to the 17th and 18th centuries, come first of all from th
Saxony mining area.

In addition to the horsemen's axe with a short handle there also appearec
as early as the late Middle Ages, axes on long staves designed for combat o
foot and wielded by both hands. The Flemish godendag, mentioned in th
early 14th century, must have belonged to this category. However, its actus
shape still remains uncertain. In the course of the 15th century we encounte
in Central Europe, particularly in southern Germany and perhaps in north
ern Italy, too, axes on long staves with the head of an almost almond-shap
extended into a point upwards and with a wide neck. Engravings of th
tree-pattern type often appeared on the blade-section. At the turn of th
15th and the 16th centuries the head adopted a more complex shape wit
spiked projections at the rear part and with a hook coming rectangularl
from it. The head was sometimes indented and decorated with perforation
on the bottom part.

At the end of the 15th century there also originated axes of the so-calle
bardiche type with a narrow arched blade section whose lower end was fixe
to the staff. This type of weapon, of Russian origin, and used by infantry an
town guards from the 15th till the 17th century, was also favoured in Polan
and in some Nordic countries, particularly in Sweden and in Finland.

The Scottish weapon called the locher or lochaber axe was of a simila
style. The head was of an arched shape of almost crescent outline whos
lower back edge, in the same way as the *bardiche*, was fixed to the pole. Th
curved hook coming out from the top of the handle is typical of this weapor
This axe was used in Scotland, but also in England, from the end of th
Middle Ages till the 17th century.

Battleaxe for foot soldiers,
c. 1500

Another type of axe for combat on foot is represented in the second half of the 15th century by weapons combining a hammer with an axe (*Mordaxt*). Their head features a blade section of almost triangular shape with straight cutting edge. The inner edges were originally concave; opposite to the head there was a hammer with a rectangular plate. These weapons, sometimes complemented with a vertical and lateral spikes,

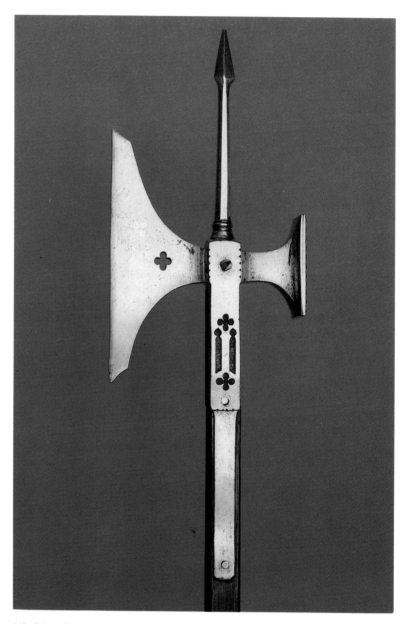

149   Poleaxe, France or Switzerland, last quarter of 15th century. Three groups of circles inlaid with copper on the axe, the hammer with diamond cut and copper band. The four-sided point on an octagonal neck.

Couse, second half of 15th century

150 Bill with a hook and a spike, the sickle-shape hook incomplete, *c.* 1400.

Glaive, *c.* 1500

used to be classified as being of French origin (J. Mann, *Wallace Collection Catalogue*, 1962). According to Wegeli (*Inventar der Waffensammlung des Bernischen Historischen Museums III*, 1939) they appeared in 15th-century Switzerland as an infantry weapon.

Some halberd types, with the spike replaced with curved sabre blades, were exclusively cutting weapons (*Säbelhelmbarte*). They appeared towards the end of the 16th century in Upper Austria and were used in relatively large numbers in Bavaria during the Thirty Years' War. The Austrian type features a fully developed axe on the halberd, which is crescent-shaped with a hook on the opposite side. The long curved sabre blade is the main characteristic of the Bavarian type whereas only the axe remained from the halberd with a relatively short neck and arched cutting edge.

Even the scythe should be ranked among weapons with a cutting effect. This farming tool, if fixed to the handle as its extension, could serve as an effective although crude weapon, and was often used by peasant insurgents from the 16th till the 19th century. In the Polish insurrections of 1794, 1831

151 Sabre halberd, Bavaria, second quarter of 17th century.

152 Glaive of palace guard of Ferdinand I (1526—54), *c.* 1550. Etched and engraved decoration with imperial arms and the letter *F.*

Glaive, second half of 16th century

Italian halberd, first half of 16th century

and even 1864 whole units, called the *Kossinierze,* equipped with these combat-scythes, participated.

The couse, in its advanced appearance predominantly a herald's weapon of the 16th and later centuries, was undoubtedly derived from the upright-positioned scythe, but its origins are somewhat different. It originated in France and was used in Flanders in the second half of the 15th century, known as a couse or *vogue française.* It was provided with a knife-like long blade with the back edge sharpened. However, this type was soon discarded. The 16th century couse featured a rather wide blade with arched cutting edge and a straight, blunted back edge from which the neck formed a socket. It was not too common as a combat weapon; however, in the richly decorated style it was a favourite weapon of the palace guards of European courts from the 16th till the 18th century. In the case of palace guards of Austrian and Bavarian rulers, called the *Hatschiere,* it remained in use till as late as the early 20th century.

The glaive (*Gläfe*) was mainly a herald's weapon. The blade featured an arched cutting edge elongated into a point. On the blunt back-edge there was usually a hook, straight, curved or crescent-shaped, and on the base of the blade there were triangular projections. After the mid-16th century this weapon, too, was of an exclusively decorative function as indicated by the frequently appearing wavy blades.

Another staff weapon, the bill, is related to the couse. Sometimes it is called the Italian halberd (*roncone* in Italian, *guisarme* in French). The long sharp point indicates that it had a thrusting function, too, but its principal purpose was cutting with the arched, later somewhat angled, blade, and the sickle-shaped hook at the foot of the blade was mainly intended to cut through the tendons of the enemy's mounts (that is where its German name comes from) and so immobilize them. From the written records it is apparent that in Italy it existed perhaps as early as the 13th century. It is also mentioned in connection with the troops of Charles the Brave in 1476 and it was in vogue practically all through the 16th century. The usual form of this weapon was still provided with a short blade only, but with a prominent hook. This variant was apparently still used in the first half of the 15th century.

The Halberd

The medieval staff weapon called the halberd was of a predominantly cutting character, but is was possible to use it for thrusting. Its origin can ◗ found in Switzerland where its basic shape played an important role in t◗ liberation campaign. It was most effective in the well-known battles ◗ Morgarten in 1315 and at Sempach in 1386. Later on, too, the halbe◗ remained a significant weapon of the Swiss infantry, but it was widesprea◗ throughout Europe.

The earliest type is a rectangular-shaped axe with a straight cutting edg◗ elongated into a spike and fastened to the staff by means of two socke◗ Somewhat later, after 1400, a rear spike appeared. The Swiss halberd cha◗ ged in the course of the 15th century. First of all, a socket appeared on t◗ lower side of the axe into which the staff was inserted. Later on, the late◗ spike was forged right out of the axe head, and, finally, the thrusting spi◗ had its final section in a prominent rhomboid or even rhombic cross-sectio◗ The next evolutionary feature of the halberd towards the end of the 15th a◗ in the early 16th century was the moving of the spike from the vertical a◗ of the staff. The cutting edge was becoming oblique, and the spike w◗ further gradually elongated. In the mid-16th century the spike length b◗ came three times the length of the cutting edge of the axe which also a◗ quired a different shape. There appear axes with cutting edges both conca◗ and also convex so as to achieve a half-moon shape. The edges of both t◗ axe and the hook are profiled and the head, including the hook, pierce◗

From the second half of the 16th century onwards, following the increa◗

Halberd, end of 15th
century

Halberd, mid-15th century

153   Swiss halberd with rear hook and prominent spike. On the blade, punched mark of rough five-pointed s◗

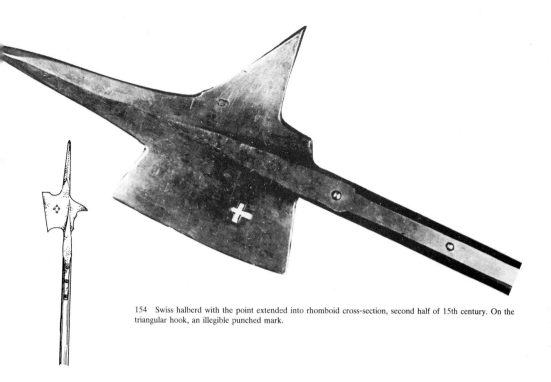

154 Swiss halberd with the point extended into rhomboid cross-section, second half of 15th century. On the triangular hook, an illegible punched mark.

Halberd, c. 1520

155 Halberd with a long spike, the edges of both the blade and the hook profiled, Germany, second half of 16th century.
Halberd with angled cutting edge and the point offset from the centre-line of the staff, Germany, first half of 16th century.

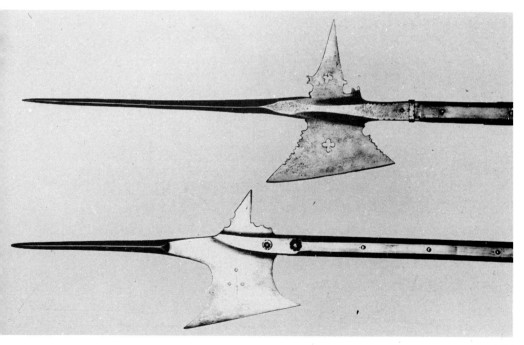

ing number of musketeers in the infantry and with the improved efficiency of their fire, the numbers of soldiers equipped with the halberd decreased and after 1600 the halberd gradually disappeared. The halberd remained in service in French infantry to distinguish sergeants, as stipulated by the regulation of 1683, and was still to be found as late as the first half of the 18th century. From 1766 on the halberd ceased to be mentioned in this function. In the Austrian infantry, too, a halberd-type weapons, called the *Kurzwehr* indicated corporals and NCOs according to the regulation of 1705. There too, it disappeared entirely in the mid-18th century.

Decorated examples of halberds featuring rich etching, engraving and

156   Halberd with a moon-shaped axe and a hook, long spike with a knob, Central Europe, late 16th century.

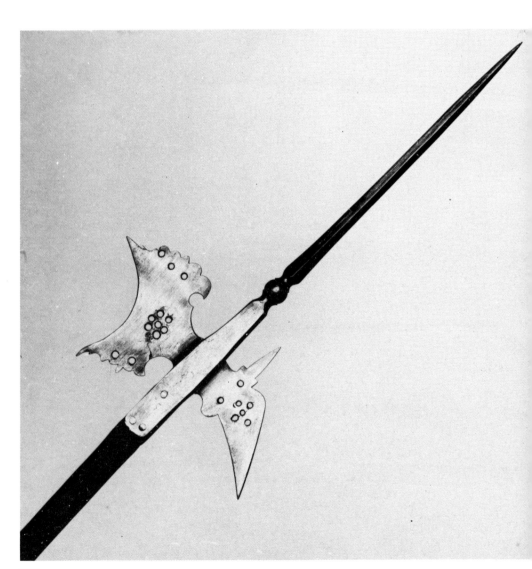

157 Italian halberd with spike and hooks, the mark of scorpio on the blade, northern Italy, probably Milan, *c.* 1500.

gilding, remained, however, for a long time to come, and not only in the 18th century, the weapon of palace guards in various European courts. Monograms and arms of the rulers or rich Church and secular magnates disclose not only the provenance, but the date of the individual specimens.

Halberd, second half of 16th century

158 Herald's halberd with etched and chiselled ornamentation, the gilded arms of Saxony, Saxony, early 17th century.

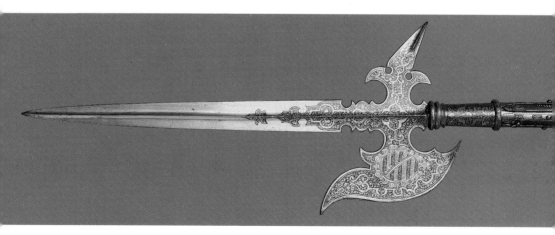

THRUSTING STAFF WEAPONS

We include the spear and the lance among thrusting weapons, along with other weapons derived from the lance, such as the runka and the spetum, the awlspear and later on the spontoon.

The Spear and the Lance

Both the spear and the lance are basically simple thrusting weapons with the point set on a long staff. Their origin is of a very early date. It cannot be ruled out that some larger flint heads or larger heads of bone known from Neolithic finds were spear parts. A developed spear point can be found as early as the Bronze and Iron Ages. In both cases the weapon should be considered as a dual-purpose one, suitable for both combat and the chase. Distinguishing between the two kinds is problematic in the earlier periods. Generally it holds true that the spear was provided with a narrow point, a longer neck and a narrow socket, and so with a thin and lightweight staff.

Framea, 5th—6th century

159   Spear of framea type, 5th—7th century.

This was connected with the fact that both in hunting and in combat the spear represented a throwing weapon which, in the hands of a skilled user, could hit the target over a relatively long distance.

The spear was a weapon of warriors on foot at the beginning of the Middle Ages and during its early phases. There were two basic types. The first is the framea featuring an elongated rhomboid head of, most frequently, rhombic cross-section with a neck running smoothly into a long and narrow socket. The other type, the ango, had the head formed as a spike with backward-running winged projections, a long neck and a conical socket. Throwing spears were in general use in the early periods of European history, particularly among Germanic tribes and the Franks, but also, much later,

160   Spear of barbed type, 6th—8th century.

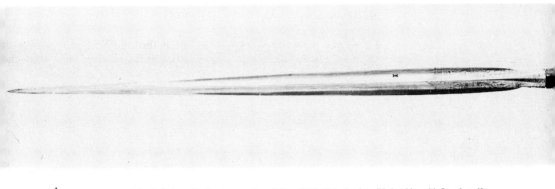

161 Awlspiess of Italian type, northern Italy, *c.* 1500. Ridged point, gilded etching with figural motifs.

Schefflin, *c.* 1500

Lance with winged projec-
tions, 8th—10th century

among the Vikings. From the 8th century on this type was becoming out-dated and disappeared entirely later on.

In a transient way, towards the end of the 15th and in the course of the 16th century, there appeared in infantry equipment a throwing weapon called the *Schefflin* (javelin). This weapon had a narrow, long and profiled head with a short socket on a lighter staff. It is relatively rare.

The lance is a weapon of both horsemen and warriors on foot in hand-to-hand combat. The early medieval spears from the 8th—11th century are typical, with relatively long knife-styled heads, and narrow, conical and sometimes edged sockets. The socket featured short, triangular projections set bilaterally (the wings). Lances shaped in such a way were still general weapons of both mounted men and infantry in Europe as late as the end of the 11th century, even though spearheads without projections can be discovered in archaeological finds.

The period of the late Middle Ages is also the period of marked differentiation between the infantry and the cavalry lance. In the 13th century the lance heads were shorter than before, but bigger and the sockets of larger diameter attest the thicker staves being used. A short but robust head, most frequently of a rhomboid or rhomboidal section, with not too long a neck and a conical socket, are characteristic features of a 14th- and 15th-century horseman's lance. Side by side, there also appeared leaf-shaped heads of rhombic cross-section. The staff, of considerable length, was provided with a vamplate, a round shield to protect the hand in the place where the lance was grasped. The long and heavy lance called for other provisions, too. From the end of the 14th century the staves of horsemen's lances were provided with hollowed-out space in their bottom third sections to allow a firm grip. In the first part of the 15th century there appeared a lance-rest for the breastplate which facilitated holding the long and heavy lance in an appropriate position.

162 Lance-head with winged projections, Bohemia, 10th—11th century.

135

163 Head of an equestrian lance, the point rhomboidal in cross-section, the socket conical, 14th century.

The tournaments necessitated the creation of other lance-head shapes, of which the coronet-shaped head is the most interesting, with a very short but strong conical socket and the head split into three or four blunted arms.

Horsemen's lances and their heads did not change much in the course of the 16th century, but towards its end they gradually disappeared from the heavy cavalry. An exception was the Polish heavy cavalry called hussaria (not to be mistaken for the hussars, light cavalry of Hungarian origin). However, the lance was preserved in the equipment of East European light cavalrymen, particularly in Poland and the Ukraine. From the 1730s onwards, there were attempts to introduce the Polish cavalry type with their lances into a number of European armies. In Prussia there was an uhlan regiment established in 1740–41, which, however, was transformed into a hussar one as early as 1743. Towards the end of the 18th century, cavalry equipped with a lance, the uhlans or the lancers, were added to most European armies.

Uhlan lances were mostly of a simple shape. Heads provided with ridges or of rhombic cross-section and with sockets most frequently complemented with langets were fitted on to a wooden staff. The Austrian uhlan lance Model 1798 and 1798/1849 was formed into an almost round shape resembling a little onion under the point. This fashion also appeared on the Bavarian lance Model 1854. Colonial armies of some nations were using lances provided with a pole of bamboo as in England, France and Belgium.

France after 1871 and Austria after 1884 discarded lances from their equipment, but after Germany introduced the lance for the entire cavalry in 1889 (replaced in 1893 by a lance of steel tube), France re-equipped all cavalry except the cuirassiers with the lance. The lance did not prove itself during World War I, and this was its final appearance in most armies. The lance with a small flag carried by Polish uhlans at the beginning of the war in 1939 was an isolated anachronism.

164 Head of an equestrian lance, leaf-shaped, Bohemia, first half of 14th century. The neck and the socket inlaid with bands of yellow metal and decorated with scale-engraved decoration.

Lance, 14th – 15th century

165   Head of a tournament lance split into four points, short conical socket, Bohemia, 15th century.

Landsknecht lance, first half
of 16th century

Before discussing the pike for infantry and its evolution, it is necessary to mention an infantry weapon which, although of territorially limited significance, is extremely interesting as far as typology is concerned. It is the awlspear (*Ahlaspiess*), characteristic of Bohemia and Austria possibly already at the end of the 14th century but certainly in the 15th century. Its very long and narrow head of square cross-section is of a prominently thrusting character. Its relatively short staff is inserted into a concave socket. Most specimens are provided with a round shield around the neck. The weapon is known from Bohemian pictorial records of the 1420s and Viennese written records of 1444 and 1497. The latter evidence shows the weapon as ranking among the basic equipment of the city's militia.

166   Infantry lance-head, 13th – 14th century.
The point of an awl, fragment, Bohemia, 14th century.
Infantry lance-head of rhomboid cross-section, conical socket, 14th – 15th century.

137

167 Infantry lance-head with reinforced point, Bohemia, second half of 15th century. Punched mark of cros: with arms of the same length in square-shaped recess.

Pike, 17th century

The infantry pike of the late Middle Ages was generally larger and heavie: than the equestrian varieties. The head was most frequently leaf-shaped reinforced in the middle, and changing into a generally conical socket which was nailed to the haft. The earlier examples of the 13th and 14th centuries were lighter and those of the 14th—15th centuries more robust. The overal length of the 15th-century infantry lance-heads (30—40 cm) as well as thei: long sockets reveal that they were a mighty weapon of a considerable effec- tiveness.

In the second half of the 15th century the penetrating power of the poin: was further enhanced by shaping it into a tetrahedral cross-section over a length of several centimetres.

In the 14th and 15th centuries there appeared large heads with a winged point, a very long neck and with a socket or tang to fix it to the pole. Thes: heads could be utilized either as lance-heads (as documented by illumina- tions of the period), but chiefly they were for missiles for ballistas and catapults. These mighty siege weapons used against fortresses utilized thes: heads as carriers of incendiary substances.

In the infantry tactics based particularly on the Swiss pattern, that is i: mass formation, side by side with halberds, long lances — pikes — wer: gaining significance. In the course of the Burgundian Wars of the 1470s a new tactic was deployed in which pikes created a thick and almost impenet- rable barrier. Their length (about 5 m) allowed not only the front rank bu: the rear ones as well to become engaged. The pike also played an importan: role with the German Landsknechts.

This weapon originated in Italy in the 14th century, but gained signifi- cance only in Swiss and Landsknecht infantry units in the 15th and 16th centuries. The head as a rule was not too large, the overall length including the socket amounted to 15—18 cm and featured diverse shapes. The poin: was most often leaf-shaped, of rhombic cross-section and with a socket, sometimes with langets. In the 17th century the heads were tetrahedral, too, with a socket and long langets. The pike was a weapon of significance throughout the 17th century. Only after the introduction of flintlock mus- kets provided with a bayonet did it start losing its status. At about 1700 (i: 1720 in Sweden) the pike disappeared from infantry equipment.

unting spear, 16th—17th
ntury

168 Head of infantry pike, second half of 16th century.
Head of infantry pike, mid-17th century.

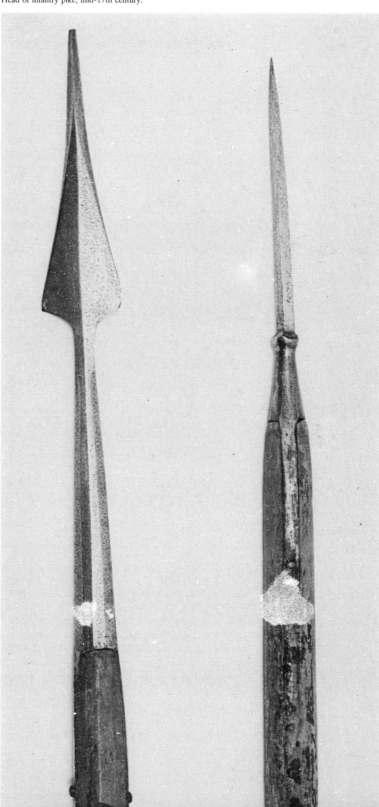

The Knebelspiess, the Partisan and the Spontoon

The weapon called the *Knebelspiess* is reminiscent of the shape of the infantry lance from the second half of the 15th century. It usually features a long and rather wide head of rhomboid cross-section, basically shaped as an elongated triangle, but under the neck, at the beginning of the socket, there are bilateral triangular projections resembling those of the Carolingian lance. Evidently it was a considerably effective weapon and it remained in use till the 16th century, often for hunting purposes.

The partisan, too, which originated at the end of the 15th century in Italy, had evolved from the lance. In the early stage it was a long tongue-shaped

Partisan, second half of 15th century

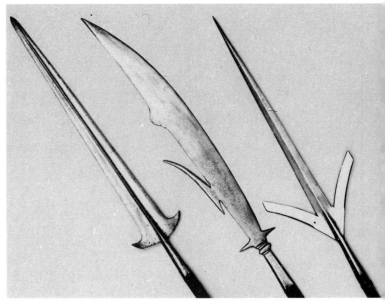

170 Partisan with a tongue-shaped head with central ridge and moon-shaped base.
Italian glaive with rear hook, early 16th century.
Runka with rhomboid head and arched flukes, northern Italy, early 16th century.

head fashioned as an elongated triangle with rather long neck and socket. From the beginning of the 16th century the base of the point over the neck was gradually extended into a moon-shaped formation. The partisan as a combat weapon did not stay in use for long, but it became a favourite weapon of heralds and palace guards. As early as the end of the 16th century there appeared a specific partisan type, the linstock, with a wide pointed blade and two arched arms ending in jaws to hold the match. Linstocks were mostly plain; however, from time to time some were richly decorated.

◀ 169 Winged spear, with leaf-shaped head and two flukes under the neck, 15th century.

From the end of the 17th century we encounter partisans with a relatively short head decorated with arms or monograms of rulers or with military symbols. They were weapons or rather marks of distinction indicating infantry officers' commanding capacity. Their scaled-down and simplified versions used to be called spontoons. They were introduced, according to the regulation of 1690, in France, and in Prussia they replaced the partisan during the reign of Frederick II. The Prussian type with a short and wide head reduced to an almost round base at the bottom was pierced with an opening in the base. A cross-piece grew out bilaterally from the neck, the concave socket being profiled with ridges. The Prussian spontoon-type was adopted by other German states, too, but also by other countries such as Denmark, the Netherlands and Russia. The spontoon was discarded in 1807 in Prussia; in England not before 1827.

Partisan, 17th century

171 Artillery partisan, South Germany, end of 16th century.
Leaf-shaped head with pierced section beneath, engraved and relief decoration.

172 Austrian officer's partisan, mid-18th century. Gilded imperial arms and monograms *MT* (Maria Theres[a]) and *FCI* (Franciscus Caesar I).

173 Prussian sergeant's spontoon, mid-18th century. Engraved monogram *FR* (Frederick II); the name of t[he] regiment on the base worn and only partly legible.

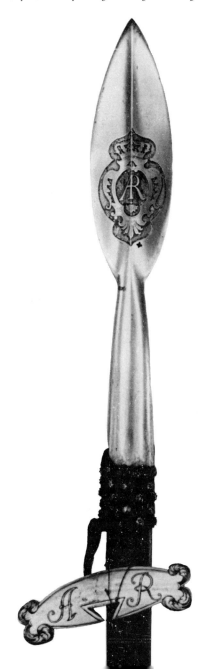

Other Types of Thrusting Staff Weapons

Other types of thrusting staff weapons developed from the lance. The runka or *corseque* can be ranked among them. It originated in 15th-century Italy, starting at the end of the century. It appeared in France, and it spread just a little north of the Alps. The runka features on the neck under the point a bilateral projection, sometimes rather large and profiled, with the points

174   Boar-spear with leaf-shaped head, Saxony, *c.* 1725.
The cross-bar held by a leather strap. Monogram of August the Strong on both the head and the cross-bar.

Runka, late 15th – 16th century

Spetum, 15th – 16th century

Awl, 15th century

bending upwards. The other version of the weapon is represented by the spetum or *Frilauer Spiess*, where the projections running out from the neck are bent (arched) down so that their points are directed downwards. The weapon is territorially limited to northern Italy and the adjacent Austrian regions where it appeared from the end of the 15th till the second half of the 16th century.

175   Mancatcher with springs, 16th—17th century.

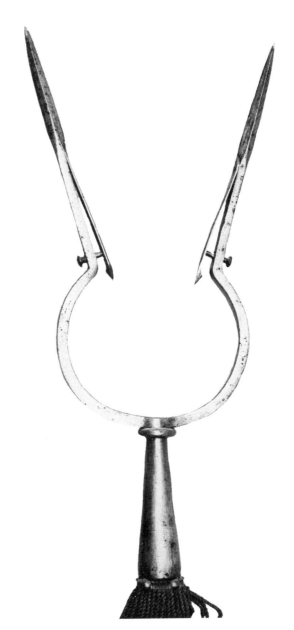

Weapons with a wide leaf-shaped head, usually reinforced with a ridge in the middle, and equipped with a prominent neck and a socket from which a cross-piece grew were used for hunting from the 16th till the 18th century. The cross-piece was mostly of bone, fixed with leather straps. On simpler examples, a plain cross-piece of iron can also be found. The staff was originally bound with leather straps to achieve the firmest grip. It was the so-called boar-spear (*Sauspiess, Saufeder*). Luxury weapons of this kind belonging to the hunting equipment of princes and other feudal magnates were often decorated on the head and on the cross-piece and also provided with tassels in the owner's heraldic colours.

Richly decorated heads of similar shape, that is, a wide leaf-shape with a ridge, were also used by the 16th-century officials. They could be found at the court of Henry VII of England in the early 16th century, but also in the equipment of Emperor Ferdinand I's guard (*c.* mid-16th century).

Starting with the second half of the 15th century, there also occasionally appeared combat forks (*Sturmgabel*), as a rule with two strong spikes, rather like an ordinary peasant's pitchfork. They were designed both for combat and for sentry duty; there also appeared examples combined, halberd style, with an axe, in the second half of the 16th century.

The so-called mancatcher, *Menschenfänger*, should be classed with edged weapons, too. Two spikes run out of a circular base in much the same way as in the combat fork, but often provided with a leaf-spring. The idea was to get the adversary's neck in between the spikes and catch it in the circular section which was sometimes provided with pyramid-shaped spikes on the inner circumference. This strange weapon was already mentioned at the turn of the 15th and the 16th centuries but it also appeared even later.

PERCUSSIVE STAFF WEAPONS

Both weapons achieving the desired effect and employing either a sho
handle or a longer staff fall into this category. The first subdivision inclu
the mace, the war-hammer and some clubs; the other the spiked 'Morni
star' (*Morgenstern*) and the combat flail, or war-hammers and clubs or
long pole designed for combat on foot.

Man discovered percussive weapons at the very beginning of his ex
tence. A simple wooden club or a fist-wedge of stone were weapons,

176 Mace head, the flanges inserted into slots on the socket and copper-soldered there. Prague, first quarter
15th century.

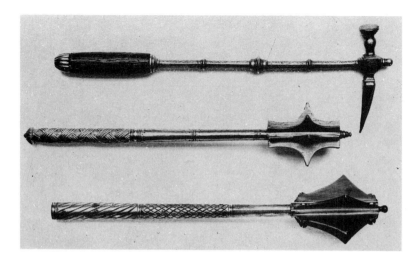

177 War hammer with profiled handle, the grip covered with wood, Central Europe, first half of 16th century.
Mace with profiled flanges and the grip with entwined decorated surface, Italy, *c.* 1500.
Mace with profiled flanges, the grip with spirally grooved surface, northern Italy, first quarter of 16th century.

matter whether used for hunting or in hand-to-hand combat. Evolution then progressed through to a stone hammer fixed to a wooden handle and from the axe/hammer combination of stone eventually to weapons of bronze and iron.

The Mace

Various kinds of clubs serving as a combat weapon appeared in the early Middle Ages. Pictorial records of the 11th century, such as the Bayeux tapestry, depict both foot soldiers and horsemen with clubs or maces. The latter use some kind of elongated pear-shaped club but no more details about it can be deduced from the tapestry. The foot soldiers use another weapon with a trefoil-shaped head. A rudimentary form of a further weap-

178 Decorative mace, Milan, 1608. The round head with pyramid-shaped spikes encrusted with gold. Among rich ornaments, personifications of the seven planets.

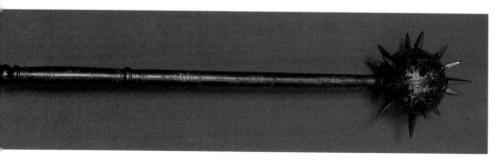

147

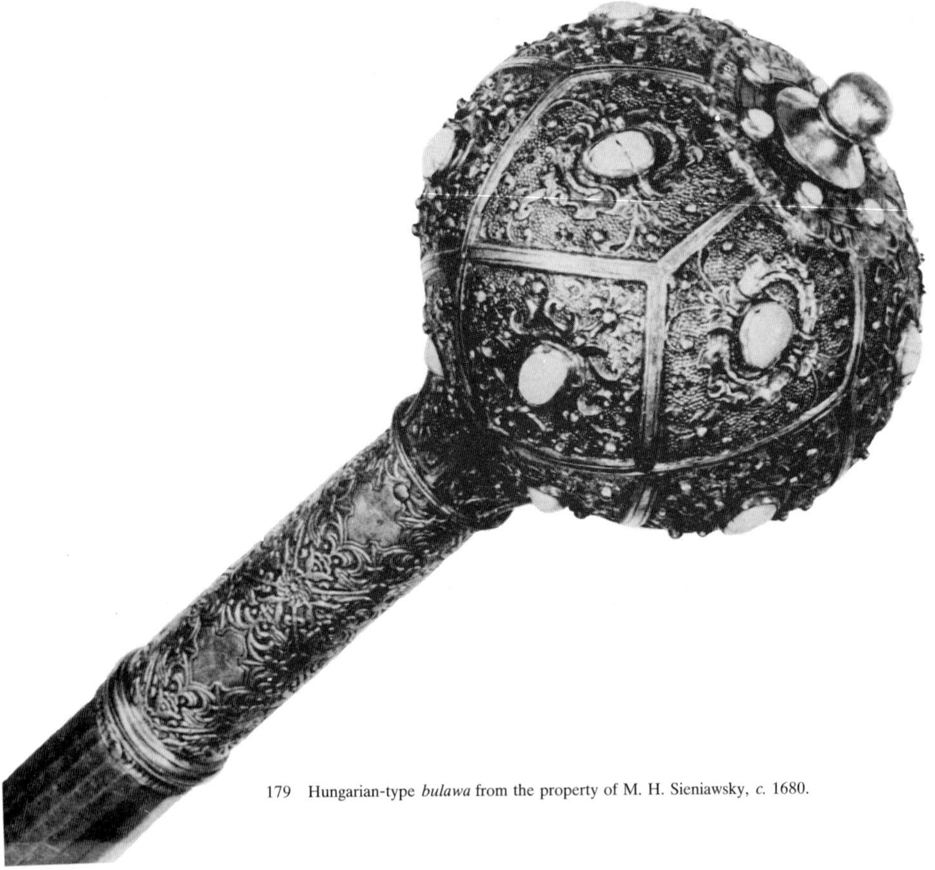

179 Hungarian-type *bulawa* from the property of M. H. Sieniawsky, *c.* 1680.

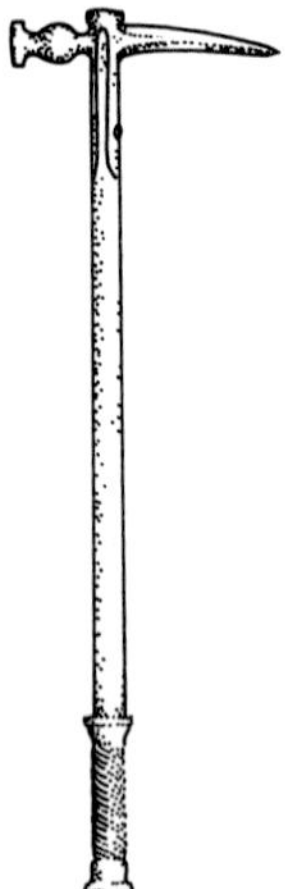

Hammer-type mace, 16th century

on, apparently a spiked club, is documented in pictorial records fro end of the 13th century. It is a case of a weapon with a barrel-shaped possibly a metal one — of iron, provided with three rows of spikes.

From the end of the 13th and in the 14th century, finds in various tions in Europe — e.g. in Sweden, Bohemia, Moravia, and Slovak contain mace heads mostly with three rows of pyramid-shaped spikes socket. The outer rows of spikes are of half-pyramid shape, the ones i inner row of full-pyramid shape. The heads, mostly of bronze, the Bohe specimen of iron being an exception, are provided with a barrel-sh socket for insertion of a handle, probably of wood.

In the course of the 14th century there evolved another mace-type the head provided with longitudinal flanges, sometimes forged, m however, copper-soldered to a short tubular socket. At the beginning 15th century there were from six to eight flanges and their shape wa veloping from a simple trapezoid into more complex outlines. At the tom, the flange at first bears on the socket directly; later on by means of or a base lug. A wooden haft was inserted into a relatively short socket was at first opened at the top, later on ending with a knob. At abo mid-15th century the socket grew longer to finally produce an all-iron either tubular or faceted; there also appeared heads with ten to t flanges. Late Gothic maces of *c.* 1500 feature flanges profiled in a

nmer-type mace, 16th tury

complex way, spiked on the hitting side and often pierced on the flat surface. Hafts are often profiled with ribs and the grip at the bottom is confined within two discs. The trend towards more decoration on the head as well as on the haft continued in the Renaissance style, in the first half of the 16th century. In the 15th century the mace became a symbol of commanding authority and maintained this character in the decades to follow.

Considerable Turkish influence made itself felt in the development of this weapon, too, in Hungary, Poland, the Ukraine and Russia. There appeared, in the 16th and 17th centuries, maces with smaller spherical or oval-flattened heads and a large number of flanges, sometimes just roughcast ones, or with smooth heads. The Hungarian *buzdygans*, the Ukrainian *piernaczes* and the Polish *bulawas* were predominantly symbols of commanding authority, and for this reason some examples feature a most exquisite workmanship. This is the case of the *buzdygan* from the so-called Hungarian set for Christian II, Elector of Saxony, or of the Polish *bulawa*, dating from *c.* 1680.

Among striking weapon we come across, in the cavalry, one with a shorter handle and a head like the morning star (*Morgenstern*). It has a globular head with a large number of radially projecting pyramid-shaped spikes.

The War Hammer

War hammers (*Streithammer*) were known from the 15th century; however, they became more frequent in the following century. The earlier type with a vertical spike at the top and a short hammer-head at right angles was used in France and Italy in the second half of the 15th century, and later mainly in 16th-century Central Europe. The blunt face is usually of a square shape and on the reverse side there is a sharp beak (*bec-de-faucon*), sometimes of a considerable length. The iron haft provided with a grip at the bottom sometimes features a hooked hanger to be attached to the belt or the saddle. The 16th-century records depict the war hammer in the hands of the commanders of Landsknechts or other mercenary troops as a symbol of their authority.

The war hammer also occurred in infantry equipment (*Fußstreithammer*) in the 15th and in the early 16th centuries. It was usually provided with a strong, vertical spike of quadratic cross-section springing from the top. The hammer face was usually split into four spikes. On the reverse side there was a slightly bent beak.

Clubs and Combat Flails

nmander's hammer-type :e, first half of 16th cen-

Clubs are weapons, mostly improvised, which combine suitable elements — a striking tool, a pole and a connecting link, mostly chain — to create an object suitable for combat.

A ball on a chain can be found more frequently, i.e. a ball of iron of about 6 — 10 cm diameter provided with a large number of pyramid spikes and suspended from a chain of suitable length which is fixed to the pole (*Kettenmorgenstern*). This weapon is already mentioned in the 15th century, but more frequently later, mostly in connection with peasant wars as a weapon of the common people. However, the striking part can be of diverse nature; weapons of this type using sword-pommels but also other iron objects are

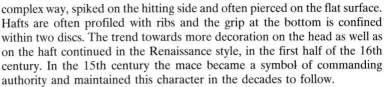

149

War hammer, *c.* 1500

180 Iron spiked ball on chain, probably 15th century.
Sword pommel on chain, 15th century.

War hammer, 15th century

known. The pole, if preserved, may be long, and intended for combat on foot, or short, designed for horsemen.

The combat flail is, from the technical point of view, closest to the foregoing weapon. As an effective military weapon it was recommended by Conrad Keyser in his manuscript called Bellifortis as early as 1402. Soon afterwards it became a typical weapon of the Hussite people's armies. In the German peasant wars (1525–26) it was frequently used by the insurgents.

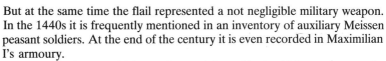

But at the same time the flail represented a not negligible military weapon. In the 1440s it is frequently mentioned in an inventory of auxiliary Meissen peasant soldiers. At the end of the century it is even recorded in Maximilian I's armoury.

Extant specimens, which may have originated in the 15th century, consist of a wooden head provided with mounts of four metal rods fastened by three or four strip sockets on which large pyramid spikes are located. The head

181 Combat flail, Bohemia, probably 15th century. Fragment of the wooden head, mounts of four twisted rods and four sockets (the spikes missing). Two chain links attach the head to the mounts of the pole.

Hitter (*Kettenmorgenstern*), 16th century

War flail, 15th–16th century

was suspended from a chain, usually of two links, whose other end was attached to a closed hook on the metal ending of the pole which was wielded by both hands. Together with this advanced form we also come across plainly improvised specimens with the spike driven right into the wood or the chain replaced with leather straps. Some of these pieces may come from the peasant rebellions of the 17th and 18th centuries.

Spiked Clubs (the Morgenstern)

These represent an exclusively popular weapon used particularly in the time of revolutionary movements and peasant insurrections or an emergency weapon employed by the militia.

The earliest type is represented by a suitable piece of wood bulkier at one end, probably root-wood, and provided with spikes, as shown in an illumination of the *Codex of Jena* (Bohemia) from the early 16th century. However, it was generally a weapon on a long pole with the head turned on a lathe into a barrel-, round- or pear-shape, most often provided with an iron band and long pyramid-shaped spikes.

The *Morgenstern* was widespread all over Europe and stayed in use for very long time. The people involved in the German peasant wars used it, and their Swedish counterparts employed it as late as 1743 (Seitz, *Blankwaffe* I), and in Switzerland militiamen were equipped with the *Morgenstern* even after 1847 (Müller, *Hieb- und Stichwaffen*).

Perhaps it could be recorded that the era of percussive weapons has not ended entirely yet. Not only the treacherous knuckle-duster, but also the police truncheon belong to this category.

DECORATION OF EDGED WEAPONS

Edged weapons were often skilfully treated as art and craft products, particularly if the customer's intention was to procure a prestige weapon. Often the weapon was of considerable artistic value as well.

The design and composition of outer rings, the arms of the hilt, the outer and inner ribs springing upwards towards the pommel of the late-Renaissance rapier certainly represent a specific aesthetic order. Naturally, the final impression may be further enhanced by the surface treatment of the individual parts. A similar situation can be encountered in the case of the 'Schiavona' basket which grew out of the fan-shaped pattern of bars around the cross-guard — to be surmounted with the sometimes complex set-up of arrow-shaped elements running towards a single point at the top of the basket.

However, in addition to the aesthetic principles which applied even to later weapons such as those from the Baroque and Rococo periods, there were other means by which the master craftsmen achieved a high aesthetic value for their products.

Chronologically the earliest decorating techniques are connected with the application of precious or non-ferrous metals. The overlaying technique using silver or other non-ferrous metal is very old, deeply rooted in the early historical era. Viking weapons were quite often adorned using this method which employed the colour contrast between dark iron and the bright shiny tones of silver, gold or brass.

Overlaying with precious or noble metals is based on a fine, dense network of grooves cut into the iron surface. A sheet of softer noble metal is then hammered on to it so that the bottom surface will get a good hold in the grooved network. This technique survived the classic Viking period and was also used for decorating the pommel and cross-guards of a sword which might have belonged to Sigvinus, Archbishop of Cologne, at the end of the 11th century.

Inlaying represents another technique for decorating iron with noble metal. Grooves are cut into iron in such a way that the bottom of the groove is somewhat widened and wire of silver or some other noble metal is hammered into them. This technique was used from the 11th till the 13th century for work on sword-blades. Ornaments and particularly inscriptions, most frequently of religious nature such as *IN NOMINE DOMINI,* sometimes groups of letters — perhaps composed of the initial letters of the individual words, were done in this way. Occasionally this decoration in silver appears also on the pommel and the cross-guard, such as a sword from Finland datable to 1150—1250.

This technique became widespread again during the Renaissance. Relatively numerous parts of swords, rapiers and daggers, sometimes also parts of maces, were inlaid with plant ornaments or figural motifs. This decorating technique was also applied to the pommel of a double-handed sword. From the 17th century on inlaying with silver was also used by the makers of Scottish and English basket-hilted swords.

In order to achieve colour shades and contrasts gilding was also used to enhance engravings of ornaments and figural scenes. This procedure employs a foil of gold laid on to the base material first, then polished and smoothed down. Blades of Italian *cinquedea* daggers from the late

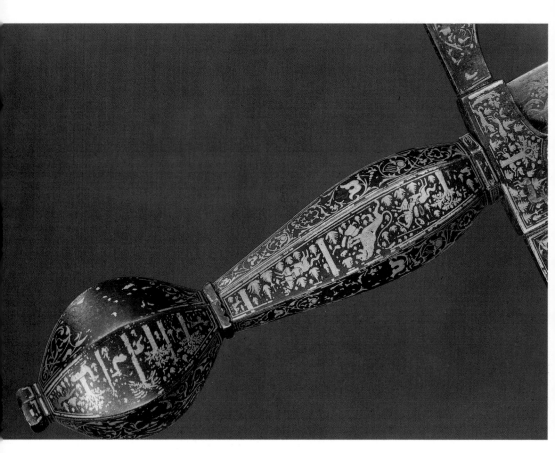

182 Sword, the blade probably of Solingen provenance provided with etching by Jan Collaert the Elder, Antwerp, c. 1540−81.
Hilt richly inlaid with gold, apparently by Damiano de Nerve, Milan, c. 1550−60. In between scrolls, hunting motifs and a fortified town. On the upper side of the cross-guard, inscription inlaid with gold.

183 *Cinquedea* by Ercole dei Fideli, Ferrara, end of 15th century. The blade with gilded engravings of mythological scenes and other figural elements. The cross-guard chiselled and gilded, the grip with lateral silver band bearing the inscription of *ERO PARCE EXICO PENAS.*

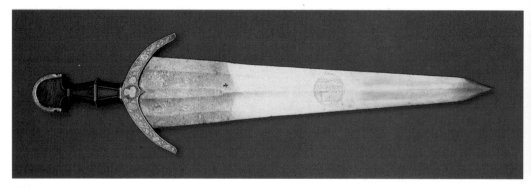

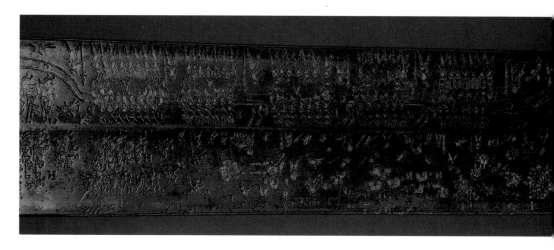

184 Detail of gilded engraving depicting the battle of Hulst in 1642 executed on a sword-blade. J. Ollich, sword-maker, Johann Cloberg, engraver, Solingen, 1643.

15th and early 16th centuries, especially those by Ercole dei Fideli from Ferrara or by others from his workshop, are not only decorated with rich ornaments but also with engraved and gilded scenes from mythology. However, depicting a complete battle scene of the Thirty Years' War as executed in a gilded engraving by Johann Cloberg, an engraver from Suhl, on a blade by Johann Ollich in 1643, is unusual.

Gilding accompanying engraved, chiselled or etched decoration was a technique frequently used in adorning ostentatious 16th- and 17th-century weapons. In the last quarter of the 18th century blades were often blued, and a fine gilded engraving of trophies and flower ornaments then stood out distinctly against such a background. The blueing process, which produces a surface layer of blue colour on steel, can be carried out using a solution of chemicals — most frequently cold, seldom hot. Blackening is a process of similar nature; the difference is in the process itself being carried out both

185 Processional glaive with gilded engraving, probably Venice, c. 1610.

by hot and cold methods. A special type of gilded engraving is typical of the masters of the Zlatoust manufacture in Russia, established in 1814. It consisted of a combination of dark-shade blueing with gilding on a grained surface (*iasczur*). On weapons by these masters of the 1820s, among whom I. N. Bushuev in particular was a prominent figure, not only ancient Greek and Roman themes were depicted, but also battle scenes of the period, especially of the 1812 war against Napoleon. A closely similar technique was also employed by a master in the Solingen workshop of P. D. Lüneschloss in 1844.

186 Halberd of Emperor Rudolph II's palace guard, Augsburg, 1577. Gilded etching, in between ornaments the *R II* monogram and signature of the author of the etching — *HS* (Hans Stromayer).

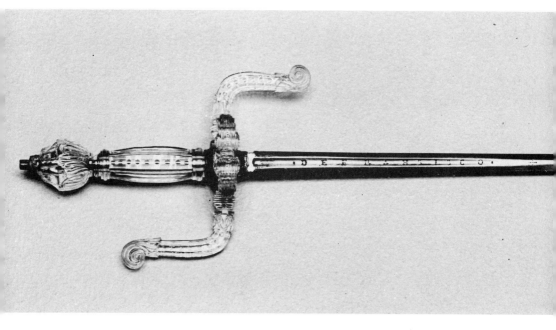

187 Rapier, probably Saxony, *c.* 1680. The hilt carved out of mountain crystal, the blade marked *IDE* (?) *Francisco.*

Etching complemented with additional chiselling or engraving of details represented an extraordinary effective way of decorating the blades of both side weapons and lances. For example, after the mid-16th century Jan Collaert from Antwerp, who marked his work by the inscription of his name in full, ranked among the foremost art and craft specialists employing this technique. Somewhat later, Hans Stromayer from Augsburg marked the weapons decorated by him with just the *HS* monogram.

Carving in iron, much favoured during the Renaissance, represents another technique of decoration of edged weapons. Many masters remain unknown but we know some by name. After the mid-16th century, Jörg Sigman from Augsburg decorated furniture with figural scenes in deep relief. In the late 16th and early 17th centuries, low relief in fine execution, often on a gilded background, was in vogue. This technique was employed by Otmar Wetter working first in Munich and then in Dresden, or by his pupil Daniel Sadeler who worked for a few years in the Prague court of Emperor Rudolph II and later on in Munich where in the mid-17th century Caspar Späth was also working. Carving in iron was also successfully applied to Baroque weapons of the second half of the 17th century.

Another way of decorating iron with carving can be encountered on Spanish-style cup-hilt rapiers and left-hand daggers belonging to them. Their furniture is pierced in unbelievably delicate ornaments complemented with motifs of animals and birds.

Goldsmiths, too, took part in the decoration of edged weapons. In important world collections we can find swords with furniture of gold decorated with coloured enamel or set with precious stones. In the 16th century they come first of all from the workshops of Spanish masters — often anony-

157

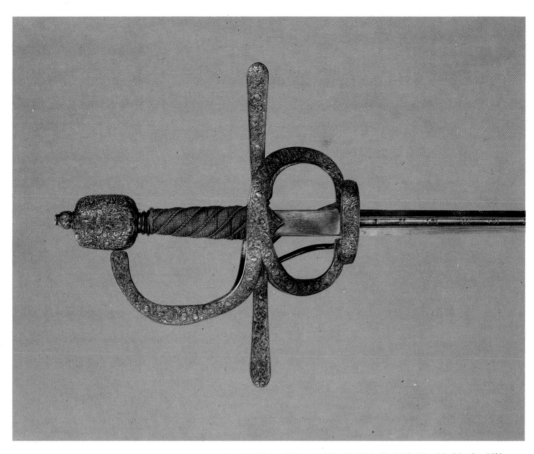

188 Rapier, blade by Antonio Picinino, Milan, *c.* 1586–89, hilt by Daniel Sadeler, Munich, after 1620. The hilt carved in iron on gilded background; ornaments, scrolls and floral motifs. Coat of arms on the pommel, probably Wallenstein's.

189 Cup-hilt rapier, the cup of iron with pierced ornament, southern Europe, third quarter of 17th century.

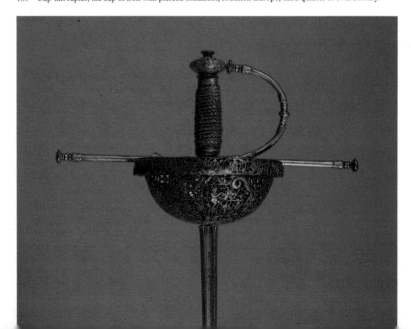

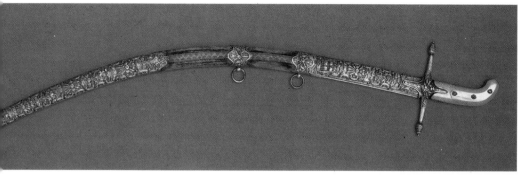

190 Sabre in Turkish style, Central Europe, *c.* 1700. The grip of green stone, scabbard mount wrought silver.

191 The so-called Hungarian set consisting of sabre, broadsword, *buzdygan* and riding equipment — by Johann Michel (Michael), a Prague goldsmith (except blade), made for Elector Christian II and delivered in 1612. Gilded silver, Bohemian garnets, topaz and amethyst stones, mountain crystal.

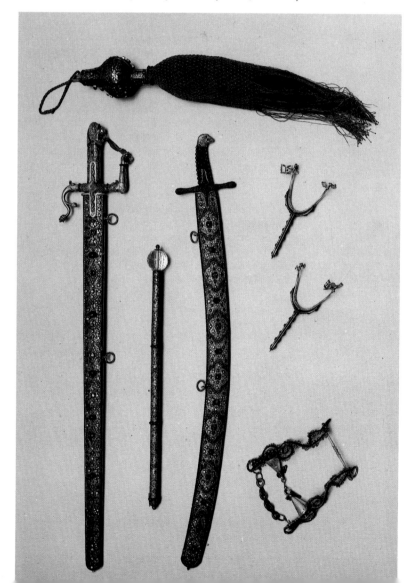

mous. Pieces by Pero Juan Pockh from Barcelona, originating in the second half of the 16th century, are among the most beautiful ones.

In the early 17th century the Prague of Rudolph II became a centre where many art and craft specialists in diverse fields were concentrated. Johann Michael, a goldsmith, was responsible for outstanding work on the so-called Hungarian garniture ordered by Christian II, Elector of Saxony, which was finished in 1612. It was not the only work by this master and somewhat later he supplied a similar set to Maximilian I, Duke of Bavaria.

On the other hand, the goldsmith who worked on the hilt and scabbard of a sabre, which, as tradition has it, belonged to Nicolas Zrinský the Younger (died 1664), a Hungarian magnate, remains anonymous. The Hungarian provenance of the weapon is attested by a hallmark with a Hungarian emblem. At the turn of the 17th and 18th centuries the victories scored against the Turks after their defeat at Vienna in 1683 evoked a fashion of copying their styles. It made itself felt in weapons, too, as documented by the onyx grip and scabbard overlaid with wrought silver plate of a sabre of Central European origin datable to about 1700.

Weapons with furniture of silver with rich relief and gilding also came from the Saxony-Polish area in the first part of the 18th century. In the 18th century even ceremonial smallswords display furniture of silver and even gold set with precious stones or decorated in relief.

Brass, which as a material for the production of furniture for side weapons was common in the early 18th century, made it possible to cast elaborate furniture — be it high or low relief. Gilding the furniture or just some areas of it then added more shine to both the whole and the detail and in a way that utilized the contrast of light and shade. The new Rococo style further loosened the grip on ornamental shapes and refined them as well. The Neo-Classical and Empire periods, although bringing about a stricter approach to fashioning shapes, also introduced new elements, and, moreover, in the later stage reverted again to rich ornamentation in gilded brass.

Bone and ivory as materials for producing parts of furniture such as grips, particulary those of hunting falchions, have already been mentioned in the preceding chapters. Mountain crystal as a material for pommels of medieval swords has been discussed as well. From this point of view, the hilt of the Baroque Saxony rapier from the last quarter of the 17th century represents a unique phenomenon, with all parts of the hilt being carved out of mountain crystal.

In the 19th century, the art and craft approach to decoration of cold weapons was coming to an end. An upsurge in the industrial production of weapons, particularly from the mid-19th century on, had an adverse effect on their artistic concept and execution. Etching on a nickelled background on the blade, no matter how showy it may be, becomes a routine technique of little artistic value lacking a creative approach. The same holds true for hilt decoration. In much the same way as in other areas, industrial production forced crafts out of business along with their artistic merits.

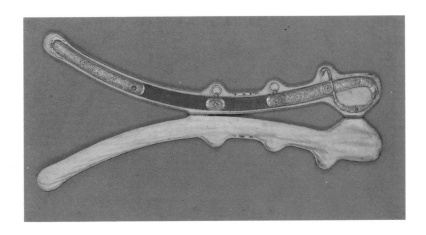

192 Commemorative Empire sabre, cased, Mainz, 1834. The blade marked *S et ZV*, decorated with ornaments, imperial arms and inscription *Die Oesterreichische Garnison Mainz 1834*. The hilt of gilded brass and the scabbard mounts decorated with coloured stones.

193 Broadsword from the area of Poland and Saxony, first third of 18th century. The hilt with chain is of silver with gilded relief. Scabbard mounts of engraved silver (probably somewhat later).

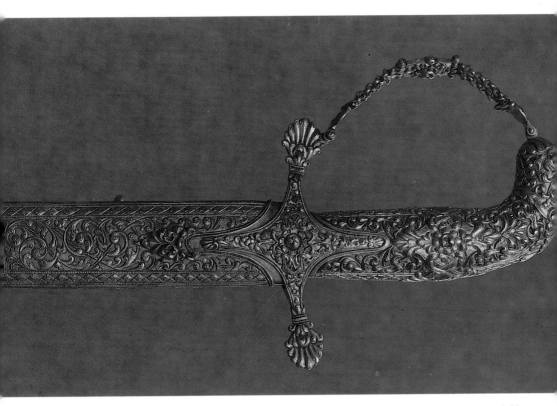

MARKS ON EDGED WEAPONS

The idea that the maker marked his product using his name or simply his mark is of a very old origin. Blades of Viking swords featured bands of soft iron showing the names of current Franconian blade-makers. The name of *ULFBERTH* is the earliest among them, being attested to as early as the second half of the 9th century. The name of *INGELRED* or *INGELR* appeared for the first time in about the mid-10th century. It is worth mentioning that both these names can be found on weapons of both the 9th and 10th centuries. It means that, after a certain time elapsed, the name ceased to be the maker's mark and became a generally recognized hallmark of quality. Other names have been found on blades, too, which can be considered the marks of master craftsmen.

It is remarkable, too, that hilts of Viking swords from time to time bear the inscription of names such as *HLITER* or *HARTOLFR*, which in connection with the words *ME FECIT* indicates that these are the names of those who made the hilt, the cross-guard and the grip. The name of *HILTIPREHT* found on cross-guards of two 9th- and 10th-centuries swords where, however, the attribution *me fecit* is missing, is the earliest one. It goes without saying that there are more names of this character; not so many, however, as there are marks on blades.

Considerably later there appeared another master's name belonging to the maker of quality blades. Master *GICELIN* seems to have been active some time between the mid-12th and mid-13th centuries.

The inscribing of names then disappeared for a long time. In the early 14th century, blades originating in the Danubian town of Passau came into vogue. About 1330, the sign of a formalized running wolf (a part of the town's coat-of-arms) appeared on them. It was inlaid in copper or in brass wire. This, however, is a mark quite different from that of the maker. By this mark the town in fact guaranteed the quality of its sword maker's products. The Passau wolf became a hallmark of quality for a number of centuries to follow. In the 1460s, the Passau town council protested to the town council of Solingen, claiming that the Solingen sword makers were using the wolf mark although they were not entitled to do so. We do not know if the protest was successful. However, it certainly did not prevent unauthorized imitations of the Passau wolf mark in Solingen or elsewhere. As late as the 17th century we can still find this mark, side by side with others, on the blades of Solingen sword makers.

In the 14th and 15th centuries blades were marked with symbols whose meaning is not clear. It cannot be ruled out that these marks indicated the quality of the weapon in question. There is for example a cross growing out of a formalized heart, frequently also the symbol of the Imperial orb which can be found on 14th- and 15th-century blades, and, of course, the Passau wolf. Mostly these symbols were inlaid with yellow-metal filling in the engraved lines.

However, mark appeared on other medieval weapons, too. The upper part of a sword in a rectangular frame, punched on the neck of a Gothic Bohemian axe from the 14th century, is undoubtedly the maker's mark. We cannot be so sure about shields with symbols on a 15th-century axe. This could well represent an approval mark of the locality where the axe was produced, perhaps Bavaria. The same goes for an equal-armed cross punched in a square-shaped hollow on the point of a Bohemian lance dating to

1414

The so-called running wolf (*Passauer Wolf*), 17th century

the second half of the 15th century. Marks on other staff weapons are quite frequent. The mark of a scorpion on halberds of Italian provenance after 1500, probably from Milan, is the most frequently occurring one. However, marks have been preserved on Swiss types of halberds as well as on other staff weapons. Their identification will be very difficult.

From the end of the 15th century in Italy, and later also in the production centres of Spain and Germany, letter marks started appearing. *O* over *T* in a shield is considered to be Toledo's 16th-century general mark. Later on there was often the inscription *EN TOLEDO* (also *NTOLO, ENTOLO*) in the fuller of the blade even if the sword maker's mark or his name were not shown. The masters of Toledo frequently used the mark of a letter under a coronet in a shield. Sometimes the letters indicated the family name (*S*-Sahagum). More often, however, they were connected with the Christian name; the *A* was used as a maker's mark by Alonso de los Ríos, Alonso de Caba, Antonio Gutierrez and others. The inscription of a full name occasionally appeared in the case of some masters in the second half of the 16th century (*Sahagun el Viejo, Thomas de Aiala*). However, it was not, until the turn of the 16th and the 17th centuries, that the inscription of the full name became more frequent and in some cases prevailed over other marks, e.g. *Francisco Ruiz*. Some Spanish sword makers were in the habit of adding a small half-moon to their personal mark to indicate they were Espadero del Rey (the King's sword maker).

In Italy, inscriptions of full names were more frequent in the first half of the 16th century; a luxury falchion of the period was marked *FAUSTINO GELPHO BRESCIANO*. The Picininos of Milan often used the mark of a tower with the name inscribed around it. But on their two-handed sword the mark of the tower is positioned separately, complemented with the inscription of *ANTONIO PICININO ME FECITE IN MILANO 1584*.

The Solingen masters often used pictorial marks inherited by the family and mostly complemented with the name. In such a way a king's head belonged to Johann Wundes. Wilhelm Wirberg (Weyersberg) and other members of the family used the symbol of nippers with full inscription of name and locality. Johann Ollich, too, used a mark of this type — with a man's head and inscription of his name and place of work — on a sword blade of 1643. Examples by a somewhat younger J. Hoppe can be identified

Sword, 14th—15th century

Italian sword, probably Milan, *c.* 1500

Rapier, Toledo, early 17th century

163

194 Marks of sword-maker Johann Ollich from Solingen on blade of a sword from 1643.

195 Marks on back edge of French broadsword of the year 1815.

⊞ ANTONIO · PICININO · MD

⊞ FECITE · IN · MILANO · 1584

Two-handed sword, Antonio Picinino, Milan, 1584.

Cavalry sabre Model 1798,
Austria, Pottenstein man-
ufacture

POTZDAM

Cuirassier's broadsword
Model 1732, Prussia,
Potsdam manufacture

FISCHER

Cavalry sabre Model 1803,
Austria, Fischer, Vienna

according to the combination of five marks with crossed arrows in a shield with the name and the date (*c.* 1650). His older namesake, and a relative, probably Johannes Hoppe (who had been working in England for some time) marked his product by a representation of a wild man. In some cases the maker added the production year on top of his name and place of work (*Weilm Rodbrass 1613*).

The system of marking developed until the early 17th century and was continued for some time even if many preserved weapons remain anonymous. Army regulation weapons of the 18th century are mostly marked with the name of the respective manufacturers. From the time that the Potsdam manufacture was established in 1722, Prussian weapons generally bore the name of *POTZDAM,* sometimes complemented with a punched eagle.

Austrian weapons, particularly in the second half of the 18th century, were most often marked by the Pottenstein manufacture in Steyr, Russian weapons by the Tula manufacture including the production year.

In the course of the 19th century (starting in 1813), Prussia was purchasing most of its edged weapons in Solingen, and for this reason Prussian weapons mainly feature marks of several Solingen makers. The Fischer company of Vienna were producing Austrian edged arms from the turn of the century, later on also the Jung company and others.

∴ ME FECIT ∴ SALINGEN ∴ 1613 ∴ ∴⅊✝∙∙

∴ WEILM ∴ ROD ∴ BRAS ∴ ANNO ∴ ⅊✝

Rapier with wavy blade,
Weilm Rodbrass, Solingen,
1613

Mᵉ Fᵗᵘʳᵉ Imple du Klingenthal aout 1813

Sabre of mounted chasseurs
of the Guard, Model AN
XI/XIII, France, Klingen-
thal manufacture

165

Златоустъ, Маія 1826 года

Cavalry sabre Model 1826,
Russia, Zlatoust manufac-
ture

From the early 19th century, the marking of French weapons included th
name of the manufacturer, the month and the year of production. Afte
1832, the model mark was added, too. In most cases it was the importan
Alsatian manufacture Klingenthal founded *c.* 1730. The early signatur
recalls the proprietor (*COULAUX FRÈRES*); during the Napoleoni
period the signature reads *Manufacture Impériale de Klingenthal.*

Production of edged weapons in Russia was taken over by the Zlatous
company from its foundation in 1814 and its marking sometimes also in
cluded the production year and month. The factory, founded in the secon
half of the 19th century, marked its products with a round-shaped symbc
depicting the tsarist eagle and the inscription of *Zlatoust Or(uzheinaya
Fabr(ika).* The production year was then indicated separately showing the
year and the letter *g* (abbreviation of *goda*, 'of the year') in the Russia
Cyrillic script.

Marks on weapons represent one of the means of determining and classi
fying the individual specimens as to their territorial origin and date. How
ever, thorough knowledge of the relevant specialized literature and studie
of the subject are a prerequisite for marks to become a reliable aid.

MECHANICAL SHOOTING WEAPONS

The need to hit a moving animal at a distance was strongly felt by primitive man. In the prehistoric period it was the bow and arrow which served this purpose. It goes without saying that none of the bows have been preserved, but their effectiveness is attested to by the fact that primeval people used to protect their left wrist against the swing of the bow-string by using plates of stone. Along with these protective plates, stone arrow-points and darts of bone represent the earliest proof of effective longer-range weapons.

The bow, needless to say, was used throughout the Bronze and Iron Ages. In the early phases of the historical era, the Huns, and later on the Avars, too, raided Europe. They left a lot of evidence in archaeological finds. As well as curved sabre-blades they were represented first of all by arrow-heads. These nomadic arrows are characterized by a three-leafed point with a tang for attaching the head to the shaft.

Bow and arrows remained the only long-range weapon of European nations in the early Middle Ages. However, the arrow types of the 8th—10th centuries changed. The development of forging techniques enabled the creation of a hollow socket into which the arrow shaft was then inserted, and the head took on a winged shape.

196 Archer's bracer of stone to protect the wrist, two stone arrow-heads and an arrow of bone, c. 2000 B.C.

167

197 Three-sided arrow heads with tang, 6th—8th century (the three on the left). Winged arrow-heads with socket, 8th—10th century (the three on the right).

From the 11th century onwards, spearheads showed considerable variations. In addition to winged heads provided with sockets there appeared flat, leaf-shaped heads with a tang or even V-split heads. However, heads with a rhomboid cross-section may be found, possessing greater penetrating power. Some of them are slim in outline, others more robust, but both are provided with a tang. In the 12th and 13th centuries these new shapes were apparently adapted for arrows to be used in another weapon for both hunting and long-range combat — the crossbow — the bolts being provided with a socket. They were in general use in the course of the 14th and 15th centuries.

The bow, however, was used both in hunting and war for a long time to come. In the 14th century it still was a common weapon in most European countries. The English longbow was one of the most famous, having proved its supremacy, in the hands of English archers, over the Genoese crossbowmen in the 1347 Battle of Crécy.

Common European bows, somewhat shorter for horsemen and somewhat longer for warriors on foot, were of the straight-pull type. The bow-string was attached to the ends of the bow which was shaped as a slightly curved convex arch. By pulling the bowstring towards himself the archer increased the bend of the bow, thus creating the energy necessary to propel the arrow. Bows were made from tough yet resilient wood, particularly yew and possibly ash — rather than maple wood which some present-day research workers seem to prefer. The English longbow, which was as long as a man, could launch an arrow over a distance of several hundred metres while maintaining a high penetrating power. However, the archer's considerable

198 Arrow-heads, 11th—13th century.

muscular strength and extraordinary skill were essential. The equipment used in today's sporting archery is derived from the shapes and properties of the longbow.

In the East, another type of bow was very common throughout the Middle Ages, the so-called compound bow. It was considerably shorter and for this reason better suited for horsemen such as the Tartars from the 13th century onwards. Its principle was that, while at rest, the ends of the bow were bent forwards, and the archer had to use considerable strength to bend the end sections backwards far enough to extend the bow-string as much as required. This variety of bow was in use throughout the Middle Ages in Tartar and

199 Hook for bending the crossbow using the crossbowman's belt, Bohemia, pre-1437.

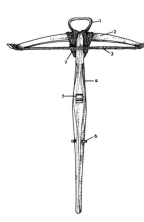

Crossbow
1 Stirrup
2 Bow
3 Bow-string
4 Stock (tiller)
5 Nut
6 Pins
7 Binding

Turkish light cavalry, and also in Hungary, Poland and Russia. It still ranked among the equipment of the Cossacks and other light cavalry warriors a late as in the 17th century. It was carried in a sheath mostly of leather, which was *en suite* with the quiver, plain in the case of rank and file soldiers. Set of luxurious execution were richly decorated in silver or gold embroider; sometimes complemented with coloured stones or ornamented with meta work of gilded brass.

The crossbow originated from the bow and its principle was known to th Romans. From its Latin name *arcubalista* the German term of *Armbru* may have been derived. It spread in Europe particularly in connection wit the Crusades from the late 11th century onwards. The process was so quic that the Church deemed it necessary to proclaim the weapon 'murderou and non-Christian' at the 2nd Lateran council in 1139 and ban it. The ban repeated again at the turn of the 12th and the 13th century, was no effective at all, and the crossbow gained in popularity as a long-range weap on.

The bow is the principal part of a crossbow. Mostly it is of a composit structure. Sometimes it was formed of stacked strips of horn and resilien wood, at other times the core of horn was overlaid with plates of fish bon The structure was then wrapped in animal sinews and covered with fin

200   Crossbow with bow of steel and windlass, Central Europe, *c.* 1500.

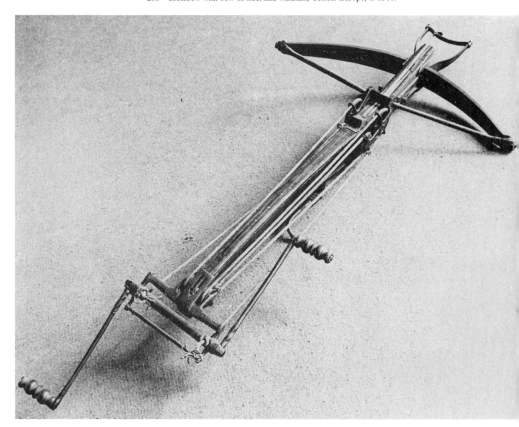

201   Bolt heads for crossbow, 15th century.

leather or parchment. The bow was fixed to the stock by hempen rope binding; the same method was used for fixing the stirrup to the central part of the bow. The bowstring was made out of several dozen jute strings coiled round by a cord, and its eyelets served for attaching it to the final hollowed parts of the bow. When drawn back, the bowstring was caught in the recess of the retaining device, the nut, which was most frequently made of bone. In addition to the recess to retain the cord the nut had another groove at the bottom to take the end of a long bar which served as a trigger. The upper part of the stock was overlaid with bone where the bolt was placed in a shallow groove. A little way behind the nut, an iron pin was transversally seated in the stock to accommodate mechanical devices for spanning the bow.

Normal manual strength was not sufficient to span composite bows, so various mechanical devices were introduced for this purpose. The *cingulum balistareum* method was the most frequent one in the 14th and in the first half of the 15th century. The crossbowman tilted his crossbow down to touch the ground and put his foot into the stirrup. Then he bent down and caught the centre of the cord using the double hook hanging down from the belt. Then, stretching himself he spanned the bow and inserted the cord into the nut. The crossbow was also bent by a device based on the lever principle (the goat's foot lever — *Gaisfuss*). Written records indicate that from the 1440s onwards steel bows started being used as well as the composite ones.

171

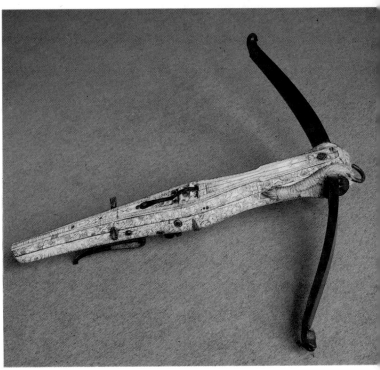

203 Richly ornamented crossbow, the bow of steel, the stock entirely covered with bone with engraved ornaments, hunting scenes and the scene of Helen's kidnapping (after Homer). At the front, inscription and dating 1592. Iron parts chiselled and gilded. On the lever-trigger, arms and date 1592.

202 Arrow-head of King of Shooters with engraving and the letter, 15th century.

204 Detail of the richly ornamented crossbow.

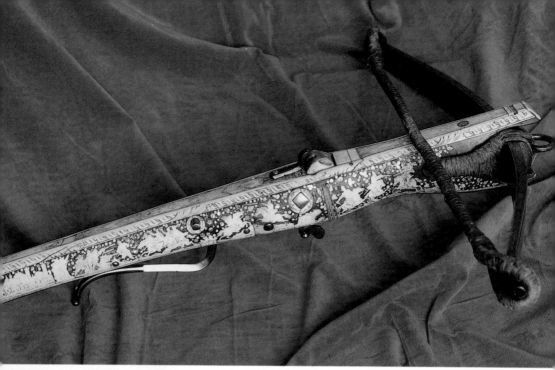

205 Hunting crossbow of Johann Georg I, Saxony, after 1612.
The stock partially covered with bone and mother-of-pearl.
Arms of Saxony and Meissen and *IGI* monogram.

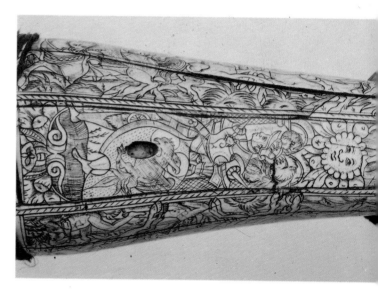

Details of the hunting crossbow of Johann Georg I.

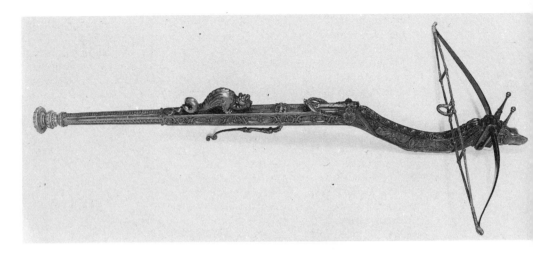

206 Crossbow of Italian type with rich carving in relief.
Front part of the stock arched with double bowstring.
The weapon belonged to William of Pernstein, Chancellor of the Bohemian kingdom at the end of the 16th century.

The current spanning methods were not strong enough to span steel bows, but the windlass was. Its longitudinal sleeve was positioned against the end of the stock, the hooks engaged the bowstring and by turning the two handles a capstan device resulted in the cord being pulled far enough to be caught by the nut.

The windlass was suitable in the defence of strongholds, etc. where the crossbowman's position did not change much. However, it was not really suitable for field warfare or for hunting.

The so-called 'German jack' or *cranequin* was primarily for mounted users of the crossbow or for hunters. It was mentioned in written records as early as the 1420s. Its principle was based on a toothed wheel positioned in a casing. The toothed wheel engaged a rack with two hooks to hold the bowstring. The archer then turned the handle set into the centre of the wheel until the bow string was engaged in the nut. Eventually this method of bending the bow became general.

Both the shape and the weight of the bolt changed, too. The bolt was provided with a relatively thick, short shaft complemented with the fletching of elongated triangular pieces of paper or parchment inserted into slots at the end of the shaft to guarantee accuracy in flight. The bolt heads were rather big, mostly of rhomboid cross-section, sometimes with a tang but more frequently with a socket. For hunting purposes in particular, large winged or split heads were used. The heads were mostly of iron, but as early as 1427 heads of steel were mentioned, sold at double the price of the iron ones.

The equipment of crossbowmen included quivers with bolts. As a rule they were of leather, provided with a wooden base and carried suspended from the belt.

Specialized craftsmen produced longbows and crossbows. In the 14th – 15th centuries they belonged to medium-sized yet generally well-to-do strata of town craftsmen, who, in addition to their work, had the duty of defending the town ramparts in case of attack. In the same way as other craftsmen, the bow-makers, too, were establishing their separate guilds. In the 15th century there also appeared specialized quiver-makers.

The crossbow as an infantry projectile weapon continued in use, along with the developing firearms, till the first half of the 16th century. However, after that date it was still used for hunting and sporting purposes. Organizations in which the burghers practised crossbow shooting began as early as the beginning of the 14th century, first of all in Switzerland and later on in most countries of medieval Europe. Festive competitions were organized whose winners, either in target shooting or 'shooting towards the bird', were celebrated as kings of marksmen. In addition to other prizes, in the 15th century, they received a bolt whose head was decorated with an engraving encircling a minuscule letter *r* (*rex,* king).

From the technical point of view crossbows for hunting purposes and shooting contests did not change much in the course of the 16th century; however, their decoration did. Facing with bone was more common until the tiller became entirely covered towards the end of the 16th century. These surfaces were then decorated with rich ornamental and figural engraving. Iron parts, such as pins and trigger, were often gilded.

The shape of the stock began changing from the beginning of the 17th century. A small protrusion at the bottom of the inner side foreshadowed the cheek-piece similar to that of shoulder arms of the period. Changes are evident in decoration, too. Parts fully covered with bone became less common and the other surfaces were inlaid with ornaments and figural scenes.

Later on in the 17th century the rear part of the tiller was replaced by a butt resembling that of the wheellock rifle. It had a normal trigger and was sometimes provided with a hair-trigger instead of a lever. After the mid-17th century, the hunting function of the crossbow ceased to exist as well. Up till the end of the 19th century sporting associations using this weapon flourished in some parts of Germany and in Switzerland. Recently, however, a renaissance of the crossbow has taken place which is so successful that regular world championships and other competitions in shooting with this weapon take place.

In the 16th century the prodd or bullet crossbow, also called the ballester or stone bow, was a variety of crossbow. Instead of a single bowstring the prodd featured a double string, in the centre of which there was a sort of basket to take the bullet. The Italian type features the tiller arched down in its front part and the foresight suspended between two pillars in the top front part of the tiller. Some German prodds, called *Kugelschnepper,* had a stock in the shape of a quadrangular iron bar and the butt was derived from the German butt of wheellock rifles.

FIREARMS

EVOLUTION OF HAND-HELD FIREARMS FROM THE 14th TILL THE END OF THE 19th CENTURY

THE EARLIEST FIREARMS

The origin of firearms, like the birth of many other branches of technology, is rather obscure. The discovery of gunpowder was an essential prerequisite, yet we do not exactly know where and when gunpowder appeared for the first time, nor we know who its inventor was. Gunpowder, used for shooting well up till the end of the 19th century, is a mixture of saltpetre (potassium nitrate), sulphur and charcoal. The formulae of the individual gunpowder types may differ, yet it can be said that saltpetre represents about three quarters of the mixture, whereas sulphur and charcoal, in an approximately equal proportion, make up the remaining part.

Some scholars suggest that gunpowder originated — possibly in Italy — from the earlier 'Greek fire' used in Byzantium, whose inflammable fluid components were replaced by solid ones with saltpetre added to the mixture. Most experts, however, believe that knowledge of gunpowder was passed on to Europe from China by the Arabs. The Chinese knew of gun powder very much earlier than the Europeans, and used it as an explosive

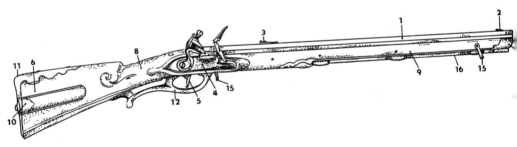

Hunting gun, 18th century
1 Barrel
2 Front sights
3 Rear sights
4 Lock
5 Trigger
6 Butt
7 Cheek-piece
8 Neck (wrist) of the stock
9 Forestock or fore-end
10 Patch-box cover
11 Butt-plate
12 Trigger-guard
13 Side-plate
14 Forestock end
15 Sling-mount
16 Ramrod
(2—3 Sights, 6—9 Stock,
11—15 Furniture)

176

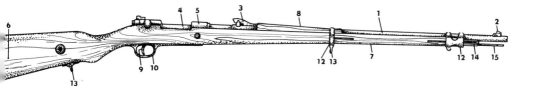

substance. Later it was used in weapons based on the rocket principle.

Gunpowder appeared in Europe early in the second half of the 13th century; here, too, it was originally used as an explosive substance. In the early part of the 14th century the first primitive firearms originated in which gunpowder provided the driving power to propel the projectile to a distant target. The blossoming prosperity of medieval European towns in the course of the 14th century, the boom in crafts and the considerable experience already accumulated in metal processing provided the expertise for this quite new way of utilizing gunpowder. The accumulation of sufficient financial resources also helped make the production of the new weapons possible.

The earliest firearms known from the pictorial evidence of the period featured a prominently extended breech section and were designed to discharge arrows. These missiles, however, were soon displaced by stone and iron or lead balls. Craftsmen possessing the greatest experience with similar techniques set about the manufacture of the new weapons. Bronze barrels, dominant in the 14th century, were cast first of all by bell-founders, and iron barrels, which were more common from the 15th century on, were mostly forged by blacksmiths. In contrast to craftsmen organized in guilds, early gunmakers worked on a contract basis, hired by individual towns or feudal lords, and their duties as a rule included not only the manufacture of weapons, but, in case of need, operating them as well.

The oldest firearms were exclusively artillery pieces and only in the second half of the 14th century did lighter, portable types appear, designed to be handled by a single soldier only. In overall appearance they resemb-

207 The earliest extant firearm, barrel of bronze, end of first half of 14th century (so-called 'Loshult gun' — named after the Swedish locality of Loshult where it was discovered in 1861).

177

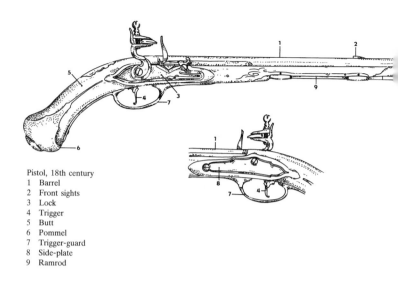

Pistol, 18th century
1 Barrel
2 Front sights
3 Lock
4 Trigger
5 Butt
6 Pommel
7 Trigger-guard
8 Side-plate
9 Ramrod

led artillery pieces, having proportionately smaller dimensions, and for t
reason the term 'hand cannon' was used for them. Before the end of t
century the barrel had been complemented with a wooden stock facilitati
easy manipulation. In this way a genuine handgun, operated by a single m
only, came into being. The stock was a straight wooden tiller which w
either fitted into the barrel-socket projection or, alternatively, set in a slot
the stock and secured there by thongs or metal straps. About 1400, a ho
appeared beneath the barrel; this protrusion was supported on a so
foundation, such as a rampart wall or a shield. This way of holding t
weapon steady must have resulted in greater accuracy, but, most importa
ly, the recoil was reduced considerably. From the hook, the outstandi
innovative feature, the term of hook-gun (arquebus) resulted.

208   Bronze barrel, second half of 14th century. Touch-hole with round priming pan situated on top of
barrel, with plug projection provided with two openings to nail the barrel to wooden pole-stock.

209 Barrel of bronze hook-gun with socket projection to accept the stock, 1400–50. Barrel of iron hook-gun, *c.* 1430, with lugs and pegs underneath for fixing it to the stock.

The first written records mentioning firearms come from England and Italy in 1326; in the following years they appeared in France, Germany and elsewhere, and by the end of the century firearms were known over practically all Europe. Even though they had already been in use for several decades, firearms were not too effective, and their application was markedly limited. Loading them was a lengthy process; the gunner had to pour gun-

210 Iron gun ('hand cannon'), *c.* 1375. Lateral wall of the barrel burst open when fired.

Tiller stock, 14th century (held under the soldiers's arm when firing)

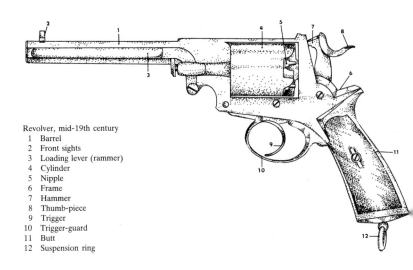

Revolver, mid-19th century
1 Barrel
2 Front sights
3 Loading lever (rammer)
4 Cylinder
5 Nipple
6 Frame
7 Hammer
8 Thumb-piece
9 Trigger
10 Trigger-guard
11 Butt
12 Suspension ring

powder down the muzzle and (using the ramrod) push the shot home. Originally, the touch-hole connected the chamber with the upper surface of the barrel but subsequently with its right-hand side where there was a priming pan with a small amount of powder. This was ignited either by a hot iron rod or a glowing piece of coal held in pincers. This restricted the discharging of the weapon to a position where fire was readily available, so that the gunner had the means of making the igniting agent burn. For this reason both artillery pieces and hand-held guns were used almost exclusively in siege warfare, or, vice-versa, in defence of castles and towns.

MATCHLOCK WEAPONS

The construction of the lock mechanism was of principal importance for the further development of firearms. 'Lock' is a collective term for the assembly of parts making the mechanical discharge of the weapon feasible. However, this word, whose etymology and meaning are identical in a majority of important European languages, was not derived from any actual locking function (there being none) but from the locksmiths who started making these firearm parts in the 15th century. They were the craftsmen possessing the greatest experience in the production of similar mechanisms.

The match, a length of cord soaked in potassium chlorate and then allowed to dry, burns slowly with a glowing end. The match replaced the heated wire in the hand of the gunner, and then it was just a small step to actually attaching it to the weapon. This happened in the first quarter of the 15th century, but wider use of matchlocks had to wait till the second half of the century. The

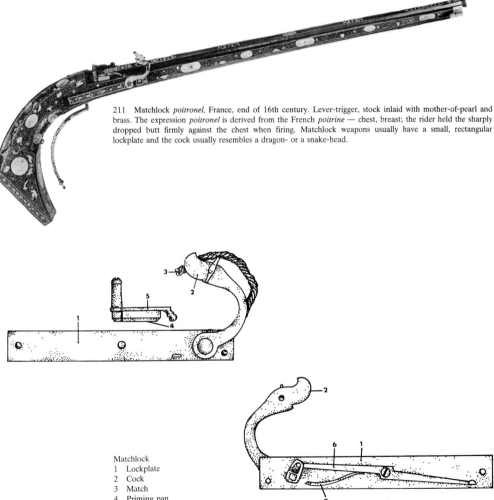

211 Matchlock *poitronel*, France, end of 16th century. Lever-trigger, stock inlaid with mother-of-pearl and brass. The expression *poitronel* is derived from the French *poitrine* — chest, breast; the rider held the sharply dropped butt firmly against the chest when firing. Matchlock weapons usually have a small, rectangular lockplate and the cock usually resembles a dragon- or a snake-head.

Matchlock
1 Lockplate
2 Cock
3 Match
4 Priming pan
5 Pan cover
6 Trigger-lever
7 Spring

181

gunner, who previously had to concentrate on igniting the charge, could now concentrate on the target and devote himself to careful aiming. That is why both front and rear sights appeared on firearms in the course of the 15th century. Further innovations were introduced, too, and from the 15th century on pins passing through protruding tangs forged to the underside of the barrel secured it to the stock. The threaded breech plug replaced the spigot in sealing the breech end of the barrel. The effectiveness of firearms was increased by lengthening the barrels and reducing their bore and also by the introduction of grained gunpowder instead of the original pulverized type used in the first quarter of the 15th century.

The earliest locks had the match fitted into the top arm of the serpentine whose lower section served as trigger. From the second half of the 15th century the cock clamping the match was held in position by a simple leaf spring whose resistance was then overcome by pressing the lever. From the early 16th century, side by side with the lever a vertical trigger appeared in the form of a short rod protected against accidental pressing by a trigger-guard. This type of trigger became more and more common, but the lever remained in use, on military muskets in particular, for another century. The cock with the match could be situated either behind the pan and tipping forward, or, it could be in front of the pan (this design became general later on) and tipping towards the gunner. It goes without saying that variants of the matchlock may feature further, less important diversities.

About 1500 a somewhat different variant of the trigger system, which is called the snaplock, appeared. Instead of the match, tinder was used as the igniting agent. It was obtained from the tinder fungus by boiling its caps along with wood ash and by further processing the resulting substance. The cock generally ended in a tubular holder for the tinder. As a rule it was necessary to cock it beforehand so that it would be caught and held by a claw on the sear lever. It could be released by pressing the other end of the lever fashioned as a button protruding on the right-hand side of the stock. Later on, about the mid-16th century, this lateral button trigger was replaced by the usual vertical trigger. Pressing the trigger of a snaplock does not over-

213 Austrian musket with matchlock, produced in Wiener Neustadt in 1657.

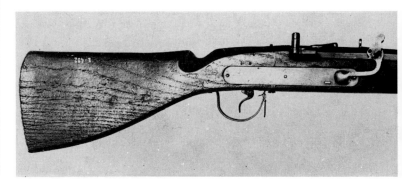

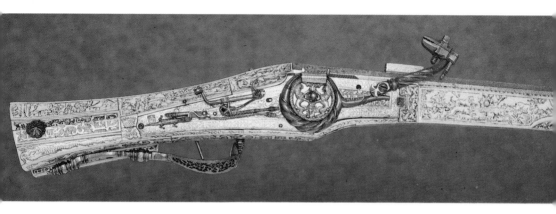

214 Gun with combined snap- and wheellock, marked *WD* (Wolf Danner, Nuremberg), 1544 (the triggerguard of a later date).
Richly decorated with engraving and gilding, the stock covered with engraved bone featuring ornamental and figured motifs.

come any resistance of the spring; the cock is swiftly tipped into the pan, powered by the spring action.

The snaplock spread far less widely than the matchlock and was used first of all on target weapons. Although it was necessary to ignite the tinder before each shot, on the other hand it did not call for the care which had to be devoted to the permanently glowing match if it was to remain fully functional. This involved keeping it burning, removing the ashes, advancing and fixing the match properly so that its glowing tip would always fall right into the priming powder in the pan when the trigger had been pressed.

Matchlocks ceased to be used in Europe at the turn of the 17th and 18th centuries. In this connection two things should be pointed out which hold true for other types of locks as well. The fact that a new, more advanced

215 Long gun with combined snap- and wheellock, Central Europe, dated 1574 on butt-plate and having no connection with the date of origin, 1620, on the barrel.

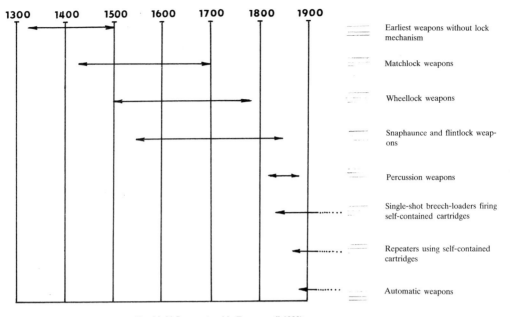

1300	1400	1500	1600	1700	1800	1900

Earliest weapons without lock mechanism

Matchlock weapons

Wheellock weapons

Snaphaunce and flintlock weapons

Percussion weapons

Single-shot breech-loaders firing self-contained cartridges

Repeaters using self-contained cartridges

Automatic weapons

Hand-held firearms (used in Europe until 1900)

system of ignition had been designed did not mean that the previous system went out of use immediately. Over the same period, weapons with different lock systems were found side by side. Sometimes the lock system depended on the weapon type, one system being geared to military weapons and another to hunting weapons. Sometimes a specific lock system was connected with a specific geographical area over a long period. Even in cases where the new design had been commonly accepted as being more advantageous some years elapsed before all owners of weapons started using it. Over the transitional period both systems were always used indiscriminately. The occurrence of two different locks systems on a single weapon, either a pistol or a long gun, has always been typical of these periods. This arrangement was to increase the reliability of the weapon which could be fired by the second method if the first failed. Alternatively it provided its owner with the choice of one system out of the two which were common at that time.

Further it is necessary to point out that information related to the years when particular lock systems were in use are valid only for Europe. Matchlock weapons saw service in many Asian countries, Japan, China, India and elsewhere, and in South America, as late as the 19th century, long after they had been abandoned in Europe. A similar pattern was followed by other later, lock systems too, which maintained their position on other continents much longer, no matter whether they were produced there or imported from Europe.

WHEELLOCK WEAPONS

While the earliest locks ignited the priming powder in the pan with the aid of a substance set alight beforehand, the match or a piece of tinder, wheellocks and later on snaphaunce locks and flintlocks produced, through their own action, the sparks which ignited the priming gunpowder. The wheellock was named after the wheel with a serrated circumference whose edge protruded through the bottom of the priming pan. After the weapon was loaded, the mainspring was compressed by means of a special key, the spanner, placed over the wheel spindle, and the cock was manually lowered so that the piece of pyrites clamped in its jaws was in contact with the edge of the wheel. When the trigger was pressed, the mainspring was released, and by means of a transmission chain caused the wheel to rotate rapidly. Friction between the wheel edge and the pyrites produced sparks which ignited the priming powder in the pan.

Leonardo da Vinci's drawing in the *Codex Atlanticus* and a somewhat later drawing, dated 1505, in a manuscript by a Nuremberg burgher named Martin Löffelholz are mentioned every time the origin of the wheellock is researched. Wheellock weapons actually appeared for the first time at the beginning of the 16th century, perhaps in northern Italy or, more likely, in southern Germany. It was there that the watchmaking trade was developing, and the local watchmakers, no strangers in the world of springs and wheels, could undoubtedly provide valuable expertise in designing and producing wheellocks.

The earliest wheellocks have been preserved on combined weapons where the firearm was coupled with a crossbow or an edged weapon. In a short time separate wheellock guns and pistols appeared, and about 1530 these weapons were being used over the whole of Europe. In the second half of the 16th century the competition of snaphaunce and flintlock weap-

216 Wheellock gun, Italy, *c.* 1580. 'Fish-tail' butt and stock inlaid with scrollwork of iron wire.

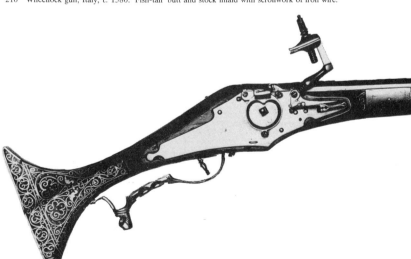

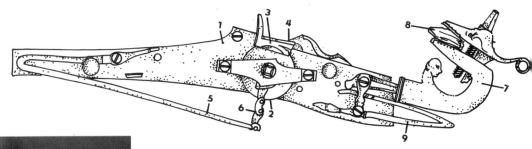

Wheellock with external mechanism
1 Lockplate
2 Wheel
3 Priming pan
4 Pan-cover
5 Mainspring
6 Chain
7 Cock
8 Flint
9 Cock-spring

ons began, which in some areas resulted in virtually the complete replacement of wheellock firearms by these systems in the course of the 17th century. In other areas, however, particularly in Central Europe, wheellock firearms continued in general use, side by side with flintlock weapons, well into the second half of the 18th century. The evolution of the wheellock over more than 250 years as well as its individual design variants can therefore be covered here only in their basic features.

The early wheellock firearms had the mainspring located outside the lockplate. From the mid-16th century it could be found inside, with the exception of some variants, such as the so-called 'Portuguese', used first of all in Italy, or the locks of so-called *tschinke* guns produced in Silesia and named after the Silesian town of Těšín.

◀ 217 Wheellock gun, South Germany, *c.* 1600. Weapon belonged to Archduke (later Emperor) Matthias. Stock inlaid with white bone (motifs from the symbolism of the Order of the Golden Fleece), spiral-ended butt, cock with thumb ring.

218 *Tschinke* gun with wheellock, Silesia (probably Těšín), mid-17th century.

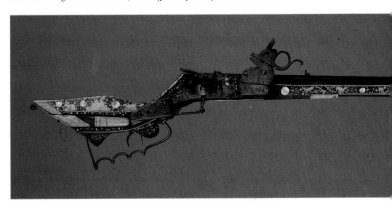

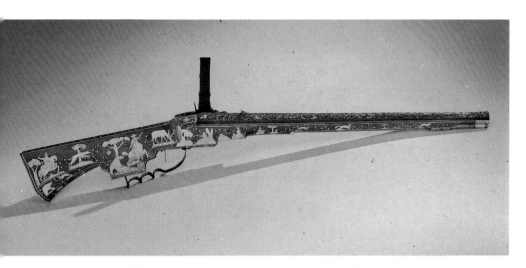

219 Wheellock gun with chimney, Germany, mid-17th century.

220 Wheellock rifle by Matheus Crannister, Central Europe, *c.* 1730—40. Wheel completely concealed behind lockplate, long thumb-piece, trigger-guard with finger-rest.
In contrast to the rather small lockplate of the matchlock the larger lockplate of the wheellock offered a suitable space for decoration. In the 18th century the cock was decorated as well. The motif used on this weapon — the enthroned sovereign with eagle tearing away his sceptre — suggests the hypothesis that it is an allegory of Charles VI (ruled 1711—40). He had no male successors and the Hapsburg rule was challenged by some neighbouring countries.

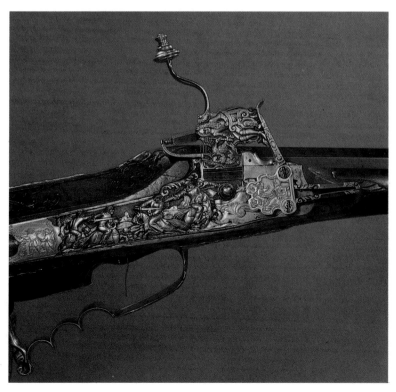

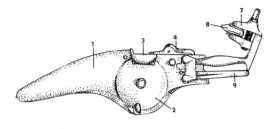

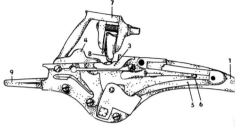

Wheellock with internal mechanism
1 Lockplate
2 Wheel
3 Priming pan
4 Pan-cover
5 Mainspring
6 Trigger-lever
7 Cock
8 Flint
9 Cock-spring

The mainspring located on the inner side of the lockplate was attached ▸
it. This is, however, not true of the French wheellock where the mainsprin▸
was seated in the gunstock. This type also featured the wheel spindle pro
truding from the other side of the stock rather than coming through th
lockplate.

In various periods and areas the shape and location of the mainspring a
well as of the lockplate, the cock and other elements of the lock mechanis▸
kept changing. After the middle of the 17th century the wheel, original▸

222 Fragments of two wheellocks with outer mainspring, datable after 1550; found in a field near the village
Mirovice in Bohemia. It may be the case of the type described in records of the period as Bohemian outer igniti▸
lock (*Handror mit aussern bohemischen Feuerschlösser*) from which the wheellock of the later *tschinke* guns m▸
have originated.
▼

◄ 221 Wheellock pistol, with monogram *FP* (the mark with a lily), France, first quarter of 17th century.

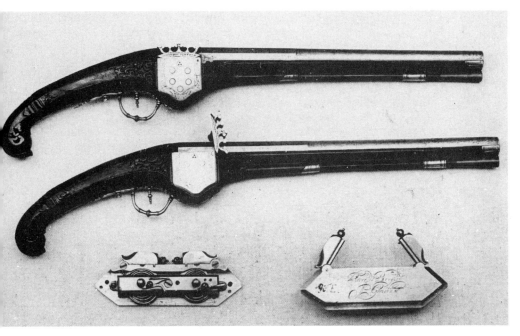

223 Pair of pistols with watertight wheellocks, Lafontaine, Mourges, 1642. Pair of double watertight wheellocks, Pierre Bergier, Grenoble, *c.* 1640. The locks have spiral mainsprings, the wheel-spindle protrudes at the left side (one of features typical of the French wheellock). Tilting pan-cover holding the piece of pyrites functions as the cock.

protruding from the lockplate, was located out of sight inside it with only the spindle coming out of the lockplate. In Central Europe this type was in general use from the second half of the 17th century and became prominent in other areas, too, where wheellocks were already being displaced by snaphaunce locks and flintlocks. To facilitate handling the cock, some specimens feature either a ring-like extension, or, more frequently, a thumb-piece, still short and seldom used in the 16th century, but considerably lengthened and almost universally used in the 17th and 18th centuries. In the later period, the cock, too, is as a rule covered by a small plate serving as an additional surface for decoration.

As long as the cock is not lowered and remains in the upright position, no accidental shot is possible, but neither is instant use of the weapon. To make it possible to have the weapon ready, a number of safety-catch devices were introduced — some of them having already made an appearance on matchlock weapons. On the other hand, to increase reliability, two cocks could be used on a single-barrelled weapon or a pivoted cock with a clamp on each side, thus providing a handy spare means of ignition in case of failure.

Besides the usual wheellock types there appeared, on a fairly restricted scale, various designs featuring different components. A coiled mainspring can be found instead of a V-spring, or just a segment instead of a complete wheel. There also were self-spanning weapons in which the wheel was wound by moving the cock, thus making the otherwise indispensable spanner redundant. Waterproof wheellocks emerged, too, which kept the powder in the priming pan dry and the weapon fully functional even in ba weather. Some wheellocks were fitted with a vertical cylinder covering tl pan and acting as a small funnel to carry the smoke produced at ignition ¶ and away so that the shooter could keep aiming at the target.

Making a relatively complex and demanding wheellock often represent an obligatory task for craftsmen wishing to join the rank of masters and th the gunmaker's guild. For this reason or as a result of a customer's specific tion a wheellock may appear even in a period when, in the particular are the system had already been rendered obsolete by evolution. In Centr Europe, however, even in the second half of the 18th century the wheello was still a commonly used weapon.

SNAPHAUNCE AND FLINTLOCK FIREARMS

Snaphaunce locks and flintlocks require the cock, with the flint clamped in its jaws, to be pulled back manually into the full-cock position before firing. Pulling the trigger then makes the cock — powered by the mainspring — swing forward striking the flint against the steel plate, producing the sparks necessary for ignition of the priming powder in the pan.

The earliest written evidence of the existence of the snaphaunce lock comes from Italy and Sweden in 1547 and in the course of the 16th century early snaphaunce locks can be found over a considerable part of Europe. The individual variants take their names from the country or area where they were used or where they originated and from whence they spread elsewhere. Sometimes, however, they were named after the place where they were first discovered by later scholars, which need not necessarily imply that they had actually originated there.

The principal distinctive features of the individual types include the loca-

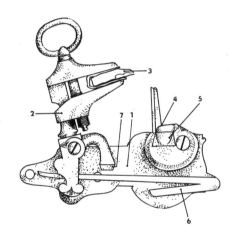

Catalan (miquelet) lock
1 Lockplate
2 Cock
3 Flint
4 Battery-frizzen (steel and pan-cover)
5 Pan
6 Mainspring
7 Trigger lever

224 Rifle with Baltic snaphaunce lock, Sweden, mid-17th century.

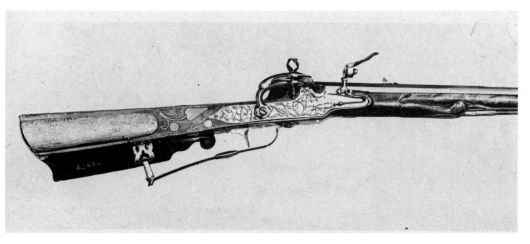

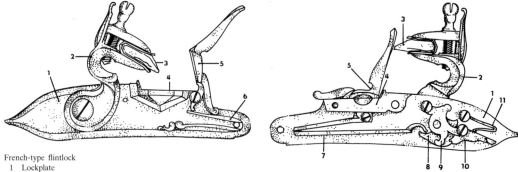

French-type flintlock
1 Lockplate
2 Cock
3 Flint
4 Pan
5 Battery-frizzen (steel and
  pan-cover)
6 Spring for steel and
  pan-cover
7 Mainspring
8 Tumbler
9 Tumbler-bridle
10 Sear-lever
11 Sear-spring

tion of the mainspring which can be found either on the outside of the lockplate (early German and Scandinavian locks, the Russian lock, the *à la Romana* type and the Catalan lock — also referred to as the Spanish lock or *miquelet* in literature), or on the inside (the Dutch lock, the English and the Scottish locks or the Florentine lock). Another factor is whether the steel and the pan-cover are two separate parts as typical of most types or combined in one functional unit (the battery). Naturally, these two criteria alone would not suffice to differentiate the many types of locks. Further design elements and details are of consequence while classifying them, e.g. the way safety-catch devices secured the cock against accidental firing or the mode of the mainspring acting upwards or downwards on the toe or the heel of the cock as well as other design details. Even the shapes of some components are of importance; e.g. those of the cock make a distinction between the

225 Italian snaphaunce weapons with *alla fiorentina* lock. Pistol with trigger-guard missing, barrel by Lazarino Cominazzo, lock by Giovanni Battista Buoni, Cavriago, end of 17th century. Gun produced in the town of Brento in 1761.

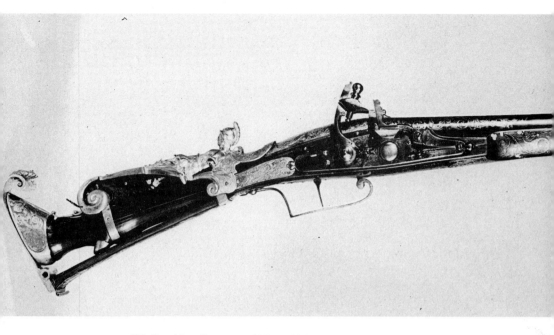

226 One of the earliest weapons with French flintlock by Marin le Bourgeoys, Lisieux, early 17th century.

Swedish, the Norwegian and the Baltic variants of the Scandinavian lock.

The final form in the evolution of locks of this type is represented by the variant which originated in France at the beginning of the 17th century and whose invention can be most likely attributed to Marin le Bourgeoys. The French flintlock has its mainspring located on the inside of the lockplate; the steel and the pan-cover are combined in one unit. The cock is firmly connected to the tumbler which features two notches to engage the trigger-lever, so that there are two positions of the cock available — the half-cock safety position in which the weapon cannot be fired, and full-cock. In contrast to all preceding types where the trigger lever was controlled by a vertically placed trigger operated horizontally, in the French-type flintlock the combined sear and trigger lever works vertically.

Shortly after its invention the French flintlock spread rapidly, first in France and then throughout the rest of Europe in the following decades, driving — with a few exceptions — the snaphaunce lock out of use. In some peripheral regions (Scotland and the Scandinavian rural areas) the local variants survived and so did, till the early 19th century, the Florentine lock in Tuscany and Emilia. To a lesser extent production of other types, e.g. of the Roman lock, went on, too. However, the only variant which represented a large-scale and lasting competition for the French flintlock was the Spanish lock — the miquelet. Till the end of the flintlock era it was used in Spain and Portugal, but it was also in favour all over the Mediterranean area. Miquelet locks can often be found on weapons of southern Italian provenance (the territory in question being politically connected with Spain over a long period) and they also had a pronounced influence on

193

227 Pistol with English snaphaunce lock, England, 1593.

228 Pair of all-metal Scottish pistols with snaphaunce locks, 1662. Some Scottish pairs of pistols feature a right-hand lock on one pistol and a left-hand lock on the other; there is no trigger-guard. Scottish pistols were not carried in holsters but hung from the belt, and for this reason they were provided with a belt-hook.

Balkan arms as well as on weapons of other areas outside Europe under Islamic influence. With the exception of southern Europe the miquelet only exceptionally achieved prominence, although its occurence is not so isolated as has hitherto been claimed. Many noble families of the Hapsburg monarchy were related by marriage to the Spanish aristocracy, and thus it is no surprise that Austrian and Bohemian gunmakers, evidently at the request of their customers, were making firearms with the miquelet lock.

Even prior to the invention of the French flintlock we can find examples where a variant influenced the design of another snaphaunce lock. Still more pronounced was the appeal of the French flintlock, some elements of which made themselves felt in the later English and Florentine locks. This influence manifested itself in the mother country of the miquelet, too, and in the 18th century there originated special constructions called *à la tres modas* (according to three fashions) combining elements of the miquelet, the Roman lock and the French flintlock, or *à la moda* lock, sometimes referred to as the Maḍrid lock.

During the more than 200 years of its existence the French flintlock itself was evolving. Its individual elements were changed as well as the shapes of some parts. Introduction of a new part, the tumbler-bridle, in the second half of the 17th century represented a significant improvement. The function of the bridle, parallel with the lockplate, was to secure the tumbler against deflection from its vertical position. In certain periods flat and convex profiles of lockplate and cock alternated in France. However, this detail can hardly be used for a more exact dating in other countries, since outside France these fashion trends were adopted after a certain delay, and, moreover, both styles can be found side by side during the same period.

229   Pair of pistols with *alla Romana* locks, Antonio Sicurani, Rome, *c.* 1700.

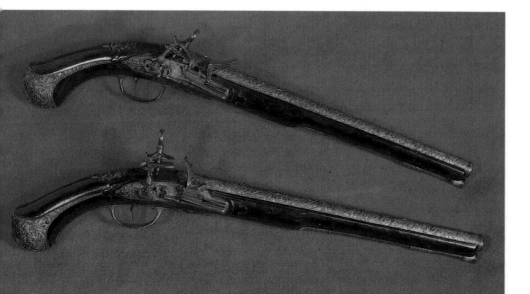

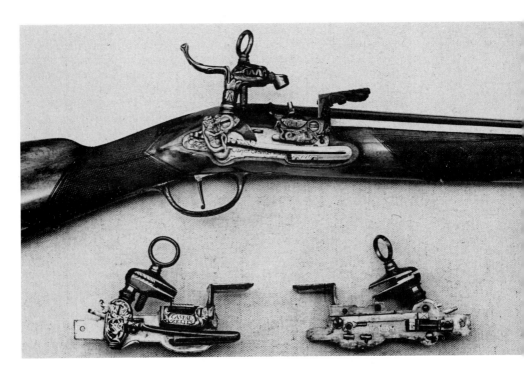

230 Specimens of *alla Catalana* locks produced in Central Europe.
Pair of locks by Caspar Zelner, Vienna, *c.* 1700.
Single-barrelled gun by Caspar Neireiter, Prague, 1673.
Neireiter's hunting gun was converted to the percussion system about 1830 — a hammer in the jaws of the c
replaced the original flintlock and a nipple was inserted into the pan; otherwise the lock was preserved, inclu
the no longer functional steel. At the same time the gun was provided with a new stock. The owner of the per
was using a weapon whose barrel and lock mechanism were already over 150 years old.

Some technical innovations introduced in the last quarter of the 18th ce
tury were of more significance. First of all it was a T-shaped link fitt
between the mainspring and the tumbler, so that the spring no longer act
on the tumbler directly, but via this link. Of course, both the T-shaped li
and the tumbler-bridle are located behind the lockplate, so that it is nece
sary to take the lock out to find them. However, the small roller beari
placed on the heel of the steel and thus facilitating its movement is visib
from outside. This small roller bearing started being used in England in t
1770s and was soon adopted elsewhere, first of all on weapons of high
quality. Various improvements, both real and claimed appeared, and at t
turn of the 18th and 19th centuries there were diverse types of 'waterpro
priming pans which were to prevent moisture from dripping inside on to t
powder. From the beginning of the 19th century, first in France and En
land, then elsewhere, along with the classical S-shaped cocks (also referr
to as 'swan's neck' type), cocks in the shape of reversed 'C' were being us

In the same way as with other lock systems, in the era of flintlock firear
we can find systems differing, albeit slightly, from the standard patte
There were, for example, weapons with all-metal stocks where the co
ponents could not be put inside the stock itself and were consequen

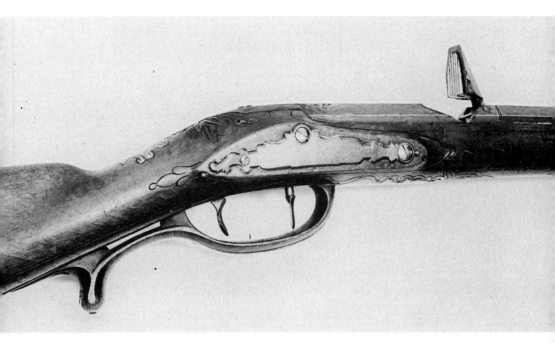

231 Single-barrelled gun with internal flintlock, by Ferdinand Morávek, Český Krumlov, end of 18th century. Its hinged steel is held flush with the barrel outline when the weapon is fired. The cock is located in a hollow chamber behind the barrel and activated by a coiled spring. The action is cocked by a vertical lever located in front of the trigger but enclosed within the trigger-guard. On some other specimens this is done by a lever projecting horizontally from a slot on each side of the stock. The weapon also features the so-called Capuchin stock with trigger-guard of wood which was carved as an integral part of the stock. This is typical of some 18th- and early 19th-century Central European weapons.
Originally the trigger-guard was all-wood; later on it was reinforced by a metal (iron and brass) band.

232 Single-barrelled gun with *à la moda* lock and Madrid-style butt, Antonio Rovira, Igualada, Catalonia, 1758.

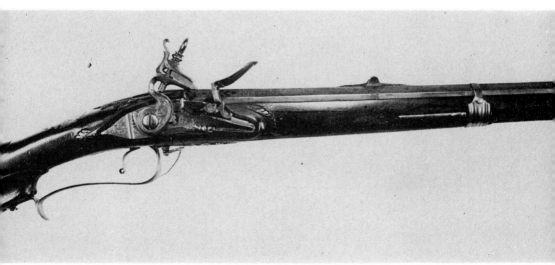

233 Short stubby pistol with Catalan lock; the weapon is typical of 17th- and 18th-century gunmakers from the Spanish township of Ripoll. Lockplates of Catalan locks were limited to the smallest possible dimensions.

234 Pair of French flintlock pistols (the cock missing on one weapon), cased, Boutet et Fils, manufacturer of Versailles, *c.* 1810. The cock in the shape of reversed *C.*

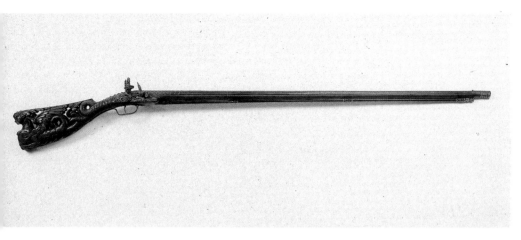

235 Gun with snaphaunce lock, Netherlands, c. 1640. Lockplate and carved butt decorated with motifs of mermaid, dragons and sea monsters.

◀ 236 Single-barrelled gun with flintlock, early 18th century, Dietrichstein coat of arms (two vintners' knives) on barrel. Coexistence of different lock-types can be seen on the weapon, too. Lock is French type, but frizzen (with grooved steel), the jaws of the cock and the connecting screw are the same as in Catalan lock.

237 Pocket pistol by Samuel Brunn, London, early 19th century.
The central cock was better for pocket pistols, as it offered less obstruction than the laterally positioned variety when the weapon was being drawn out of the pocket. From the same reason the pistol is provided with a pivoted trigger which jumps out of its slot in the stock when the action has been cocked.

placed on both its sides; there were firearms with under-hammer action (to prevent the cock from obstructing aiming). Weapons with internal (or concealed) lock, apparently a Czech invention, were a predecessor of the much later hammerless guns. The whole lock mechanism was located in a hollow chamber behind the barrel. Box-lock pistols spread in England in the second half of the 18th century. These were equipped with a central cock and a priming pan over the breech, without a tumbler (the mainspring acted directly on the heel of the cock), and were provided with a sliding safety-catch above the top of the butt behind the cock. Pistols of this type were later produced in Belgium and elsewhere.

238 Single-barrelled gun with detonator lock, Joseph Contriner, Vienna, c. 1820. The fulminate container is interconnected, via a tie-element, with the hammer. After the hammer has been cocked the small pan is filled with the fulminate into which the hammer strikes after the trigger has been pulled.

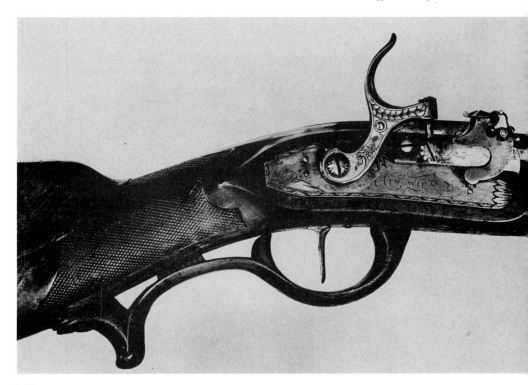

PERCUSSION WEAPONS

Fulminates, substances detonating on impact, were first used towards the end of the 18th century. Although they could not replace gunpowder in the breech they made themselves useful as an agent for igniting it and consequently they replaced fine gunpowder in the priming pan. The early variants of the percussion system are called detonating locks. The first weapon of this type was patented by A. Forsyth, a Scottish clergyman, in 1807. The 'scent bottle', a shaped pivoted magazine filled with fulminate was the basic part of the lock. It deposited the necessary quantity of fulminate into the pan where the hammer exploded it by means of a separate firing pin. Forsyth's invention was soon imitated in many countries on the Continent and within a short time less sophisticated, safer variants appeared. These used deposits of fulminate fitted into various metal or paper tube primers, discs and pills and later fashioned as tape priming on a movable strip of paper.

The copper percussion cap containing the fulminate, fitted over the end of the nipple, proved itself the most advantageous system. In comparison with the flintlock, the cock of the percussion lock had no jaws, but struck the cap in a hammer-like action. The steel, pan and spring were removed from the lockplate and replaced by the nipple. About 1820 this percussion-lock became known in England; several English gunmakers claimed its invention, and in the course of the 1820s it spread to the Continent. The older detonator lock was used in some areas for some time; then, however, the percussion cap gained dominance and remained in use till the end of the muzzle-loader era.

Conversion of the flintlock to the percussion system was a relatively simple task, and many military or civilian weapons were provided with a more advanced ignition system. As a rule, today's collectors hold the opinion that weapons converted in such a way are less valuable than if they had been left in their original flintlock state — which is true in most cases. Some

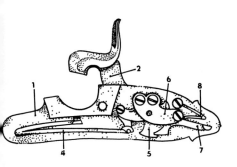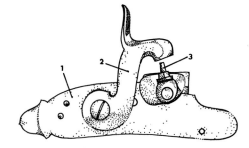

Percussion lock
1	Lockplate	5	Tumbler
2	Cock	6	Tumbler-bridle
3	Nipple	7	Sear-lever
4	Mainspring	8	Sear-spring

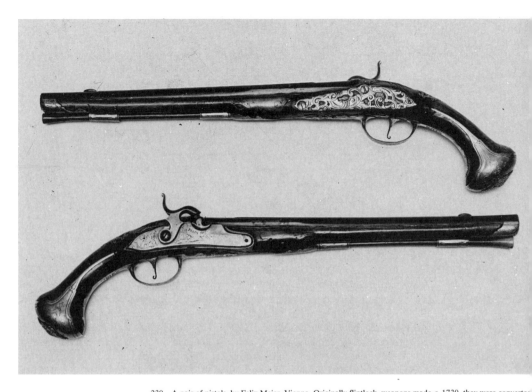

239 A pair of pistols, by Felix Meier, Vienna. Originally flintlock, weapons made *c.* 1730, they were converted to the percussion system about a century later (*c.* 1840).

240 Single-barrelled gun with percussion box-lock, A. V. Lebeda, Prague, 1829. The box-lock, patented by A. V. Lebeda in 1828, did not have the mechanism mounted on the inner side of the lockplate, but set into a box inserted into the stock from above, behind the barrel (or barrels). In such a way the mechanism was better protected againts damage or other adverse effects, and dismantling it was easier, too.

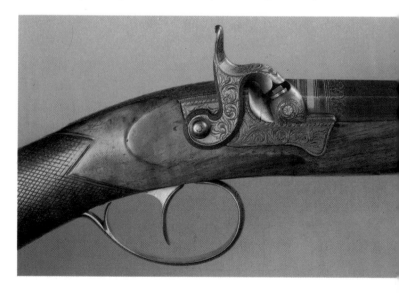

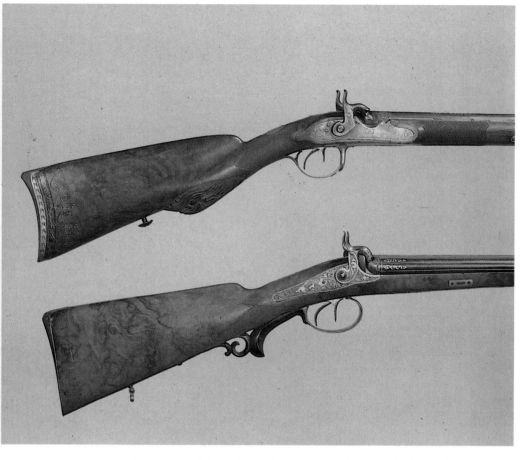

241 Double-barrelled gun with percussion lock and forward-oriented mainspring, Fabrik zu Suhl, *c.* 1830. Double-barrelled gun with percussion lock and back-action mainspring. Jọhann Leonhardt Dotter, Würzburg, 1854.

people try to re-convert the original — a course not to be recommended. Conversion of flintlock weapons to the percussion system was mostly carried out by gunmakers and examples of a sensitive approach to the task are not uncommon. Moreover, each weapon was maintained in use for its entire life. The original owner, as well as his successor, not only required the necessary maintenance and repairs, but often had the lock mechanism, the sights, the stock or other parts reshaped or replaced according to their own demands. All this should be taken into account when considering the validity of a re-conversion.

The era of the percussion lock in Europe lasted no longer than about 50 years. The percussion lock therefore was not developed into as many variants as its longer-used predecessors. Under-hammer action enjoyed wider application than with flintlock weapons, and a side-action lock appeared, too. There exist weapons with top action and hammers positioned centrally over the barrel as well as other special designs, such as the box-lock by the

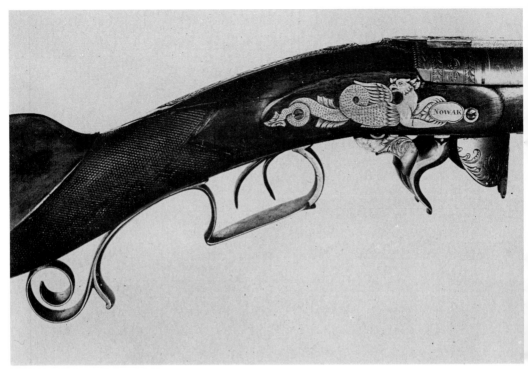

242　Percussion double-barrelled gun with under-hammer action, Joseph Nowak, Vienna, *c.* 1840.

243　Double-barrelled gun with percussion locks of special design, by Pottet-Delcusse, Paris, *c.* 1835. The central hammers are the end sections of the mainspring which, at the same time, act as the trigger-guard. After screwing off the wing screw (behind the hammers) the lock can be dismantled without any tools.

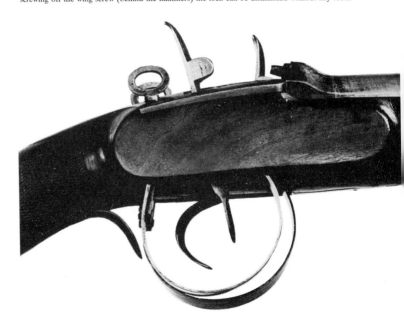

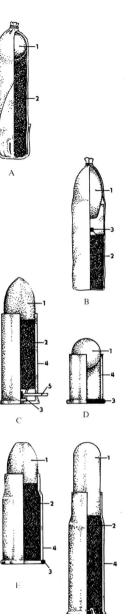

Prague gunmaker Lebeda. Fashion influenced the shapes of lockplates and some other details, and side by side with locks where the mainspring was located in front of the hammer, back-action locks (with the mainspring directed backwards behind the hammer) can frequently be found. Although back-action locks were already used with flintlock systems, their application was then limited to cases where the weapon design called for it, as in shoulder guns and pistols with drop-barrel action or over-and-under turn-over barrels.

In most of Europe percussion weapons went out of use in the 1870s. However, for export to other continents as well as to some peripheral corners of Europe (mainly the Balkan area) not only percussion weapons, but flintlock ones continued to be produced, primarily in the Belgian town of Liège, well into the 20th century. It is quite understandable, since modern weapons using cartridges cannot take anything else but the specific ammunition for which they were designed. There was certainly no problem in obtaining the appropriate ammunition in Western or Central Europe where a wide assortment of commercial ammunition was available in every little town. In other areas, however, where it was not so, an owner of a modern weapon was forced to keep a considerable supply of ammunition; running out of it rendered the weapon unusable. A flintlock weapon could manage with a sufficient supply of gunpowder only; the owner could make the projectiles himself, or, in case of need, even use some locally available substitutes.

Principal types of cartridges
A Paper cartridge for muzzle-loaders
B Paper cartridge for Dreyse needle-guns
C Lefaucheux pin-fire cartridge
D Flobert cartridge
E Rim-fire cartridge
F Centre-fire cartridge

1 Projectile 2 Powder charge 3 Priming cap (fulminate compound) 4 Cartridge case 5 Firing pin

CARTRIDGES

The further development of firearms is connected with the development of self-contained, self-primed and self-obturated cartridges. In all the previous systems the three basic components necessary for a round — gunpowder, igniting agent (a little priming powder in the pan or a priming cap for percussion weapons) and the projectile — were loaded separately. As early as the 17th century — particularly in the armies of the period — the desired amount of gunpowder was measured beforehand and put into tubular wooden container and later into a paper wrapping. From the turn of the 17th and 18th centuries onwards the paper cartridge contained both the gunpowder and the ball. During the percussion era priming caps were often attached to the paper 'cartridge'. These arrangements could speed up the loading process since the shooter had all the components he needed put together beforehand. Yet he had to load each of them separately.

One of the first self-contained cartridges was developed by J. S. Pauly, a Paris gunmaker, in 1812; ball, gunpowder and fulminate compound were enclosed in cardboard cartridge case with brass base. Because of a labour-intensive and costly production process the Pauly cartridge did not see much practical application. The task of developing an integrated self-contained, self-primed and self-obturated cartridge occupied the minds of many inventors in the course of the 19th century. Only the milestones can be discussed, even though other inventors, not mentioned here, contributed to the final solution of the problem.

In the mid-1830s the Lefaucheux pin-fire cartridge originated in Paris. Its paper cartridge case had a brass base from which a short metal rod, with the cap set at its base, protruded laterally to be struck by the falling hammer. Later on the cartridge was provided with an all-metal casing to obturate the escaping gas, and from the 1850s the Lefaucheux cartridge became the first

245   French revolver Model 1858 (Lefaucheux system).

244   Breech-loader with breech tilting upwards (using a lever set into the neck of the butt), 1812 patent by Johannes Samuel Pauly, Paris.

246 Single-barrelled needle-gun, Nicolaus Dreyse, Sömmerda, *c*. 1865.
Double-barrelled needle-gun, Rudolf Berger, Köthen, *c*. 1870.

integrated, self-obturating and self-primed cartridge to be produced commercially.

From the 1840s cartridges for the Dreyse Prussian needle-gun enjoyed great popularity. In the same way as some other designs of the period they had only combustible paper wrapping which was to be consumed in the explosion. However, after a number of shots the remnants of the incompletely burnt wrappings could hinder the function of the weapon. Escape of gas from the breech was another inherent weakness of the needle-gun and its cartridge.

247 Wheellock breech-loading pistol with the breech tipping to the side, South Germany (probably Augsburg), mid-16th century. The earliest pistols used to have straight stock resembling dagger hilts and only later on were they developed into curved stocks.

207

A rim-fire cartridge was developed at the end of the 1840s by another Frenchman, Flobert, and in this the fulminate was deposited around the inside rim of the cartridge base. There was no gunpowder in the Flobert cartridge and the projectile was propelled simply by the energy provided by the fulminate compound. At the end of the 1850s, the Smith and Wesson Company introduced rim-fire cartridges on the U.S. market for their first revolvers. From the 1860s on there began large-scale manufacture of various cartridges, not only rim-fire but centre-fire, too (with the priming cap inserted in the centre of the base of the case). Metal cartridges created another problem not known before — the necessity of removing the spent cartridge case from the chamber. This meant that additional parts were added to the breech-loaders of the period in the form of various types of extractors or ejectors. On the other hand, the introduction of a self-contained, self-primed and self-obturating cartridge was an inevitable prerequisite to the development of effective and reliable breech-loaders and repeaters as well as of automatic weapons later on.

248 Pair of French flintlock pistols, breech-loaders with screw-on barrels, R. Hewse, Wooton Basset, England, c. 1660. (The upper jaw of the cock missing on the lower weapon.)

SINGLE-SHOT BREECH-LOADERS

Illustration of some breech-action systems

Obviously, loading a firearm from the breech is much less complicated and faster than loading it through the muzzle. Breech-loaders started appearing in the second half of the 15th century. The earliest examples often feature a reloadable chamber system in which the chamber can be removed from the weapon, loaded and reinserted. Sometimes hinged breech-blocks were used, opening either laterally or upwards. In the second half of the 17th century drop-action barrels, and also turn-off barrels, widespread in England, were introduced. The vertical screw-plug and a number of other designs were used. All breech-loaders were more complicated to manufacture and consequently more expensive than the contemporary muzzle-loaders. The available technology could up to the mid-19th century guarantee neither secure obturation of the breech nor prevent partial escape of the gas produced by the burning of the gunpowder. This to a certain extent reduced the effective range of the weapon; moreover, it represented a potential hazard for the shooter, which was even more important.

Around the mid-19th century there originated dozens of capping breech-loader designs — with drop-action or forward-shifting barrels, barrels swivelling open to the side or upwards, with pivoted chambers, block action etc. J. N. Dreyse considered his concept of the needle firing-pin and the cartridge design to be his principal contribution, and at first he tried using

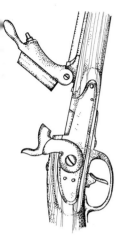

Tip-up breech-block
(Wänzl)

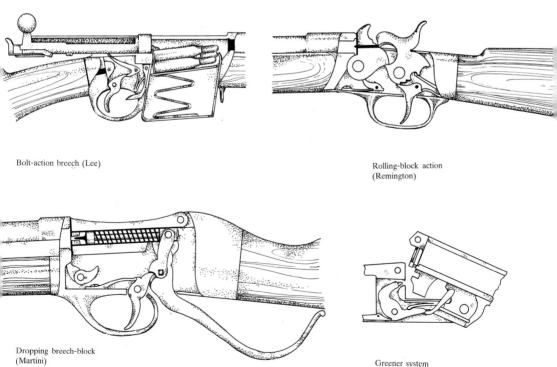

Bolt-action breech (Lee)

Rolling-block action
(Remington)

Dropping breech-block
(Martini)

Greener system

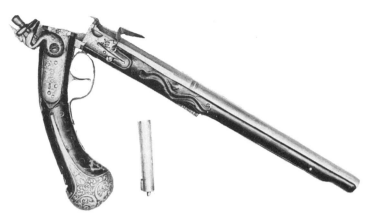

249   Pistol (one of a pair) with French flintlock, breech-loader with tipping barrel, France, c. 1670. The iron cartridge loaded beforehand is inserted into the barrel from the rear. It is typical of shoulder guns and pistols that the pan and the steel are a part of the iron cartridge case. The depicted example is an exception since these parts are mounted on the lockplate.

it to design muzzle-loaders. The occurrence of accidents during the testing of his weapons made him design a breech-loader fitted with a bolt action, a highly promising system, which secured him a place among the foremost weapon designers. The Prussian success in the war with Denmark in 1864 and particularly victory over Austria in 1866 signalled a definitive break

251   French-style lock rifle, breech-loader with vertical breech-plug operated via movement of the trigger-guard, Johann Adam Knodt, Karlovy Vary, Bohemia, c. 1730.

250   Revolving gun with match-lock, eight chambers in the cylinder, Germany, early 17th century.

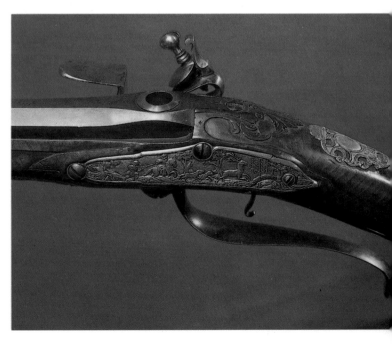

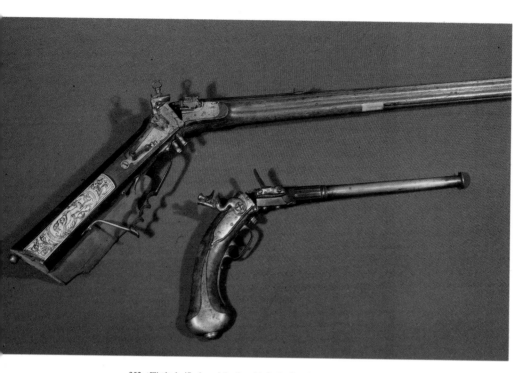

252 Flintlock rifle, breech-loader with tipping barrel, Hans Ernst Jaidtl, Brno, Moravia, *c.* 1660. Unsigned pistol of the same type, somewhat later.

through in breech-loading firearms design. In the course of a few years dozens in breech-loader designs came into being, featuring a hinged breech-block, tilting, rolling or falling block actions, bolt action both straight pull-back or rotating, as well as drop-action barrels. Many of these designs never got further than the experimental stage or were produced in small numbers; only a few saw large-scale production. It goes without saying that all these weapons were designed for self-contained, self-obturating and self-primed cartridges; moreover, single-shot weapons were already facing the keen competition presented by repeaters.

epeater with a cylindrical
ansversal) breech-block with
er and tubular magazines for
th balls and powder in the butt

REPEATERS

The endeavours to design and construct repeating firearms began at a very early date. Accelerating the rate of fire was of unquestionably great importance if we take into account the time spent loading. Yet the technological problems involved were even bigger than in the case of single-shot breech-loaders.

The simplest solution was to use a large number of barrels discharged either one after another or simultaneously in a volley. Even in the early stage of firearms development there was the so-called 'organ gun' and multi-barrelled weapons occur in later periods, too. The more barrels, the heavier the weapon, and for this reason among hand-held firearms which were to be portable, double-barrelled weapons are most common. In the earlier periods they mostly have the over-and-under barrel arrangement and only in the second half of the 18th century and in the 19th century, did the number of weapons with side-by-side barrels increase. There exist examples with more barrels; pistols are represented here more frequently than shoulder guns, since, after all, the increased weight was more acceptable in the case of a shorter weapon. On weapons firing one barrel after another either each barrel could be fitted with a separate lock mechanism, or there was just one lock on the weapon — connected with each barrel in turn through a system of cut-off touch-holes.

Later, weapons with a revolving cluster of barrels appeared and at this stage the concept of a weapon with a single barrel and a revolving cylinder with chambers was no longer far away. The term of 'revolver' or 'revolving gun' is derived from the Latin verb *revolvere*. The earliest examples go as far

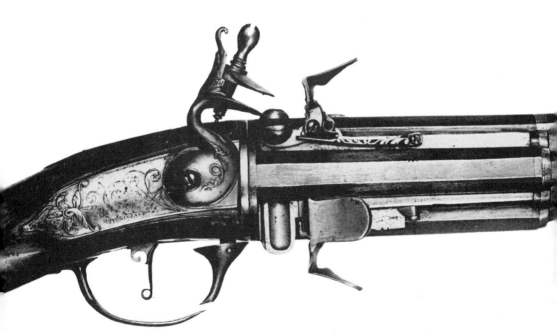

253 Revolving gun with French-style flintlock, four-chambered cylinder rotated manually; the weapon belonged to Count F. A. Sporck, Bohemia, end of 17th century.

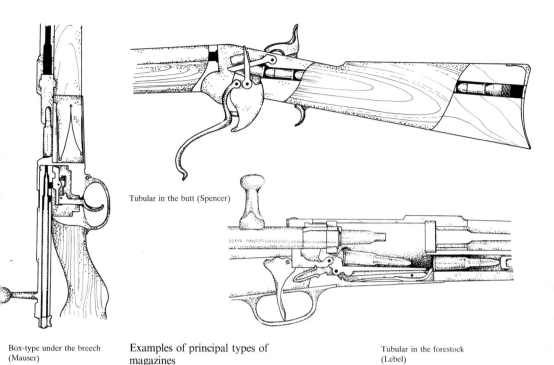

Tubular in the butt (Spencer)

Box-type under the breech
(Mauser)

Examples of principal types of
magazines

Tubular in the forestock
(Lebel)

back as the 16th century and until the 18th century revolving shoulder guns
were more common and the revolver principle was only occasionally applied to pistols. It was not until the 19th century that there was a tremendous
upsurge in the production of pistols with revolving cylinders, i.e. revolvers
— the advent of first the percussion variants, and then the breech-loading
cartridge revolvers. Credit for this development is mostly due to gunmakers

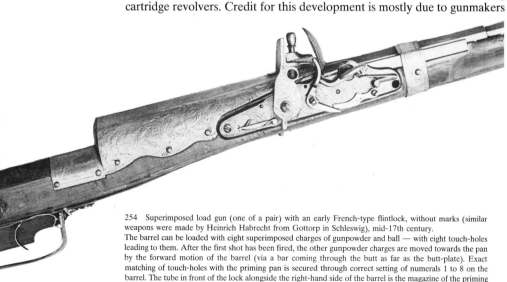

254 Superimposed load gun (one of a pair) with an early French-type flintlock, without marks (similar
weapons were made by Heinrich Habrecht from Gottorp in Schleswig), mid-17th century.
The barrel can be loaded with eight superimposed charges of gunpowder and ball — with eight touch-holes
leading to them. After the first shot has been fired, the other gunpowder charges are moved towards the pan
by the forward motion of the barrel (via a bar coming through the butt as far as the butt-plate). Exact
matching of touch-holes with the priming pan is secured through correct setting of numerals 1 to 8 on the
barrel. The tube in front of the lock alongside the right-hand side of the barrel is the magazine of the priming
powder opened manually and cut off automatically (via two levers on the lockplate) when the action is being
cocked.

256 Four-barrelled shotgun with French-style flintlock, revolving barrels, Pierre Barroy, Paris, c. 1660.

of the American continent (Samuel Colt, Messrs. Smith and Wesson, and others), but Europe, too, recorded many a remarkable design: Adams and Webley in England, Gasser in Austria, Chamelot-Delvigne in France, Nagant in Belgium, and others. The earliest revolvers employed a cylinder that had to be turned by hand, but as early as about 1680 snaphaunce revolvers appeared, attributed to John Dafte, a London gunmaker, in which cocking the action at the same time advanced the cylinder.

Revolvers can be divided into two basic categories — single-action and double-action or self-cocking; the former requires the hammer to be cocked by hand and then released by pressing the trigger, whereas just pressing the trigger suffices for firing the latter. It is true that this increases the rate of fire but the accuracy suffers. For this reason there originated revolvers whose systems enabled the action to be cocked and the cylinder advanced by either just pressing the trigger, or, in a more relaxed situation where accuracy was the top priority, by pulling the hammer back. Revolvers can also be classified using other, less significant criteria, e.g. solid frame versus open frame etc. There also appeared some designs employing magazines differing from the usual revolver barrel, but these weapons did not gain much success.

Even over the years of the growing popularity of revolvers, weapons with revolving cluster of barrels survived. Shoulder-gun varieties were rare, but pistols of this type, called 'pepperboxes', were produced in the 18th century in England, in the 19th century in Belgium and in smaller quantities elsewhere, on a comparatively large scale.

◀ 255 Revolving gun with snaphaunce lock, cylinder with nine chambers rotated by hand (the top of the patch-box in the butt not original), Central Europe, end of 16th century.

The so-called 'Roman candle' weapons offered another way of accelerating the rate of fire — a single-barrelled weapon loaded with several consecutive charges. The projectiles had blast channels drilled through them, so that the individual powder charges were interconnected and the ignition of the first shot was followed by a series of discharges in a row. This chain-reaction once started, the firer had no way of stopping it. Other superimposed types of gun employed powder charges with no interconnection, so that each of them could be discharged separately. There were double or multiple locks (one for each loaded charge) fitted along the barrel or there was a sliding lock, or alternatively a fixed lock and a movable barrel. There also existed weapons with one fixed lock and a shut-off touch-hole for each charge of powder.

Side by side with revolvers, repeaters of other systems were being produced as early as the 17th century. The principal challenge was the design of magazines. At least two were required, one for powder and one for bullets, and the mechanism to transport the projectile and the powder charge into the barrel. Some designs employed magazines fixed in the central part of the stock; others had both magazines, or at least one, in the butt, or alternatively in the forestock. In comparison with the single-shot weapons of the period these repeaters had a much higher rate of fire; on the other hand they were naturally not only much more expensive, but also over-complex from the technical point of view and prone to malfunction. The only relatively widespread variant, of which several dozen examples have been preserved, is the repeating system employing a transversal cylindrical breech block. The invention is attributed not only to the Italian gunmakers Lorenzoni or Berselli, but to other masters as well; some of them claimed

257 Four-barrelled boxlock pistol with two central cocks, England, early 19th century. Barrel plug with two touch-holes in the pan; adjusting the plug selected the upper or the lower barrel as desired.

258 Superimposed load pistol with an early type of flintlock, Netherlands, *c.* 1650. The brass pommel shaped as a human head. Four superimposed charges of gunpowder and ball can be loaded into the barrel. From the pan the touch-hole leads to the first gunpowder charge. In this space there is also an opening to the tube set alongside the opposite side of the barrel, and from this tube the touch-holes lead to the second and the third charge of gunpowder. The last (the fourth) charge has an independent shut-off touch-hole.

authorship in the marking of their weapons. Repeaters with a transversal cylindrical breech block had two tubular magazines in the butt, which fed a ball and a charge of powder into the chambers of the breech block when the weapon was tilted muzzle downwards. When the block was revolved via the lateral lever, the ball fell out of the first chamber recess into the breech part of the barrel while the powder chamber remained positioned behind the ball. Weapons of this type were produced by many gunmakers — during the last part of the 17th century in Italy, in the 18th century first of all in England, and then also in Austria, Germany, Switzerland and even Russia. This would seem to justify the conclusion that the system — no matter how complicated it may seem — must have functioned without any major trouble.

The problems of repeaters, too, could be definitely solved only after self-primed and self-obturating integrated cartridges were introduced. The designers of the second half of the 19th century launched a new version of their predecessors' ideas and fitted tubular magazines, this time for rim- and centre-fire cartridges, into the butt or the forestock. Both variants were widespread particularly in the U.S.A. (Spencer, Henry, Winchester, and others). However, starting at the end of the 1860s till the mid-1880s similar weapons were constructed by many European designers — Vetterli, Fruhwirth, Kropatschek, and others — including those who later on became famous because of their designs of repeaters with the box magazine under the breech, such as Mauser and Mannlicher.

The latter arrangement proved itself to be the most advantageous one for rifles. Prior to its introduction, various 'quickeners' and 'cartridge carrier

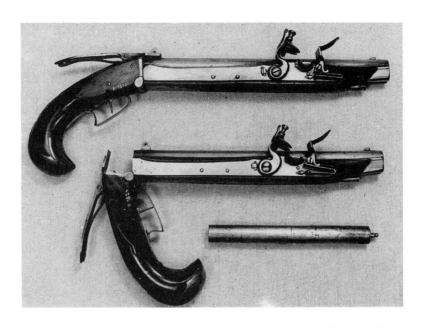

259 Paired superimposed load pistols with French-style flintlocks, *c.* 1770. Tipping barrel accepts a cylindrical magazine consisting of six screwed-together interconnected chambers. The cock will fire the first shot, and at short intervals the others will follow in sequence.

260 Flintlock repeaters with transverse breech-lock. Unsigned specimen dated 1699.
Antonio Costantini, Bologna, end of 17th century.

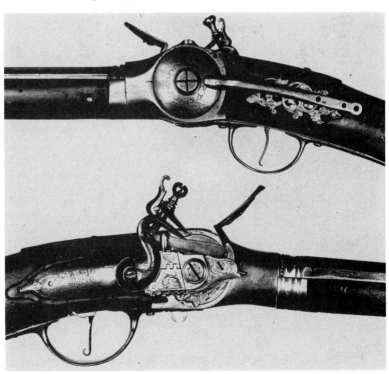

261 Detail of the foregoing weapons. Tubular magazines in the butt are marked *B* (balle, ball) and *P* (polvere, powder) in the Italian work by Costantini, while the screws shutting off the magazines are marked *K* (Kugel, ball) and *P* (Pulver, powder) in the unsigned weapon of German origin.

262 Le Mat revolver for centre-fire cartridges, *c.* 1870. The weapon is provided with two barrels — the upper one for firing bullets from the nine-chamber cylinder and the lower one for a one-shot cartridge situated in the centre of the cylinder. A lever on the hammer adjusts the striking on the upper or the lower barrel. A patent covering weapons of this system was procured in the U.S.A. by J. A. F. Le Mat in 1856; the weapon was produced in Paris and also in England and Belgium, first as a percussion revolver, then converted to Lefaucheux pin-fire cartridges, and at the end of the 1860s the designer converted it to take centre-fire cartridges.

263 Adams percussion five-shot revolver with self-cocking action, produced by A. Francotte, Liège (licence of R. Adams, London).
Six-barrelled percussion pepperbox with under-hammer action and ring-like trigger, G. Mariette, Liège.

were attempted, patented by S. Krnka in particular, whose basic feature was positioning the magazine on the central part of the stock next to the chamber. Loading was certainly accelerated, but compared to a magazine as a permanent part of the weapon this solution would just not do. Use of repeaters with the magazine situated under the breech, from the 1880s onwards, was almost universal. In England versions of the earliest design of this type by the American designer L. P. Lee were adopted, and in other countries solutions by continental designers — Mauser, Mannlicher, Mosin, and others — with vertically or just occasionally horizontally arranged magazines, e.g. Krag-Jörgensen. Weapons designed at the end of the last century were used, with minor improvements, by soldiers for over half a century, and these designs have been used for sport and target shooting up till now.

AUTOMATIC WEAPONS

Not even repeaters could fully satisfy the demand of the military for an increased rate of fire. From the 1860s on there originated various machine-guns with a mechanical function — weapons with a cluster of barrels, basically updated variants of the venerable organ guns. In Europe they were used during the 1870—71 Franco-Prussian conflict. Then, in the 1880s, the first automatic weapons proved successful. What the operators of mechanical machine-guns had had to secure by their own activity was now carried out

264 Russian infantry gun Model 1870 (Berdan II) with quick loader patented by Sylvestr Krnka, the type of quick loader dating to 1875.

265 As early as the period of single-shot breech-loaders attempts at making some lock functions automatic in order to increase the rate of loading were carried out. In Karel Krnka's experimental adaptation of Austro-Hungarian infantry gun Model 1873 (Werndl) releasing the hammer not only fired the weapon, but also opened the breech automatically.

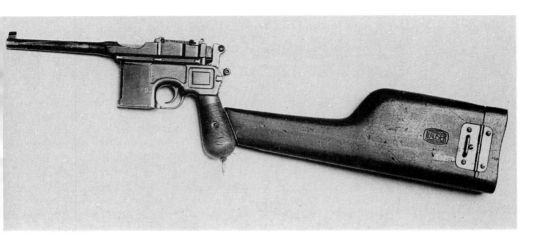

266 Mauser Model 1896 ranked among the most popular self-loading pistols of the 19th century. In the later variants, starting with 1898, the wooden holster could be attached to the butt and used as a shoulder rest.

automatically, using a part of the energy generated by the explosion of the gunpowder. While machine-guns fired bursts, 19th-century automatic hand arms were self-loading weapons, automatically ejecting the spent cartridge and transporting a new one from the magazine into the chamber. It was necessary, however, to pull the trigger for each shot. Besides a number of development models the first successful types of self-loading rifles and above all pistols (Luger, Krnka, Mauser) achieved success in the late 19th century, yet the heyday of automatic weapon design and manufacture was to be the 20th century.

The enormous technological progress of our century has naturally made itself felt in the sphere of hand-held firearms, too. However, as far as their basic design goes, no revolutionary ideas have been introduced and essentially it has been a matter of the exploitation and development of systems already known at the end of the 19th century.

CLASSIFICATION OF FIREARMS

MILITARY FIREARMS

Over the first two centuries of their existence firearms were probably an exclusively military affair, because their technical inadequacy made them practically unusable in other areas of human activity. In spite of the fact that the earliest hand-held weapons could match neither the accuracy nor the effective range or rate of loading of the crossbow or longbow, they gradually gained ground and improved. The impact of their military exploitation was immense. Gunpowder caused the knightly way of waging wars to disappear, and the social structure of armies, as well as combat methods, to change. Obviously these radical changes did not take place overnight. It was a long-running process in which a not insignificant part was played by the Hussite Wars and the spread of the Hussite combat experience from Bohemia to the surrounding countries. In the early 15th century the armoured cavalry was still the dominating factor on battlefields; a hundred years later mercenary infantry were dominant.

Matchlock weapons spread very quickly and remained in service until the turn of the 17th and the 18th centuries. The principal reason behind such longevity, even when the technically more advanced wheellocks and flintlocks had been around for some time, was their simplicity and much lower production cost. Wheellock weapons — pistols and carbines — were employed by cavalry which had not disappeared from the battlefield with the advent of mercenary infantry, but now represented a numerically smaller part of armies compared with the past. Cavalrymen were recruited from the richer strata of society and so could afford more expensive weapons; moreover, handling the glowing match was not really practical for a man on horseback.

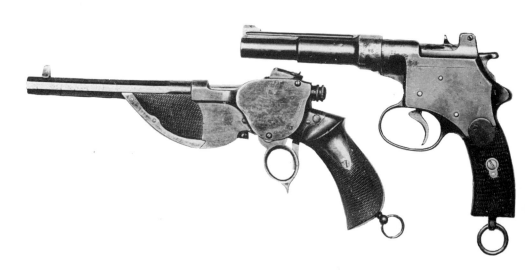

267 Five-shot pistol, design and production by Gustav Bittner, Vejprty, Bohemia, end of 19th century. Experimental model of Mannlicher pistol, 1894, five-round magazine in butt.

268 Warriors with hand guns and crossbows (incendiary arrow not only on the crossbow, but in the hand-gun barrel as well), drawing from so-called Viennese Codex, *c.* 1430 (according to *Armáda a národ*, Prague 1938).

Musketeers still represented only about half the strength of mercenary infantry of the second half of the 16th century. The properties of the fire-arms of the period, the lengthy loading in particular, made the musketeers fight in tactical formation along with the pikemen who prevented the enemy cavalry from attacking the foot soldiers before they managed to reload. The musket became a typical infantry gun; its origin is usually attributed to Spain in the second half of the 16th century. The musket barrel was set in a wooden stock which was slightly curved to form the butt. When shooting, the butt was propped against the shoulder and pressed to the cheek. The design of the stock as well as the way of holding the weapon when shooting, which became both almost universally accepted later on for shoulder guns, re-presented significant progress in the use of firearms. Curved stocks were further developed in Italy and, especially, in France.

Certain events took place in the second half of the 17th century which

269 Hussite *píšťala* (light hand gun), Bohemia, first quarter of 15th century.

270   Hook-gun, barrel from the end of 14th century (mark of the town of Vienna on the barrel), 15th-century stock.

influenced the equipment of soldiers in a significant way. Previously, military units had been formed just for the duration of the conflict, only to be disbanded after the campaign. The armament of the individual units had been their respective commanders' responsibility or had been taken care of by military entrepreneurs who hired out the enlisted soldiers for the sovereign's service. Standing armies were now created, serving in peacetime as well as in war. Demand for weapons increased, standardization was developing and state bodies began taking control of armament production. Some weapon-producing factories were established in the 17th and 18th centuries, but the major part of production for armies remained dispersed among smaller private makers. Even when army regulation models had been officially introduced, the required uniformity was not always achieved. In the records of the period we come across numerous complaints by army inspection bodies concerning the individual makers whose weapons differed from model specification in some details or even in their dimensions.

Bayonets were introduced in the second half of the 17th century. A long gun with a bayonet replaced the pike and the division of infantry into musketeers and pikemen disappeared. The firearm became the universal weapon of all infantry. It does not mean, however, that aimed firing prevailed in the infantry; in some armies the bayonet attack was considered the decisive form of infantry combat until the mid-19th century.

As already mentioned, the matchlock was the dominant military weapon till the end of the 17th century. The wheellock found favour with the cavalry — on pistols and short shoulder guns, arquebuses and the later carbines. Infantry muskets from the second half of the 17th century with wheellock and matchlock combination remained an isolated exception. Early snaphaunce locks were used by the army, too, for example on some Swedish or Russian muskets, but there were no major changes until the French flintlock came into being. From the early 18th century this variant became almost universal among military weapons of Europe, to continue dominant for over 130 years to come. The first quarter of the 18th century at the same time marked a significant dividing line when the standardization of weapons in European armies made headway, the weapons being represented from then on by regulation service models. According to generally accepted practice a model was marked by the year when its introduction was decided upon; the weapons however did not often reach to the individual military units until a few years later when sufficient numbers had been produced.

France set the pace for the manufacture of firearms in the 18th century, and its army weapons, too, were imitated elsewhere. The French infantry gun Model 1717 was a pattern for the Austrian gun of 1722 as well as for the weapons of other countries. In a number of European countries the French Model 1777 gun was imitated, including such details as the heart-shaped cut-out section of the cock; the weapon was at the same time one of the first unified systems of army firearms including different variants of the identical basic design (shoulder guns for infantry, artillery, navy, cavalry musketon and pistol).

In the 18th century the individual models of infantry shoulder guns saw service for a relatively long time without any change or with only minor modifications. This was true for England, too, where the service weapon was nicknamed 'Brown Bess', as well as for France, Austria and other countries. Details were improved, though, and iron ramrods were introduced in the course of the 18th century to replace the original wooden ones whose breaking rendered the weapon useless. Although weapons of different armies had the same type of lock mechanism and were often similar both as to their overall design concept and a number of diverse details, weapons of some countries showed features making them recognizable at first sight.

271   Hook-gun, Central Europe, 1440−60. Barrel of so-called socket type (set on edge in functional position so that the upper edge could be used for aiming).

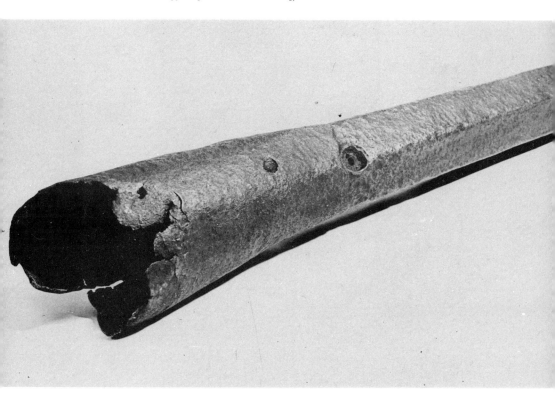

272   Musketeer by Jacob de Gheyn, 1608, coloured copperplate.

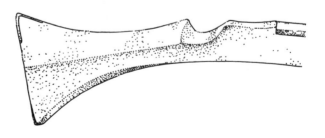

Butt typical of muskets, 17th century.

226

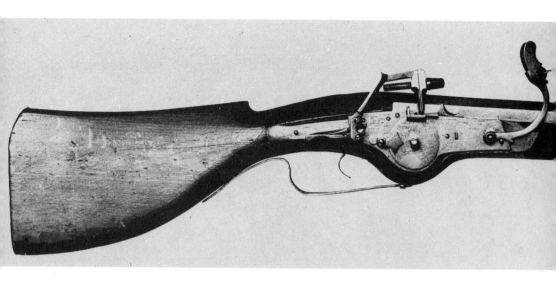

273   Austrian musket with combined match- and wheellock, design of 1686, Suhl, end of 17th century.

Prussian weapons are characterized by the special shape of the butt, a robust lock and the oval plate on the neck of the stock bearing the initials of the sovereign ruling at the time of production.

A new type of infantry — the skirmishers — originated in the second half of the 18th century. The deep 17th-century battle formations were aban-

274   Matchlock musket, Suhl, Thirty Years' War period.

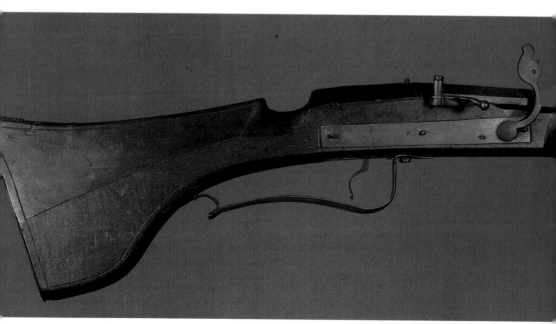

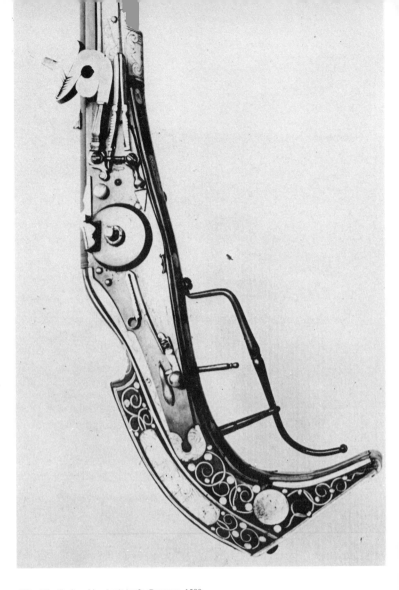

275 Wheellock carbine (*poitronel*), Germany, 1589.

doned and a linear formation was typical of the 18th century. The soldiers advanced closely side by side, in several long lines, firing volleys on order. After the first row had fired, the second and third rows fired while the first row was reloading. After the opening volleys, the bayonet attack took place. Skirmisher units, although a part of the infantry, did not advance in linear formation, but singly, seeking cover in the field, choosing their targets and firing individually at selected targets. If possible, they tried to eliminate first of all the important enemy personnel — officers, couriers and gunners. Compared to general infantry it was necessary for them to have better weapons and to be better marksmen. The first units of this type were re-

276 French cavalry musketon Model 1777, Manufacture Royale de Charleville.

cruited from game keepers and kept their name even after this new infantry component increased in numbers, having been joined by other soldiers with specialist knowledge. Jaeger guns were somewhat shorter than general infantry weapons, but they were provided with rifled barrels. Although the

277 Two weapons from the period of Napoleonic Wars: Russian infantry gun Model 1808, Tula, 1812. English infantry gun (pattern musket with 39-inch barrel), late 18th century.

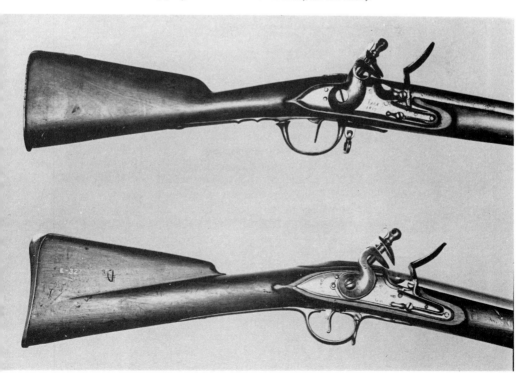

278 The Austrians fighting the Turks on the outskirts of Belgrade in 1789, coloured copperplate. Pictorial evidence of 18th- and 19th-century battles records unexpectedly frequent use of army long guns as clubs, not firearms, or, with the bayonet attached, as thrusting weapons. In man-to-man combat there was no time to reload, and so a gun held by the barrel was turned into a club.

significance of rifling had been known for a long time, the military did not put much emphasis on accuracy of fire. Army weapons were still smooth-bore and naturally also cheaper than the rifled guns. Jaeger rifles were also provided with better sights and the octagonal barrel was fixed in the fore-stock by pegs, while many other military firearms had cylindrical barrels held in the forestock by barrel-bands.

The cavalry put wheellock weapons aside at the beginning of the 18th century and started using flintlock weapons. Specialization was greater in the cavalry of the period than in the infantry. Heavy cavalry included cuirassiers. There were dragoons — originally mounted infantry using horses en route but fighting in the same manner as the rest of the infantry. Hussars came from Hungary and uhlans from Polish territories, but hussar and uhlan units were created even in countries geographically remote from these areas.

Cavalry firearm equipment included both pistols and short shoulder guns, musketons and carbines, differing for the individual types of cavalry in calibre, length and overall execution. The shortest carbines used were hussars' equipment.

Various technical units also originated in the armies of the second half of the 18th century, such as miners and sappers. Specialization in military activities went on in the first half of the 19th century, too, and ordnance specialization along with it — sometimes in an exaggerated way not justified

279 Austrian hussar carbine Model 1770, saddle bar and ring on the left side of stock.

by the actual needs. While basic design of army guns was identical in the given country and period, a host of variants could exist, differing in length or in various details. In such a way as well as infantry guns and cavalry carbines there originated variants not only for skirmishers, fusiliers and pioneers and cadets at military schools, where the variation was justified by their shorter stature, and also for artillerymen, the medical corps and other services.

280 The battle of Waterloo, June 18th, 1815 (Emperor Napoleon in the left foreground), coloured aquatint, Johann Lorenz Rugendas, 1816.

281 Austrian dragoon carbine Model 1770. Breeech-loader with chamber tipping upwards, designed by Giuseppe Crespi, Milan.

In the percussion era other significant changes took place. Rifled barrels previously used for skirmishers' guns and some carbines only, became more widespread, starting, in the 1830s, to dominate the army equipment of about the mid-19th century. However, rifled muzzle-loaders were more difficult to load. It was necessary to force the bullet into the muzzle, and its passage down the barrel was far from being easy. For this reason it was loaded with a greased wad which facilitated the passage and at the same time protected the rifling against damage. When the shot was fired, the wad prevented part of the gas from escaping around the bullet, in such a way increasing the effective range of the weapon.

The percussion system itself, widespread in hunting weapons of the 1820s and 1830s, became supreme in armies only in the 1840s. In a way similar to civil life, in the army there was a period of conversion, during which flintlock weapons were being transformed into percussion ones. It is interesting to note that the proper percussion system with nipple and priming cap sometimes made slow headway in the army. Preference was often given to the earlier variants at that time already superseded and abandoned in civilian weapons. In the Hapsburg army, for example, the Console or the Augustin systems were superseded by the actual percussion system only after the mid-19th century. The reason may have been the evidently easier and less costly conversion of flintlock weapons into these systems, as both the original pan and the touch-hole remained.

Empiricism was being superseded by scientifical achievements in the mid-19th century. The round ball previously used for centuries was replace with ogival bullets and muzzle-loading was facilitated by various types of compression or by expansive bullets, which, with their diameter smaller than the bore, passed smoothly through the barrel all the way from the muzzle to the chamber. Only there were they expanded — either by the impact of the ramrod forcing the bullet on to a mandrel placed in the chamber, or at the moment of the explosion through the impact of the gases on the base of the bullet.

As early as the flintlock era, military breech-loaders appeared, although only on a limited scale. Percussion breech-loaders became more widespread, notably as cavalry carbines in particular; designs of these weapons originated mostly in the U.S.A., but also in England (W. Terry, W. Richards, and others). However, an important change was brought about by the Dreyse needle-gun. Nicolaus Dreyse designed a new paper cartridge with the igniting fulminate pellet fitted in between the powder and the bullet. This

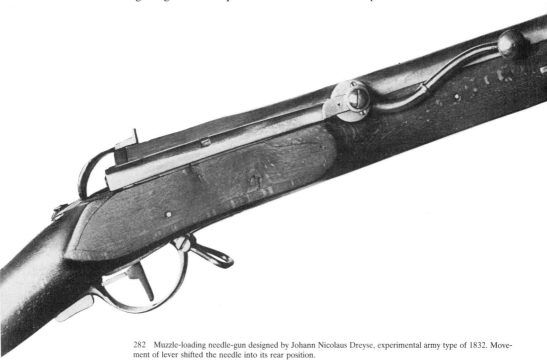

282 Muzzle-loading needle-gun designed by Johann Nicolaus Dreyse, experimental army type of 1832. Movement of lever shifted the needle into its rear position.

283 Prussian infantry gun, second half of 18th century. Cylindrical smooth-bore barrel without rear sights, ramrod of iron.
Austrian jaeger gun Model 1838 (conversion of jaeger flintlock gun Model 1795 to Console system). Octagonal rifled barrel with rear sights, patch-box in butt, trigger-guard with finger-rest; ramrod was carried separately.

position, he discovered, could produce detonation, as the hammer strike on the cap could be replaced by just piercing the fulminate pellet with a needle. He applied this idea to weapons with a needle-like firing pin named after this part. Prussia was the first country in the world to rearm its army with breech-loaders — infantry guns Model 1841 and the subsequent models of Dreyse needle-guns.

In the mid-1860s some officers in European armies, mostly the younger and low-ranking ones, were aware of the experience gained during the American Civil War, where breech-loaders and repeaters had been used on a limited scale. The effect of Prussian needle-guns in the conflict with Denmark in 1864 encouraged the introduction of breech-loaders into the army. However, it was not until the lightning victory of Prussia over Austria in 1866, attributed to different firearms, that a general change of opinion took place. At the same time the Austrian muzzle-loaders were more accurate and had a longer effective range than the Prussian needle-guns, whose rate of fire, however, was approximately three times higher. Exploitation of the other tactical advantage of breech-loaders — ease of loading and combat action while in the prone position — was appreciated by the rank-and-file far more readily than by the commanders. (In the battle at Česká Skalice in 1866 when soldiers facing enemy fire started lying down, Prussian General Steinmetz declared that no one was to lie down before being killed.)

After the Austro-Prussian war the general introduction of breech-loaders took place in European armies. Needle-guns appeared in France (Chassepot 1866), in Italy (Carcano 1867), in Russia (Carlé 1867), but on the whole other breech-loaders' designs prevailed. In many armies the accumulated stockpiles of ballistically adequate muzzle-loaders together with reasons of economy resulted in conversions to breech-loaders while brand new models were originating at the same time. Dozens of inventors and designers were offering the most diverse designs, but only some of them actually saw practical application. Various types of hinged breech blocks tilting to the side (Snider in England, Krnka in Russia) or forward (Wänzl in Austria-Hungary, Berdan in Russia and Albini-Brändlin in Belgium) appeared. Diverse kinds of breech-block action were also used by Martini in England,

284 Austrian skirmishers in action, 1820s, coloured lithograph. Unlike general infantry, jaegers advanced individually, seeking cover and fighting by aimed fire. On the left the skirmisher is loading his weapon.

Turkey and Romania, Werndl in Austria-Hungary, Remington in Denmark, Sweden and Spain, and Werder in Bavaria. Bolt-actions were used by Mauser in Germany, Berdan II in Russia and Gras in France. It goes without saying that all these weapons used integrated cartridges. Single-shot military breechloaders of the 1860s and 1870s were used only briefly and were replaced by repeaters within a short time.

285 Austrian pistol Model 1798, produced in 1831.

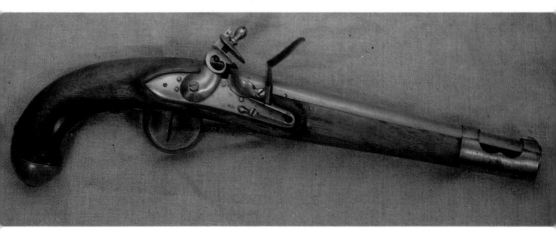

286 Prussian infantry Model 1841 (Dreyse). Made by N. Dreyse Co., Sömmerda, in 1846. It is an earlier variant of infantry gun Model 1841 with round opening in the large shield of the rear sights which was later a sector of a circle. The scrolled end of the trigger-guard was later replaced by a straight bar.

In the earlier periods, before self-primed, self-contained and self-obturating cartridges were introduced, repeaters rarely appeared in army equipment and then in negligible numbers, as, for example, the Kalthoff repeater in Denmark in the second half of the 17th century. The American Civil War of 1861−65 was largely waged with percussion muzzle-loaders, but, on a lesser scale, repeaters were used. These had a tubular magazine in the butt (Spencer) or under the barrel (Henry). The American Winchester, the successor to the Henry and Spencer guns, also appeared in the Turkish and French armies. The first army repeaters of European origin also had tubular magazine under the barrel. These included Vetterli in Italy and Switzerland, Jarmann in Sweden and Norway, Fruhwirth and Kropatschek gendarmery guns in Austria-Hungary, the Kropatschek navy gun in France and Lebel in France. The best designers of army guns of the later 19th century, Paul Mauser and Ferdinand Mannlicher, at first used tubular magazines and only later switched to box magazines fitted in the central part of the weapons. The first patent for a gun of this design was granted to J. P. Lee, an American

287 Short gun (so-called Justiz-Gewehr) for armed men of the Ministry of Justice is one of the variants of Austro-Hungarian gun Model 1867 (Werndl). Depicted example comes from collection of Franz Ferdinand.

236

288   Mont Storm English percussion gun (British patent of 1857, introduced into the army in 1864 but due to design and production drawbacks replaced by Snider gun in 1865).
Danish cavalry carbine Model 1867, Remington system (patent granted 1864, produced in Copenhagen arms-works Kjøbenhavns Tøihuus in 1871), magazine with tilting cover to hold ten rounds is situated in the butt. The first breech-loaders of the 1860s and 70s, both percussion ones and those firing cartridges, still featured external hammer and only later did firearms with internal firing mechanism appear.

whose repeater was introduced into the British army. Bolt-action guns with the magazine directly adjacent to the breech were then widespread, in fact almost universal. They were used first of all in the Mauser system, and in the Mannlicher system in Austria-Hungary and some other countries. At the end of the 19th century the first automatic weapons were adopted by armies — heavy machine-guns and self-loading pistols — whose development, however, was already linked to the following period.

Short firearms, pistols, were primarily the weapons of officers and some cavalry troopers; later on also some infantry and artillery specialists were equipped with them. Officers' pistols were not originally regulation weapons and the first models of army pistols appeared as late as the 18th century. In the 19th century the rank and file were equipped with regulation weapons but officers generally purchased, at their own expense, a pistol differing from the regulation model. Single-shot pistols were replaced with revolvers in army equipment of the second half of the 19th century. In the 1850s and 1860s mainly Lefaucheux revolvers were in use in France, Italy, Spain and Norway, which was the only instance of the military adoption of the earliest integrated cartridge, since as far as rifles were concerned, the Lefaucheux cartridge did not have any success at all. Colt and Adams percussion revolvers were used mainly by the British army, and to a lesser scale by some other countries (Austria, Prussia), first of all in the navy. From the 1870s, there began the widespread use of revolvers using centre-fire cartridges and occasionally rim-fire cartridges. In a few instances revolvers of American origin were officially adopted, e.g. Smith and Wesson in Russia or Saxony, but mostly various European designs were involved. These were Adams and Webley in England, Gasser in Austria-Hungary, Chamelot-Delvigne in France, Italy and Switzerland, and Nagant in Belgium and later on in Russia.

In addition to the guns and pistols described so far, various special weapons also found a limited military application. Blunderbusses are guns or pistols with flared muzzles, sometimes ellipsoid in shape, which fire a number

237

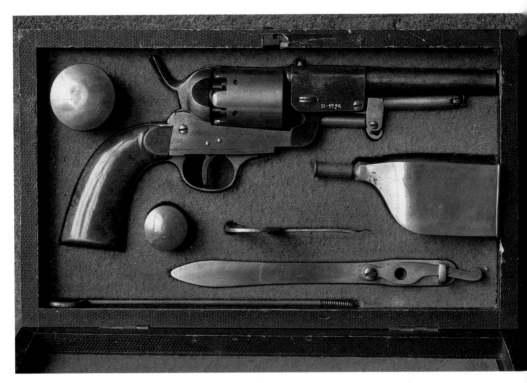

289   Austrian revolver patented 1849 was the first Colt-licensed revolver produced in Europe. It was introduced into the Austrian navy and also used as a personal, civilian weapon. Specimen cased along with complete accessories is marked *J. PETERLONGO ./. INNSBRUCK*.

of smaller balls so that a larger target area is covered with a single discharge. The blunderbuss appeared in the second half of the 16th century and remained in use till the 19th century for the protection of stage-coaches, banks, the guarding of convicts and in the armed force. Blunderbusses were particularly favoured by the Royal Navy, but in the second half of the 18th century some Austrian cuirassiers were issued with them, and in the early 19th century so were the Mameluke Guard of Emperor Napoleon. Blunderbusses were fitted with a spring bayonet and their naval varieties with barrel of brass, more resistant to the corrosive environment than iron barrels. When hand-to-hand combat began on board, these weapons were of indisputable advantage compared with ordinary guns.

Guns and pistols for launching grenades over a longer distance rank among unusual types of military weapons, together with wall guns used in defence of strongholds and signal guns. There were also army pistols with attachable butts which could be used as carbines. Multi-barrelled army shoulder guns were rare since the infantry controlled the rate of fire according to the number of men shooting and sequential fire following the officer's orders. The navies of some countries introduced volley guns with the cluster of barrels being discharged simultaneously. The Austrian border-guards over-and-under gun of 1768 was another oddity, too, with one barrel

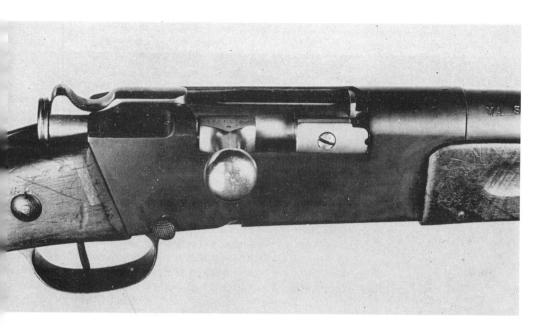

290 French gun Model 1886 (Lebel) — the last and longest-serving military repeater with tubular magazine under barrel and at the same time the first army weapon with reduced calibre (8 mm) using cartridges with smokeless powder.

291 Austro-Hungarian revolver Model 1870 (Gasser).

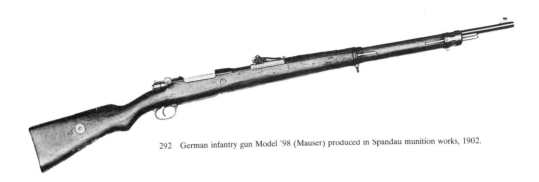

292 German infantry gun Model '98 (Mauser) produced in Spandau munition works, 1902.

smooth-bore and the other one rifled. Attention should also be paid to the frequent procedure of providing some troops with shoulder guns captured in large numbers from the enemy, either without any change at all or after some modifications such as conversion to take the standard ammunition.

Although the development of military firearms did show minor variations in various countries of Europe, only one area, the Balkans, became distinctly separate from the overall common trend. The local guns and pistols differed from the other European weapons in appearance and decoration, while no division into military and hunting weapons ever took place. Both edged weapons and firearms were an indispensable part of male attire, which was a fact that even the Austrian monarchy was forced to accept, particularly after some South Slav territories became part of the empire. The Arms Act (Imperial Patent dated October 24, 1852) did not require a licence for carrying service weapons while on duty, but, among other exceptions, it also stated that those citizens for whom a weapon was a part of their

293 Austrian Cuirassier blunderbuss Model 1759 (cock of a later type with ring-neck, the hook-shaped safety-catch situated behind the cock is missing).

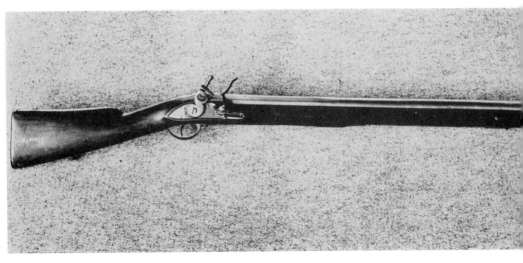

regional folk costume could carry it freely without any permit being necessary.

In the Middle Ages the burghers had the duty of ensuring the defence of their town. Town armouries were built for this purpose and burghers even kept weapons of military character in their households. Subsequently this practice continued only in Switzerland. Burgher militia was gradually losing its combat value, particularly after standing armies had been introduced, yet in the form of a municipal corps it survived in many European countries. In wartime such militia safeguarded law enforcement and order within the town, carried out sentry duty and performed other related tasks; in peacetime its members mostly neglected military training and sought achievement in various social celebrations and parades. Alongside the traditional sharpshooter and grenadier corps, in the 19th century there originated new, semi-military formations, and various paramilitary and physical education groups which provided rifle training for their members. Government bodies as a rule favoured and supported this activity by issuing older, out-of-date army weapons to organizations of this kind.

294   Detail of foregoing weapon (width 46 mm, height 25 mm). Muzzle of elliptical shape.

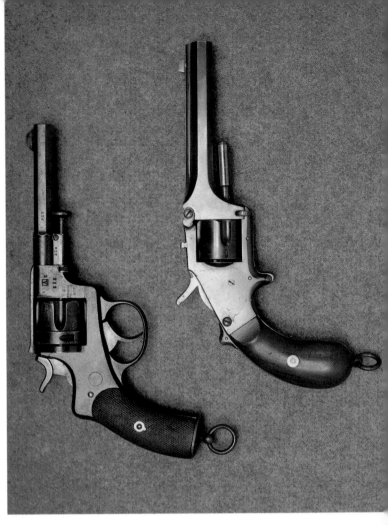

295 Belgian officers' revolver Model 1878 (Nagan[...]
Saxon revolver Model 1874 (Smith and Wesson).

296 Blunderbuss with French flintlock, Ketland, London, *c.* 17[...]
Barrel of brass flared out to 41 mm diameter at the muzzle.

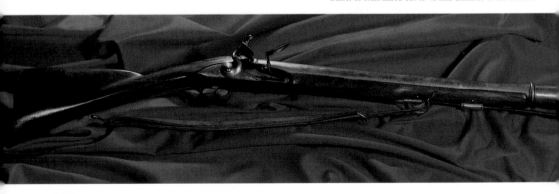

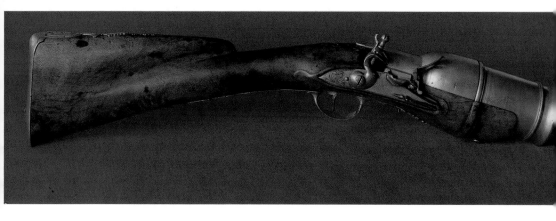

297 Grenade-launcher flintlock gun with French flintlock, Barrey, Besançon, second half of 18th century.

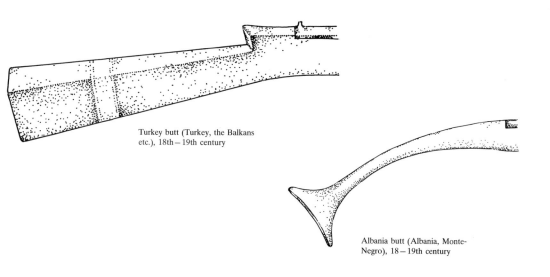

Turkey butt (Turkey, the Balkans etc.), 18th—19th century

Albania butt (Albania, Monte-Negro), 18—19th century

298 Over-and-under gun Model 1768 for Austrian border-guard units, produced by Joseph Heizenberger, Wiener Neustadt.

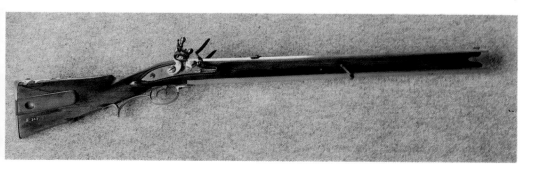

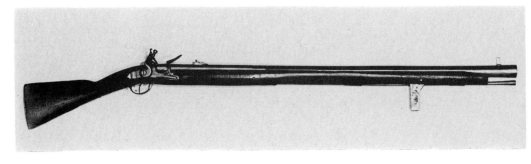

299　Prussian wall-gun with French flintlock, calibre 23 mm, overall length 162 cm, mid-18th century.

300　Gun of Prague corps (Austrian army gun, Wänzl system of 1867).

301　Volley gun with French flintlock, Philibert Chenevier, Saint-Étienne, 1786. All seven barrels are interconnected via touch-holes so that they are discharged simultaneously.

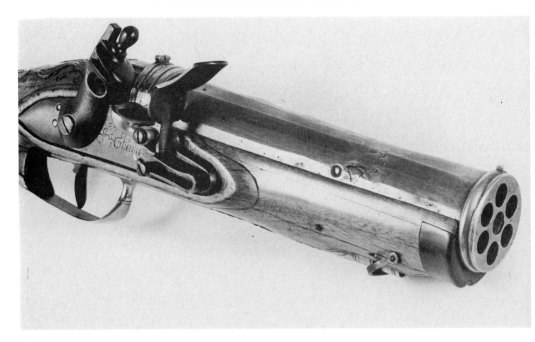

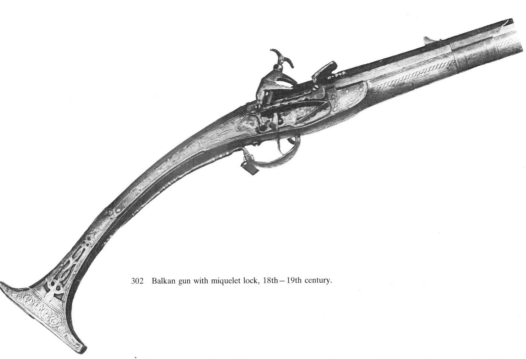

302 Balkan gun with miquelet lock, 18th—19th century.

Long guns of a military type were also part of the equipment of noble-mens' guards in the households of important rulers. In the same way that armour had been specially created for the young sons of noble families, military-type guns were now made for young boys. Even though the weapons mentioned at the close of this chapter represent rather a marginal issue, the intention is to make it clear that the topic of military weapons is somewhat more extensive and does not include just regulation models.

245

II. BÜRGER GR. ENADIER DIVISION.

303   Members of 2nd Grenadier Division of Viennese burgher corps, coloured lithography partly hand coloured, 1840s.

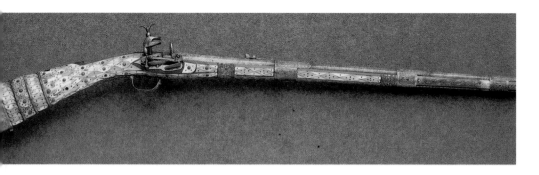

304 Balkan gun with miquelet lock, lockplate dated 1864, stock overlaid with mother-of-pearl, adorned with pieces of red coral, barrel-mounts of brass sheet.

HUNTING WEAPONS

Using firearms for hunting became possible only after the first locks had been constructed. In the 16th century the crossbow still competed with firearms in hunting equipment, but from the 17th century on the shoulder gun became the principal weapon of huntsmen. It is true that some hunting methods not requiring firearms continued, such as falconry, ferreting (chasing wild rabbits out of the warren using a ferret), and catching game in nets and other trapping gear. Moreover, a new type of hunt with horses and hounds originated in the 17th century. However, hunting using firearms has steadily gained ground since the 17th century.

Up till the 19th century hunting guns had enjoyed a dominant role in the

305 Child's gun with French-type flintlock, calibre 10 mm, overall length 90 cm (98 cm with bayonet), weight 820 g, probably a weapon belonging to later Austrian Emperor Joseph II, dated 1750. Barrel marked *Nicolaus Nisel a Wien,* lockplate *Wen. Fingelandt Prag,* furniture and bayonet of silver, weapon decorated with military motifs, Austrian eagle and *J II* initials, Austrian eagle and names of Joseph II's parents on both sides of the bayonet.

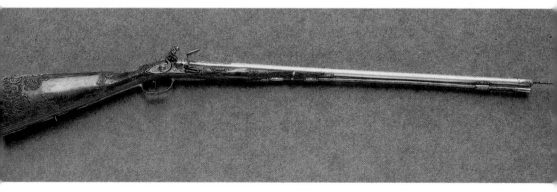

Firearms — nomenclature (according to number and type of barrels)

Single-barrelled, smooth-bore

Single-barrelled rifle

Double-barrelled side-by-side smooth-bore

Double-barrelled rifle

Double-barrelled gun (one rifled, one smooth-bore barrel)

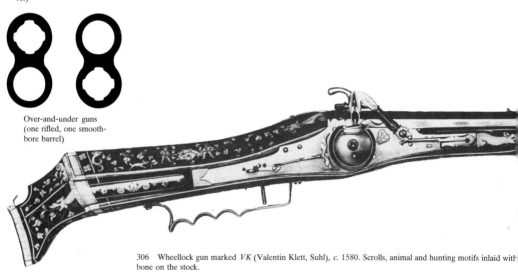

Over-and-under guns (one rifled, one smooth-bore barrel)

development of firearm technology. In the 20th century we have been used to the fact that most discoveries and new techniques get exploited first in the military sphere and are only later on adapted for non-military purposes. It was not so in the past. Army guns, produced in bulk, were subjected to cost-saving tendencies, and most technological innovations and new materials first appeared on civilian weapons and only later on military ones.

Shooting different types of game called for different types of weapons. Smooth-barrelled shotguns were used for shooting hare and birds while rifles were designed to fire bullets when big game was involved. This division, however, did not always hold true in earlier periods, even though rifling has been known from as early as the first half of the 16th century. Most soldiers fired balls from smooth-bore barrels till the middle of the 19th century and sportsmen, too, although to a lesser extent, could use smooth-bore weapons for firing balls even in the 19th century.

Matchlock muskets saw army service over a long period, but the era of matchlock hunting firearms was very short. The principal reason behind it was not the fact that the glowing match was visible over a long distance, thus disturbing the game. Matchlock weapons actually began to be used for hunting, but as soon as the more advanced, although much more expensive wheellock and somewhat later snaphaunce and flintlock weapons appeared, they found favour as hunting weapons because of their considerable advantage in comparison with the matchlock.

In Western and Southern Europe wheellock weapons served hunters for a comparatively brief period, to be soon replaced with snaphaunce and flintlock guns. Particularly from the 17th century on the French flintlock proved superior. In the Mediterranean area the miquelet was used as well as local variants of the flintlock in other areas. The situation was quite different in Central Europe where the wheellock was used on hunting firearms, or rifles in particular, quite commonly up till the second half of the 18th century. Central European wheellock hunting rifles mostly feature the so-called German stock, either straight or just slightly bent, with a short angular butt which was not propped against the shoulder but against the cheek while aiming and firing. The trigger-guard was usually shaped as a finger-rest and

306 Wheellock gun marked *VK* (Valentin Klett, Suhl), *c.* 1580. Scrolls, animal and hunting motifs inlaid with bone on the stock.

Over-and-under, smooth-bore

Over-and-under rifle

307 Shooting waterfowl (hunters with wheellock guns), Jost Amman, 1582 (according to Schuss und Waffe, Vol. III), woodprint.

Different types of triple-barrelled guns

Triple-barrelled smooth-bore

Triple-barrelled rifle

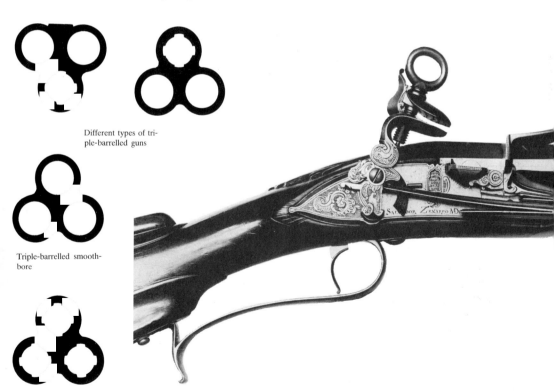

308 Single-barrelled gun with miquelet lock and Madrid-style butt, Salvador Zenarro (Cenarro), Madrid, c. 1780.

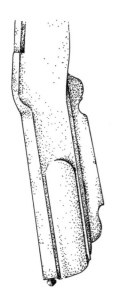

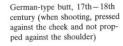

German-type butt, 17th—18th century (when shooting, pressed against the cheek and not propped against the shoulder)

309   Wheellock rifle, Lorenz Neireiter, Prague, 1727. Counter plate adorned with motif of chased stag.

there was normally a patch-box in the butt. In Western and Southern Europe another type of gunstock was developing from the 16th century onwards — with a bent butt of rounded outline propped against the shoulder. In addition to the French butt there existed also diverse local variants — usually less widespread, such as the Madrid or the Catalan butts.

310   Lightweight hunting gun with French-type flintlock, not signed, some decoration (e.g. brass and gild lockplate and furniture) corresponding to production by Karlovy Vary gunmakers of first half of 18th century

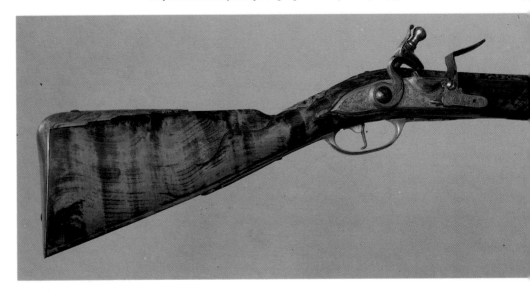

250

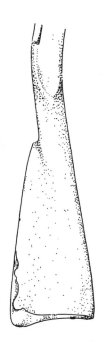

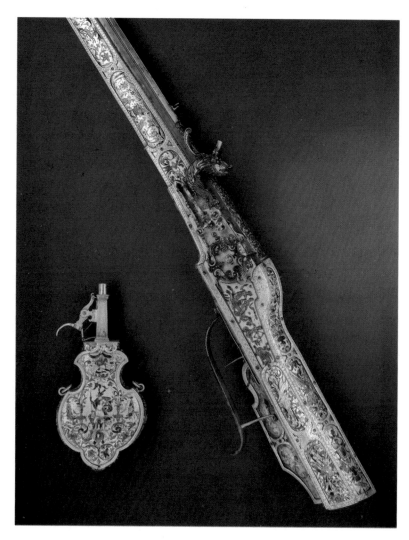

311   Decorative wheellock gun and powder flask made for Emperor Rudolph II, decoration (gilding, silvering, carving, enamelling etc.) by David Altenstetter and Daniel Sadeler, Prague, c. 1608.

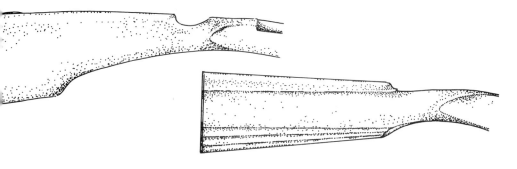

alan-type butt, 18th–19th
ury

Madrid-type butt, 18th–19th
century

312 Shooting birds (hunter with a French flintlock gun), Johann Elias Ridinger (1695 – 1767), engraving by son Martin Elias Ridinger (c. 1730 – 80).

Cylindrical barrel (common among earlier weapons, later on smooth-bore firearms)

The diversity in technology between hunting weapons from Central Eu...ope and those originating in western or southern parts of the contine... cannot be explained only through the different gunmaking traditions ... hunting styles. They were rooted in different conditions and the conseque... methods of hunting. In the rich hunting grounds of Central Europe de... hunting predominated and from the 16th century on shooting on enclos... grounds was becoming more popular. The sportsmen, and often the o... lookers, too, waited for the game in a space enclosed by a fence, canvas ... nets, and servants drove hundreds of deer or black boar in front of the... muzzles. The object was to get the maximum amount of trophies and this l... to senseless killing, since the game did not have any way of escaping from t... enclosed area.

Multi-sided barrel (common on rifled barrels)

313 A hunter in the mountains with a wheellock rifle, Johann Elias Ridinger (1695–1767), engraving by his son Martin Elias Ridinger (*c.* 1730–80).

Two-stage barrel (i.e. angular around the breech, cylindrical in front, a favoured 17th- and 18th-century variant particularly on barrels of Italian provenance)

Deer were not so common in Western and Southern Europe, and for this reason using shotguns became more widespread there: shooting hare and flying birds became a Mediterranean speciality. This hunting style called for lightweight guns, and front sights were sufficient, since aiming required only the upper edge of the barrel and the rear sights were no longer essential.

Deer being scarce in Western and Southern Europe, chasing a single item of game became widespread, which, of course, does not mean that the 'Central European' style of shooting in enclosed grounds did not appear there. In the second half of the 17th century there originated in France another style of hunting with hounds, a strictly regulated way of chasing the selected stag or roebuck till the final exhaustion of the prey. Over the same

253

314 Double-barrelled gun with French-type flintlocks, Nicolas Boutet, Versailles, c. 1810. A present fro
Emperor Napoleon to Austrian ambassador in Paris — Prince Schwarzenberg.

period hunting a single fox or hare was becoming popular in England. Th
hunting style did not consider the number of trophies important. The quarr
was given the chance to escape, and the hunt was a sporting event whic
demanded both the riding skills of the hunters and the training of the moun
and hounds.

Depending on the type of game, sportsmen used either a rifle or a sho
gun. Rifled barrels were most popular in Central Europe and in a part of
Northern Europe from the 16th till the 18th century, while in the other par

315 Over-and-under rifle with turn-off barrels, Ignaz Koppensteiner, Gmünd, first quarter of 19th century. T
original flintlock weapon was converted to the percussion system and the new owner had the stock lengthen
by 3 cm. In a way similar to some other 19th-century muzzle-loaders the weapon has the ramrod head screw
on to the butt from underneath, since because of its dimensions it would have hindered firing if it had be
attached to the ramrod. The head can be screwed on to the ramrod and a better grasp on the ramrod with a lar
head then facilitates loading the weapon.

316 Percussion triple-barrelled smooth-bore rifle, Jan Burda, Prague, second quarter of 19th century. Detail of decoration on patch-box cover in the butt depicting two hunters, the man to the right loading a muzzle-loader. The former longitudinal rectangular patch-boxes in the butt with wooden sliding cover had been replaced by metal tilting covers, frequently round or oval in shape.

of Europe they had just a modest share — the smooth-bore barrelled weapons being there due to the prevailing type of game. The common way of hunting also influenced the choice of weapons — either with the wheellock and the German-type butt or with the flintlock and French-type butt. Of course, while choosing from these two possibilities, other criteria could play their role, be it the greater readiness of the weapon for immediate fire or the better dispersion of the shot.

New ways of hunting found their enthusiasts even in regions with a different tradition. At the end of the 17th century shooting at flying birds was found in Central Europe, too, whereas before, birds were shot while at rest or were caught in nets. Hunting with mounts and hounds was promoted by such people as Prince Karl Eusebius Liechtenstein or Count F. A. Sporck. Although the aim was to hunt a single item of game, the cost often exceeded that necessary for other styles of hunting, because it called for a number of well-trained personnel, and many mounts and hounds, as well as for the creation of forest paths wide enought for the huntsmen to ride through. For this reason in the Central Europe of the 18th century the older way of hunting in the enclosed area was still common.

Collective hunts were always an important social event. Those sportsmen who preferred the individual enjoyment could choose either waiting for the game in a hiding-place or stalking it. For the latter choice, a short rifle was used — being more easily manageable in the dense forest.

In the 18th century the unification of basic European hunting-weapon types took place. Although rifles with a wheellock and German butt continued to be used in Central Europe, there, too, the flintlock began to take over and the French butt also gained favour. Besides rifle-shooting at stags, roebucks, fallow deer, bears and other game, shotgun-shooting at small game was attracting more attention. Lightweight fowling pieces as developed in France and elsewhere in the 17th century were suitable for this kind of shooting.

About 1820 variants of the detonator lock began to be used in hunting guns, and somewhat later the percussion lock with the cap on the nipple, the latter being the system prevailing from the 1830s till the 1860s. The 1830s and 1840s were also the main period for converting flintlock hunting weapons to the percussion system.

Hunting breech-loaders using self-obturating cartridges started appearing in the 1840s and spread to a large extent from the 1860s on. The Lefaucheux system, which was only occasionally used on other firearm types, either military or target weapons, became the dominant design of hunting weapons in the second half of the 19th century. In the 1850s the Lancaster system began and competed successfully with the Lefaucheux weapons somewhat later. Towards the end of the century hammerless guns began to spread. They no longer had the outer hammer the way the Lefaucheux or

317 Percussion double-barrelled gun with four hammers, Dewalle Frères, Liège, c. 1850. Two superimposed charges loaded in each barrel. Pulling the trigger releases the forward trigger first (the rear one being blocked at the time) and repeated pulling releases the remaining charge.

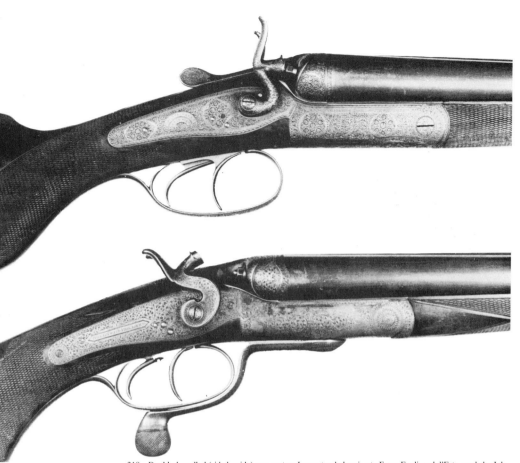

318 Double-barrelled (side by side) gun, system Lancaster, belonging to Franz Ferdinand d'Este, made by Joh. Springer's Erben, Vienna, end of 19th century, barrels by A. Francotte, Liège.
Double-barrelled rifle, Lancaster system Holland and Holland, London, end of 19th century, a weapon of Prince Colloredo-Mansfeld.

Lancaster weapons used to, but the firing pin was set inside the weapon. Break-action is typical of hunting weapons, even though other designs were employed, too, e.g. bolt action or sliding barrels and others. Automated ejection of spent cartridges appeared on hunting weapons, and choking of the shotgun barrels as well. The latter, a reduction of the bore at the muzzle section, gave better results. The principle itself was patented in England in 1866 by William Pape, even though it had been known and used by some gunmakers a few decades earlier.

As already mentioned, hunting weapons of the period from the 16th till the first half of the 19th century were the principal area where diverse technical innovations were tested, including attempts at breech-loaders and repeaters of different design. Many breech-loaders with varied breech-action have been preserved as well as repeaters with several barrels or with one barrel and various magazines for balls and powder. This kind of weapon was mostly produced for sportsmen who at the same time were enthusiasts for interesting designs and technical innovations. In the 18th century Count F. A. Sporck ranked among them, and a number of varied breech-loaders and repeaters were constructed for him or for Ernst Ludwig, while Ludwig

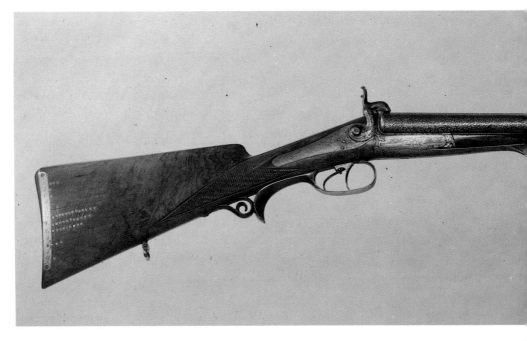

319 Double-barrelled Lefaucheux gun (one rifled, one smooth-bore barrel), Johann Springer, formerly Novotny, Vienna, c. 1860.

320 Single-barrelled gun with chemical lock, Adalbert Fridrich, Roudnice, 1820.
Lancaster rifle, Josef Gutwirth, Orlík, end of 19th century.

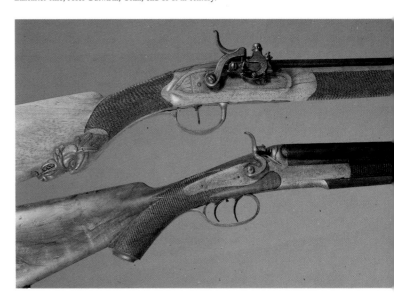

VIII of Hessen-Darmstadt favoured air-operated hunting weapons. The way of hunting in the period in question called for neither quicker loading nor repeated fire from the same weapon.

Hunting was the sovereign's or the aristocracy's privilege, and the other strata of the society either did not participate in it at all, or only on a limited scale. Feudal magnates had their personal gunmakers, chasseurs, whippers and other servants. In the course of a hunting event they did the shooting while the servants took the discharged weapon out of their hands, handed them another and took care of the reloading. The rate of fire was maintained by having a large number of absolutely identical weapons. Identical models were produced so that the sportsman had the weapon he was used to available all the time. For this reason the 18th- and 19th-centuries gunmakers produced series of identical hunting guns usually numbered on the screw-plug projection behind the barrel — sometimes only four or six pieces, but sometimes a dozen and rarely more. Frederick William I, King of Prussia from 1713 to 1740, fired over 600 shots during a single hunting day. Helped by servants and loaders, he achieved a rate of fire which would have been out of the question for any repeater of the period in view of the contemporary state of technology.

Multi-shot hunting weapons started appearing, in small numbers, from as early as the 16th century. Multi-barrelled production considerably increased the weight of the weapon. For this reason mainly double-barrelled guns were still acceptable for hunting, even though examples with more barrels appeared. Over the earlier periods single-barrelled hunting guns were general, and if double-barrelled weapons appeared, it was the case of an over-and-under barrel arrangement. The barrels were either fixed, in which case the weapon required two locks, or turn-over, where one lock sufficed. About the mid-18th century there appeared in France guns with a double-barrelled side-by-side arrangement, but their number was small and started increasing only after 1800. Both in the over-and-under and in the

321 Double barrelled gun with hammers striking on to separate horizontal firing-pins, Heinrich Barella, Magdeburg and Berlin, 1860—65.

322 Shooting out of a moving waggon, Wolff Pirckner, Jagdbuch, 1639 (according to *Zeitschrift für historische Waffenkunde*, Vol. IV). In order not to alert the game too early the waggon is disguised as an ordinary farm waggon; the long barrel and large bore of the shotgun guaranteed a higher effective range.

side-by-side arrangement the barrels could be of a different type, with one rifled and the other smooth-bore, so that the owner could use the same weapon for shooting all types of game. Both barrels could also be either rifled or smooth-bore to provide the sportsman who had missed the game with the first shot with the possibility of firing again immediately.

Double-barrelled guns in a side-by-side arrangement became common for hunting during the 19th century, and the reasons behind it were first of all social development. Important events such as the 17th-century Civil Wars in England and the French Revolution exerted a great impact upon the further development of hunting. In Central Europe, only the revolutionary year of 1848 brought about the abolition of the hitherto exclusive hunting privilege reserved for the aristocracy. Along with increasing participation of the burgher class in hunting the need for a double-barrelled weapon began making itself strongly felt. The new sportsmen recruited from the ranks of clerks, doctors and magistrates simply did not have large numbers of servants about supplying them with freshly loaded weapons in case they had missed the game. They thus needed another shot quickly, before the game disappeared. The other reason behind the quick spread of double-barrelled guns was of a technological nature. As early as the 18th century production of better-quality barrels started in Europe, and the improvement increased still more in the century to follow. As a result, a double-barrelled gun with the lightweight Damascus barrels was not any heavier than the earlier single-barrelled weapon with its massive heavy barrel. Introduction of the half-stock, with the forestock not reaching all the way up to the muzzle, also contributed to the reduced weight of hunting weapons.

323 Shotgun with French-type flintlock, calibre 28 mm, overall length 231 cm, barrel 177 cm, weight *c.* 20 kg, Suhl barrel dated 1605, lock and stock of a later date, the latest modifications datable to 18th century, the frizzen missing.

The appearance of the middle-class sportsmen also resulted in an increase of small-game hunting events after such prey as hare, duck as well as a decreased number of elaborately decorated hunting weapons. The decrease was also contributed to by the boom in the industrial manufacture of fire-arms taking place in the course of the 19th century. Although various military repeaters originated in the second half of the 19th century, hunting firearms of this design rarely appeared. In contrast to the U.S.A. where the Winchester hunting repeaters gained wide popularity, it was the double-barrelled gun which remained the typical weapon of the European sports-man.

Besides ordinary rifles and shotguns there originated different weapons designed for specific sorts of hunting or for special users. From the late 16th century and throughout the 17th century, in Silesia, and then in other areas, *tschinke* guns were produced, which took their name from the Silesian town of Těšín. They were lightweight hunting guns using an out-dated variant of the wheellock with an outer mechanism. There, however, this type of lock was vital in view of the slim stock curved down prominently at its neck into which no lock mechanism could be inserted. The *tschinke* stock is noted for the rich ornamental decoration of bone inlay with figural and animal motifs and frequent application of mother-of-pearl and brass. Compared with other weapons of the period, the *tschinke* rifles are lightweight and have an unusually small calibre, 6.5 — 9 mm. Today's experts consider *tschinke* guns to have been fowling pieces, designed for shooting birds, which theory can be

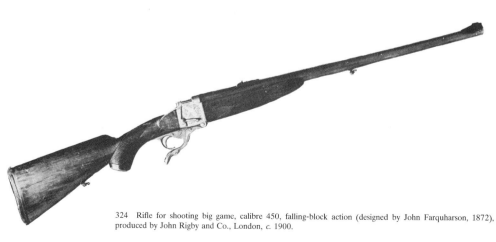

324 Rifle for shooting big game, calibre 450, falling-block action (designed by John Farquharson, 1872), produced by John Rigby and Co., London, *c.* 1900.

325 Two single-barrelled guns (No. 3 and No. 12) out of the series of twelve identical flintlock guns, Fran Adam (gunmaker to Prince Liechtenstein), Valtice (Feldsberg in German), *c.* 1780.

supported by the sources of the period, or else, taking into account their ligh weight and rich decoration, weapons designed for ladies. Some experts take both the above variants into account while maintaining that the weapons originally produced for shooting sitting birds, later on, in the course of the 17th century, became ladies' guns.

Hunting in the past was first of all an all-male affair, but some wome indulged in it. Elizabeth Christine, wife to Charles VI, Holy Roman Em peror and King of Bohemia, may be mentioned as an example. On Křivoklá hunting grounds in 1721 she shot 138 stags in a mere 5 hours.

Long and heavy fixed guns mounted on horse-drawn waggons rollin across the hunting grounds were a very particular type of hunting weapon They were used for shooting birds such as bustards or cranes, while the bird were motionless, sitting on the ground or on the water. These waggon-moun ted guns were used in the course of the 17th and 18th centuries; their boa mounted variants were used in France and England during the 18th and 19t centuries. The expression 'shot cannon' or punt-gun, sometimes used to describe this kind of weapon, was not unjustified.

The rather small carriage gun was used particularly in Eastern Europe — in Poland and Russia, where travellers in winter faced the possibility of being attacked by a pack of wolves. For such an emergency a weapon of smaller dimensions was required which would be reasonably manageable within the confined space of the carriage.

As early as the 18th century there occurred isolated cases when, at the

326 *Tschinke* gun, with initials *PK* (Pavel Kalivoda), Těšín, *c.* 1640.

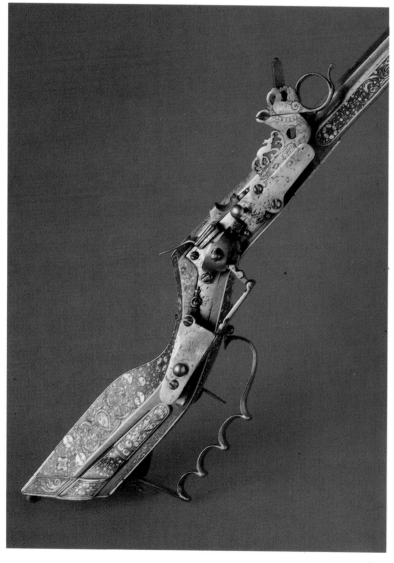

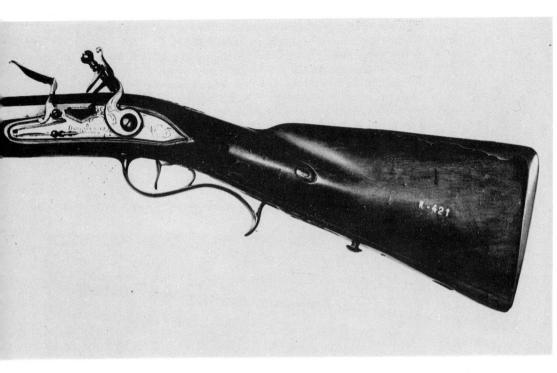

327 Flintlock rifle, Bartholomäus Daisenberger, Munich, *c.* 1760. The weapon, produced for a left-hander, has lock and cheek-piece situated on the opposite side to usual.

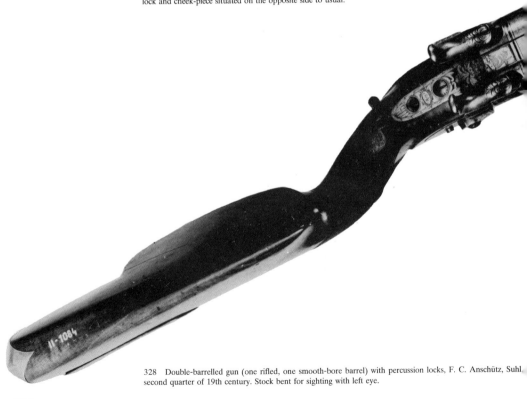

328 Double-barrelled gun (one rifled, one smooth-bore barrel) with percussion locks, F. C. Anschütz, Suhl, second quarter of 19th century. Stock bent for sighting with left eye.

courts of sovereigns and magnates, imported exotic game was released from cages in front of the sportsmen to become trophies. In the 19th century, and in the second half in particular, hunting expeditions began to other continents, mainly to Africa, but also to America and Asia. Side by side with predators such as lions and tigers, elephants, rhinos, giraffes, zebras and buffaloes were much sought after. For shooting of this kind heavy-duty, effective weapons were required to fire high-powered ammunition. Production of these special rifles for shooting big and dangerous game was developed especially in England.

The shoulder gun was the firearm typical of hunters; short firearms, pistols or, in the 19th century, revolvers, formed only a very limited part of hunting gear. While hunting with hounds and mounts, pistol shots were used to urge on the stag, and when the chase was over, a hunting falchion was used for the *coup de grâce* as a rule, but a pistol shot could be used to kill the prey. Pistols and revolvers in the 19th century served primarily as back-up weapons, when hunting predators. If the hunter was attacked by the beast of prey and could not use his rifle, either because he was too close or because he had already fired it and had not managed to reload, the pistol could be used. Pistols for this function were of relatively larger calibre, both in the case of percussion muzzle-loaders and the later breech-loaders using metal cartridges.

329 Flintlock rifle, breech-loader with tilting barrel, barrel with square bore, Jan Michael, Kuks, Bohemia, c. 1730. Weapon belonged to Count F. A. Sporck, proprietor of the Kuks estate.

In the same way as today, left-handed people were a minority group. Previously this phenomenon was considered abnormal, and the left-handers or, similarly, others who deviated from the usual standard, were seldom treated with tolerance. However, in the moneyed classes whose privilege included hunting, this deviation was mostly respected, and for this reason we may occasionally encounter hunting weapons for left-handers. They were usually guns of the period whose mechanism was a mirror image of the standard arrangement. The lock was situated on the left side and the cheek-piece on the right side of the gun. Guns with the cheek-piece on each side of the butt are rare. They could be used by both left-handers and right-handers.

Sometimes guns may be found among other hunting firearms which have the stock bent for sighting with left eye and these are called *Krüppelschaft* (stock for a cripple). Such a gun was used by a right-hander propping the gun against his right shoulder but using his left eye for sighting either because he had lost his right eye or because it was considerably weakened.

A special group of hunting weapons is typified by poachers' weapons used by people who were shooting game illegally. Quite often military weapons were used for this purpose, since a lot of them remained on battlefields after the fight enabling the local population to get hold of them. It was essential for such a gun to be portable and carried unnoticed, and so both barrel and butt were shortened, or even made detachable, so that they could be carried separately and attached to the barrel when required.

Apart from examples which are interesting from a design or technology point of view, hunting weapons also include pieces attracting attention through a certain peculiarity or unusual feature. Rarely occurring 17th- and 18th-century weapons with a different cross-section of the bore (e.g. square, triangle or heart-shaped) can be ranked among oddities. These weapons required special bullet-moulds for casting the appropriate shapes instead of balls. Another example of an approach which was not to result in functional improvement, but simply caused amusement or surprise, is represented by guns whose barrels are set in a casing of glass. Johann Gsell from Schleiz in Germany produced them in the 1660s, inspired by his noble master who had once asked whether it was possible to shoot out of glass.

SPORTING WEAPONS

The universal increase in sporting activities started in the last quarter of the 19th century, but some disciplines have a much older tradition, and shooting ranks among them. Unquestionably, even during the early period of fire-arms those men who were supposed to operate them in combat had to prepare themselves, improve their skill and practise their marksmanship. However, we have no detailed information on the subject, and ordinary combat weapons were used for training purposes.

Only the manufacture of non-military firearms after the earliest locks were designed stimulated the creation of special firearms intended primarily for target shooting. Shooting competitions using guns gradually displaced the earlier crossbow competitions; although the weapon itself was different, in many respects the organization of the competitions was similar to that of the ones they replaced.

Numerous improvements of target guns naturally could not be limited just to these, but could be used on military or hunting weapons as well. The fact, however, remains that in the 16th century, among other terms describing firearms, a new expression 'rifle for aiming' appeared, applying to a weapon designated specifically for target shooting.

During the short period of civilian matchlock and snaplock weapons the latter in particular was typical of target guns, since the need to ignite the tinder again after each shot did not matter much at the shooting range. For

330 Snaplock target gun, the Netherlands, 1580. The protrusion under the central part of the stock was supported on a rest while shooting to achieve greater accuracy.

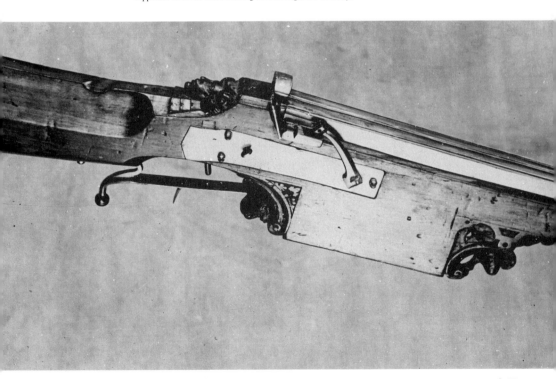

a long time afterwards target guns were dominated by the wheellock and as early as the 16th century many improvements were introduced for these weapons with the intention of ensuring the utmost accuracy. The first improvement was the rifling, typical of target guns in particular, although some towns prohibited the use of rifled barrels at shooting ranges in the 16th century.

Simple sights — at the muzzle and a notch at the breech — occurred on firearms as early as the 15th century, to be further improved in the 16th century, when leaf and tube sights appeared. The tube sight, in particular, although its occurrence cannot be limited to target guns only, was the most advantageous type when shooting at a stationary target since the marksman did not need to watch the area around the target, contrary to hunting, particularly when shooting at game in motion. The hair-trigger had been known from the 16th century — a device reducing the resistance of the trigger to a negligible level, thus accelerating the discharge and preventing movement of the weapon by pulling the trigger. If there are two triggers within the trigger guard, the arrangement now called the German hair trigger, the rear 'trigger' cocks the action while the other, the actual trigger (sometimes of a needle-like shape), is used to fire the weapon. The later hair trigger, the so-called French one, has one trigger only whose forward motion cocks the action and, pulling it in the usual way, fires the weapon.

Some 16th-century target rifles were provided with a projection in the central part of the stock, which was either placed on a rest or held in the left hand while shooting. This feature, however, did not spread widely; on the contrary, some rules prohibited the use of any kind of rest. Shaped trigger-guard with finger-rests were more common. The same goes for dioptric sights on the neck of the stock, substantially closer to the eye than the rear sight, which lengthened the line of sight. Gradually heavy octagonal barrels were commonly fitted on target rifles.

From the 16th till the early 19th century, a typical target gun was a wheellock or, later on, a flintlock rifle equipped with dioptric sights and a hair-trigger. Shooting for sport was widespread at that time. Competitions were organized by rulers and the nobility, but they were primarily a feature of town life. On Sundays and holidays, but most of all during the annual 'King's' competitions, large numbers of contestants competed on town shooting ranges located in moats below the fortification walls or in other places, such as parks or islands where shooting could not endanger anyone.

The wooden targets were square-shaped or, less frequently, round, white with the centre black, but without numbered circles, since all hits on the target were of the same value regardless of their distance from the centre. The targets were painted from the 18th century onwards, the artists being as a general rule local painters, often amateurs. However, there are also targets painted by the foremost artists of the period. Besides target-shooting, the so-called 'shooting towards the bird' was favoured, originally a cross-bow contest, which, from the 16th century onwards, was organized for riflemen, too. The target in this case was a bird its wings outspread — made out of wood. He who shot the last remnant of the bird from the high pole where it had been placed was proclaimed the king of shooters. The shooting off of either the right or the left wing was awarded by the title of marshal.

Marksmen from other towns, sometimes even from abroad, were invited to take part in important contests. These competitions were great social events, accompanied by processions, various attractions and feasting which often drew criticism.

331   In June 1585, on the occassion of the Order of Golden Fleece being conferred on Emperor Rudolph II, a shooting competition was organized in Prague. The movable target representing a rider was moved by means of a cord. As reward the contestants received the original of what they had hit on the target — Emperor Rudolph II won the rapier and the dagger, other contestants the horse, the saddle, pistols, etc. The movable target with observers and musicians is depicted on a detail from the print of the period by Antoni de Boys.

Besides square-shaped and round targets, another type was in use from as early as the 16th century, and this was a representation of human figures made out of wood. Turkish expansion was the principal danger that Christian Europe was facing, and therefore it is not surprising that these targets often represented a Turk. Targets representing human figures were used even later, first of all for rifle practice in the army, and there, too, the representation as a rule included the enemy uniform. As early as the 16th century there was shooting at moving or tilting targets which the marksman could see only for a short time. Also other, less usual types of target existed, but generally shooting at an immovable target was the normal practice.

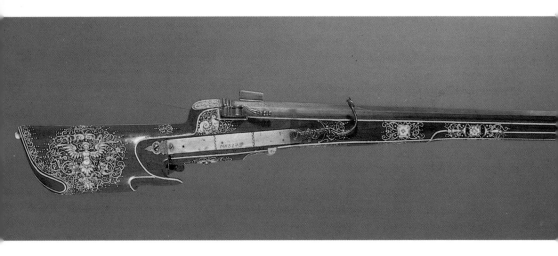

332 Snaplock target gun, with initials *HS* (Hans Stockman, Dresden), 1618. Weapon equipped with tube sights

Differentiation between target rifles and other types of gun became even more pronounced in the percussion era, particularly as regards the shape of the butt. The butt became heavier, the cheek-piece distinctly larger and the weapon was provided with a massive deeply curved butt plate (the so-called Tyrolean butt or the somewhat lighter Swiss butt featuring a smaller cheek-piece). These modifications were aimed at increasing the accuracy of the weapon through improving the aiming conditions and reducing the recoil, since neither the increased weight nor the poor manageability caused such difficulties on the shooting range as they would have on a hunt in the woods.

The manner of loading changed with the advent of breech-loaders, but

333 Snaplock target gun, with initials *GT*, Central Europe (probably Silesia), 1614. Wheel on lockplate bearing coat of arms of Duke of Brzeg-Legnica, stock inlaid with bone and white horn.

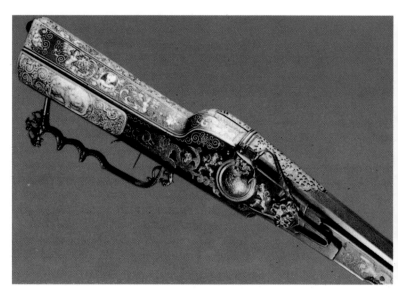

334 Wooden painted target, Jičín, Bohemia, 1861.

335 Patch-box cover of a wheellock rifle, Leopold Becher the Elder, Karlovy Vary, Bohemia, 1726–28. Relief carving of a shooting range of the period depicting a lady shooting, a servant passing loaded weapons and an observer standing behind the barrier near the target.

Examples of sights

336 Blessing the standard of the sharpshooters corps in Jihlava on May 30th, 1843, copperplate by Josef Klauser.

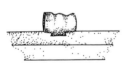

Tube sights (frequent on 16th- and 17th-century civilian weapons)

Frame sights (frequent on military guns of the second half of the 19th century)

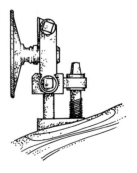

Dioptric sights (frequent on civilian, predominantly target, weapons)

Leaf sights (with one solid and one folding leaf — frequent on hunting rifles)

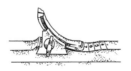

Sliding sights and arch sights (used on some army regulation weapons in the mid-19th century)

European target-rifles maintained their outward appearance. The stock still featured a sizeable butt with prominent cheek-piece and the deeply curved butt plate. Some weapons were equipped with a recess for the thumb of the right hand or with a ball-shaped rest under the forestock for the left hand. The rear sights of target rifles were already adjustable at that time and the diameter of dioptric sights increased.

The Martini dropping breech-block became the most favoured system of target rifles in Europe from the 1870s on, even though there existed target rifles employing many other systems, too. Designs by the Suhl gunmakers F. W. Kessler and R. Stahl represented variants of the Martini system; wide popularity was also enjoyed by single-shot target rifles using falling block action, particularly the system designed by C. W. Aydt, also a Suhl gunmaker.

Target rifles were weapons for sport almost exclusively from the 16th till the 18th century. In the 19th century, particularly in the second half, the assortment of sporting weapons increased considerably and new types of competitions appeared.

As early as the 18th century air-operated guns were used for short-range shooting, especially the bellows guns. These weapons brought a double advantage at the same time: the cost of shooting was reduced substantially and it was no longer necessary to walk to the shooting range since weapons of such short range and limited effect could be used even at home — both indoors and outdoors. In the 19th century the variety of these 'saloon' rifles increased and other weapons began being used along with air-operated guns. First of all they were represented by weapons of the Béringer system, a French invention, which was, however, widespread in Central Europe far more than in its mother country. Rifles and pistols equipped with this system

337   Wheellock gun, South Germany, mid-16th century (sickle-shaped spring of the outline used between 1545 and 1560). Tubular rear sights.

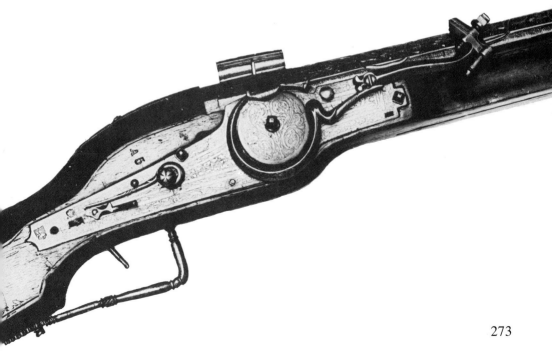

338 Wheellock rifle (one of the pair) with dioptric sights and German hair-trigger, Christoph Ris, Vienna mid-18th century.

Hair-trigger mechanism

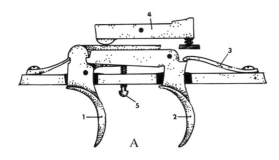

A

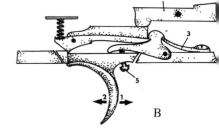

B

A   German-type
B   French-type

1   Hair trigger
2   Winding lever
3   Spring of the mechanism
4   Trigger-lever (acting on sear-
    lever of the lock)
5   Adjusting screw

employed a breech, which could, via a lever, be tilted 90 degrees (as a rule horizontally, less frequently vertically). The ball was then inserted into the front part of the breech and a special priming cap containing an increased amount of fulminate into the rear part of it. The system did not use any gunpowder, and the energy provided by the fulminate was sufficient to transport the ball to the close target. There are also a small number of Béringer-system weapons with the barrel tilting sideways; in such cases the cap only was inserted from the rear while the bullet was loaded through the muzzle.

Percussion target rifles or former hunting weapons with sleeved barrels were used for short-range shooting, too, in the second half of the 19th century. A short small-calibre barrel of about 20 cm ending with a nipple was inserted into the front part of the original barrel. The ignition cap was pushed on to the nipple through a slot in the original barrel, the bullet was loaded through the muzzle in the same way as in percussion muzzle-loaders. Inside the original barrel (sometimes also alongside it instead) there was a draw rod connected with the hammer; the rod hit the cap after the trigger

339   Target rifle, Martini system, Jan Novotný, Prague, *c.* 1880.

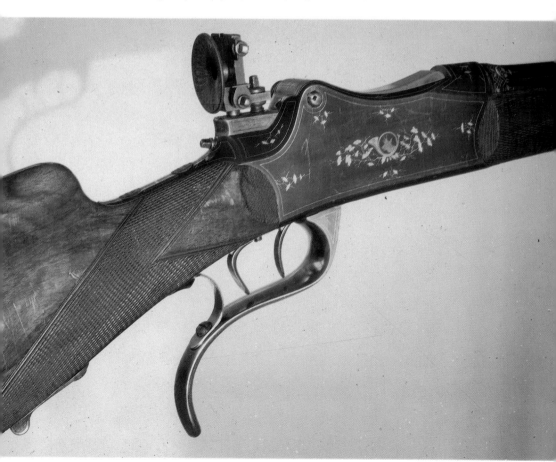

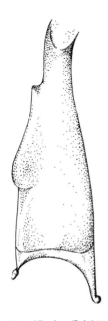

had been pulled. Target rifles with inserted barrels offered the same benefit as the other systems described, i.e. short range and cost-effective operation. Moreover, the weight and dimensions were identical with heavy target rifles used on shooting ranges, and for this reason simulation of actual competition conditions was better than in case of air-guns or the Béring system. When self-contained cartridges had been adopted, weapons using Flobert or various other small-calibre cartridges found favour. In the second half of the 19th century production of air-guns of various designs was widespread. All the 19th-century weapons for indoor shooting, either the percussion or the breech-loading variety, served for rifle practice only and for hobby shooting on various family occasions or at friendly meetings. Official competitions for small-calibre or air-operated weapons developed only in the 20th century.

Improvements of firearms in the 19th century and their increased effective range enabled the creation of a new sporting discipline, long-range shooting. These competitions began in England — from the 1860s in Wimbledon and, starting in 1890, at Bisley — and from there they spread to other countries, too. Distances of 800—1000 yards were common in England, 300 metres and more in Continental Europe. In the early days of the competitions percussion weapons were still put to use — target rifles by John Rigby from Dublin were particularly successful; in the later breech-loader era no special target rifles were used, just standard army rifles.

340 Percussion target rifle with side hammer-action (V. Wenzel, Znojmo, c. 1860), provided with dioptric sight and German hair-trigger, roughened thumb-rest in the butt, hooked butt-plate.

276

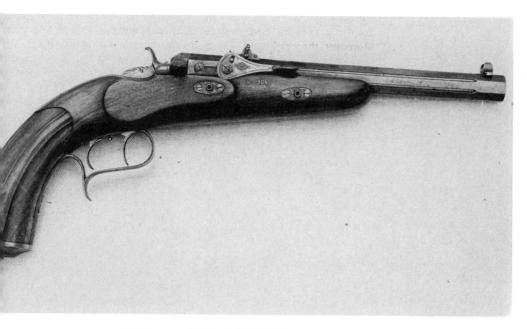

341 Target small-calibre pistol, H. Rödl, Prague, c. 1870. Breech-loader with hinged breech-block, lever alongside barrel actuates spent-cartridge extractor. Trigger-guard with finger-rest, German hair-trigger.

It was in England, too, that another new sport was born. In all previous competitions targets had been shot at from rifles, and only in the early second half of the 19th century did shotgun competitions start being organized in England — shooting at live pigeons flown out from cages. The novelty spread rapidly to France, Monaco, Italy, Spain, Germany and other countries, and besides pigeons other sorts of bird, e.g. swallows, were also used. The new competition was at the same time strongly opposed by environmental protectionists and in the late 19th century it was banned in Holland and subsequently in other countries as well. Living birds started being replaced by glass spheres, rubber balls and other objects thrown upwards and in various directions with the aid of special devices. Clay pigeons (a small disc made from clay and later on from asphalt) started replacing live birds as flying targets at competitions. There also developed shotguns designed exclusively for this type of competition.

Target pistol-shooting appeared as a new type of competition only in the last quarter of the 19th century, even though there were earlier muzzle-loading percussion pistols, equipped with a hair-trigger and adjustable sights, and intended for target shooting. From the 1870s on there originated single-shot target breech-loaders, as a rule with block breech-action and tilting barrels, equipped with a hair-trigger in Central Europe and without one in Western Europe. Revolvers, too, were modified for target shooting, but standard army revolvers without any special modification proved successful, e.g. the Russian revolver Model 1871 (Smith and Wesson system 1869), French revolver Model 1892 and other types. The development of target pistols and

342 Pair of Béringer-system pistols, cased with accessories, J. Lhotský, Prague, c. 1850.

343 Tranter-type target revolver cased with accessories, C. A. Fischer und Sohn, Lübeck, c. 1870.

344　Pair of target pistols, J. Schulhof system, produced by J. Postler, Vienna, *c.* 1880. Revolving block action cocked and breech opened via a lever on back-edge of the butt.

revolvers was in progress at the end of the 19th century and more particularly in the 20th century.

Special arms for target shooting, differing in some details from hunting or army weapons, had their origins in the 16th century, yet marked differentiation from the latter only took place in the 19th century. It was connected not only with progress in arms manufacture, but also with developments in the social sphere. Townspeople's militia which were supposed to carry out some tasks of military character in wartime and were consequently issued with military weapons, were losing their practical significance. The former sharpshooters' societies, too, either ceased to exist altogether or merged with

345　Hunting weapon from first half of 19th century adapted in second half of 19th century for short-range target-shooting. In the muzzle section of the original barrel there is a 20 cm long barrel inserted of 4 mm calibre, ignition cap inserted through a slot in bottom part of original barrel.

sports and physical education organizations originating in new areas where shooting for sport became an almost exclusive activity. In modern shooting competitions a contestant could succeed equipped with a weapon whose parameters best suited the demands of the particular discipline. Single-purpose target weapons of the second half of the 19th century thus differed from other firearm categories more sharply than their forerunners.

OTHER FIREARMS

Firearms which cannot be classified into military, hunting or sporting weapons are not numerous; as a matter of fact the only large group among them consists of weapons intended for personal protection, first of all pistols. Short arms appeared in isolation even before the advent of wheellock, but its invention enabled their large-scale production. Wheellock pistols were a new quality of firearms determined by their small dimensions which made it possible to carry the pistol secretly under one's clothing, loaded and ready for instant fire without any lengthy preparation. This provided favourable conditions for effective self-defence, but unfortunately at the same time for criminal activity as well. As a result numerous bans on using or carrying firearms appeared in various European towns over the first decades of the 16th century. The bans, however, prevented neither production nor the rapid spread of firearms.

The pistol saw service in cavalry units from the second half of the 16th century on, and became the weapon of some infantrymen, too, only much later. To a limited extent they were used for hunting purposes and in the 19th century for target shooting. Most pistols, however, preserved the character of a weapon intended for self-protection, because their small dimensions and weight, easy portability and operation were most suitable for this purpose and the shorter effective range was sufficient. In contrast to cavalry pistols of larger dimensions, which were mostly carried in leather holsters, pistols for personal defence were smaller. Later on some of them were called travelling pistols, as the weapon, cased or in a cloth bag, accompanied its owner on journeys, or pocket pistols, since a weapon of small dimensions could be easily carried in the pocket.

Pistol lock mechanism changed along with advancing firearms technology; the shape of the butt, too, can enable approximate dating of specimens not otherwise marked. Besides pistols with a wooden butt, numerous all-metal pistols are represented in the 16th century production of German

346 Wheellock pistols.
Specimen of probably French provenance, early 17th century. German pistol, *c.* 1575, barrel marked *PD* with a snake (Peter Danner, Nuremberg), lock marked *ZS* with a lily.

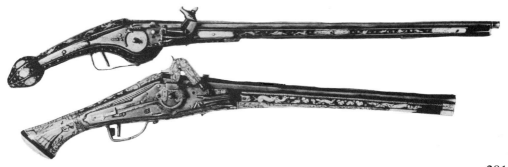

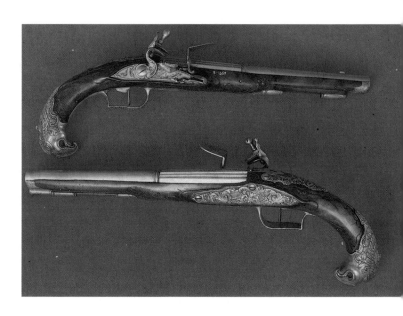

347 Pair of French flintlock pistols, barrels marked *LAZARO LAZARINO*, butt ends shaped as eagle heads. Leopold Becher the Younger, Karlovy Vary, Bohemia, *c.* 1770.

348 Varying dimensions of revolvers from the last quarter of the 19th century can be seen in these two Belgian weapons: army issue of Warnant revolver, and pocket revolver. Manufacture Liégeoise d'Armes à Feu.

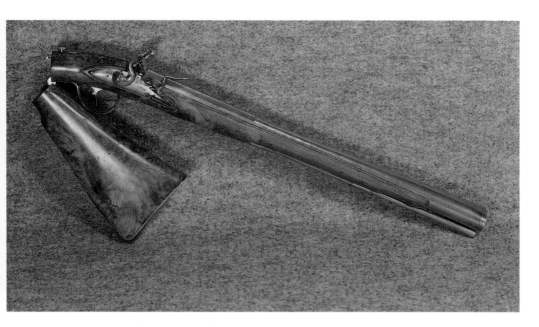

349   Blunderbuss with French-type flintlock, S. Fachitti, Brescia, last quarter of 18th century. Civilian blunder-busses of Italian provenance are often provided with tilting butt (to facilitate transport or to conceal the weapon).

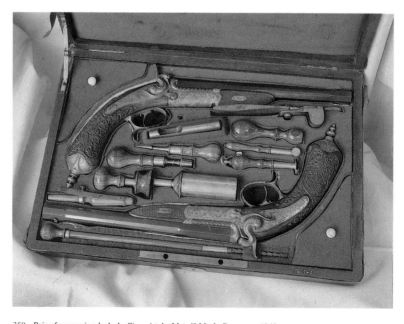

350   Pair of percussion-lock duelling pistols, Matyáš Mach, Prague, c. 1860.

Pistol butts

Mid-16th century

End of 16th century

Mid-17th century

Mid-18th century

Early 19th century

Mid-19th century

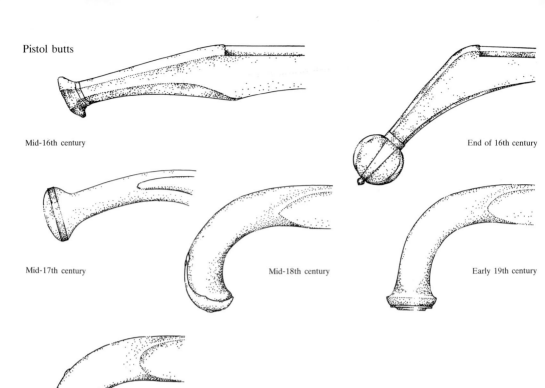

351 All-metal wheellock pistols.
Nuremberg, *c.* 1580 (above).
South Germany, *c.* 1570 (below).

Revolver, second half of 19th century

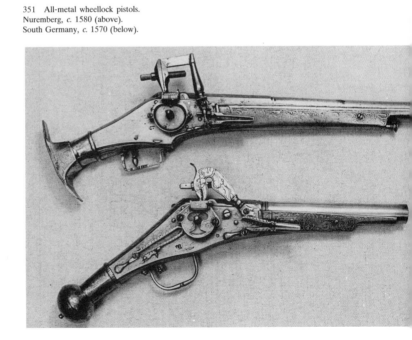

gunmakers, particularly those working in Nuremberg and Augsburg. All-metal pistols can also be found later on and in other areas, this style being typical of Scottish pistols in particular. In Continental Europe a new range of this type of stock emerged, for example, about the mid-17th century in the Rhineland area, particularly in the work of members of the Cloeter family in Grevenbroich near Düsseldorf, and later on in Mannheim; besides pistols they also manufactured shoulder guns with all-metal hollow stocks.

The technological development of pistols was similar to that of shoulder guns. Here, too, various breech-loader and repeater designs originated, but up till the second half of the 19th century single-shot muzzle-loaders were in an absolute majority. In the second half of the last century revolvers played the most significant role among weapons intended for self-defence. In addition, various designs of repeating pistols were competing for the customers' favour, but did not spread on a large scale and only the advent of self-loading pistols towards the end of the century was of prime importance. Many weapons having neither military nor hunting or sporting character also belong to this chapter. It is understandable that pistols originating in diverse periods and areas differ both in appearance and in technical concept.

Duelling pistols are a special group of weapons. Duels have been known since the Middle Ages, originally as the means of expressing God's will in

352 All-metal single-barrelled gun with French-type flintlock, Cloeter, Mannheim, c. 1680.
All-metal flintlock pistol, the Rhineland, c. 1660.

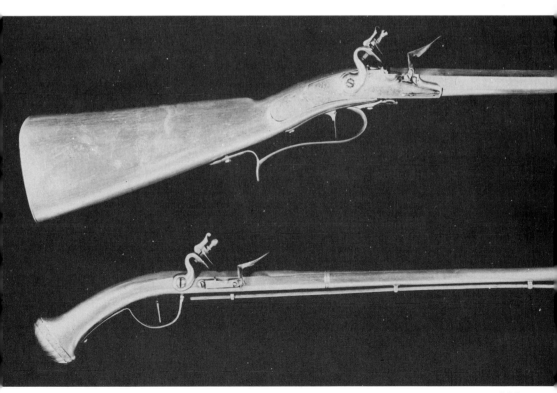

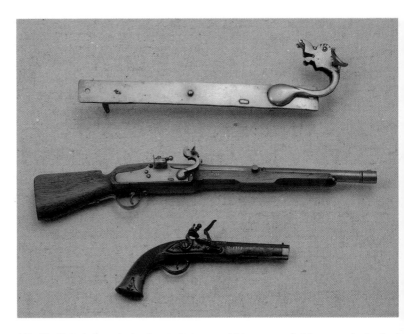

353 Wheellock pistols can be found most often among miniature weapons, but there were also functional weapons of minute dimensions employing other lock mechanisms. Miniature matchlock gun is 315 mm long (for comparison there is a standard 16th-century matchlock in the picture — 260 mm long), overall length of French flintlock pistol is 155 mm.

judicial duels, to prove the guilt or innocence of the defendant. Duels provoked by insults, no matter whether real or just imagined, were fought in various ways in 17th-century France in particular, but in other European countries as well. To defend one's honour in a duel was a noblemen's privilege and duty, and only from the end of the 18th century did duels become established in a middle class milieu, too, at first among persons with university education and later on among other members of the bourgeoisie. Duel between officers were particularly numerous, but journalists, writers, politicians and others also ranked among frequent duellists.

17th century duels were waged primarily with edged weapons, but duels on horseback occurred where standard cavalry pistols were used. As well as duels on horseback carried out in the same manner as in combat, pistol duels on foot with exact rules established beforehand took place in the 18th century. The conditions of the duel were negotiated by the seconds, and towards the end of the 18th century and later, in the first half of the 19th century, many printed rules and duelling codes were issued.

Duels were most common during the last quarter of the 18th century and in the first half of the 19th century. Although duels using edged weapons were still taking place, pistol duels were increasingly preferred during this period. In theory, both adversaries had the same chance with pistols, where-as in a rapier or sabre duel the younger duellist possibly had an advantage

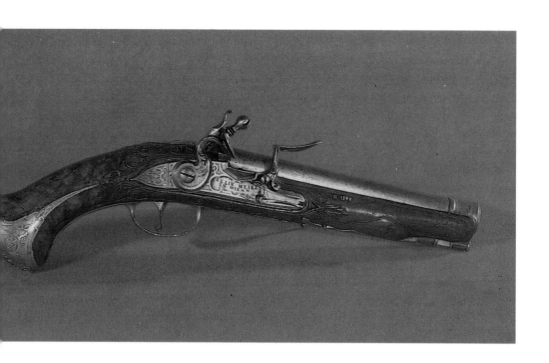

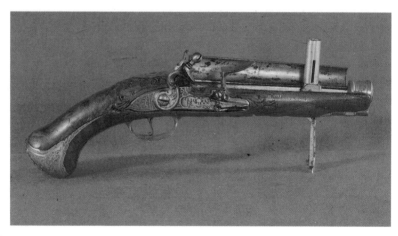

354–355 Seemingly a French-style flintlock pistol, actually candlestick with lighter, Felix Meier, a gunmaker, Vienna. *c.* 1730. When the trigger has been pulled, powder in the priming-pan will catch fire in the usual way. Simultaneously, however, the upper part of the 'barrel' will be tilted and, after the trigger reverts to its forward position, the tube with lighted candle will be raised perpendicularly and the support set in the forestock tilted automatically so that the candlestick can be put on the table.

over his older adversary, as did the taller person with a longer arm over an opponent of shorter stature.

From the 1780s special duelling pistols were produced. Pistols used in a duel were to be unfamiliar to both adversaries; only in exceptional cases were the duellists allowed to use their own weapons. Duelling pistols were identical

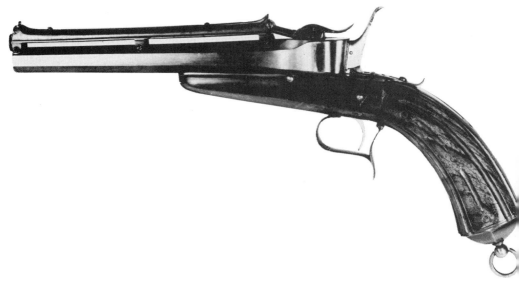

356 18-round repeating pistol for special hollow bullets holding the powder charge and a priming cap, designe
by Herman, Liège, 1852, produced by Victor Colette, Liège, c. 1855. The magazine over the barrel w
muzzle-loaded (after the covering cap had been swung off). Movement of the hammer raises and lowers the blo
breech with a chamber into which the cartridge falls through its own gravity. The lever over the breech serves
push the cartridge home into the chamber.

paired pistols cased along with loading and other accessories. During th
first fifty years of their existence they were flintlock pistols; from the 182C
percussion pistols for duelling were produced. Sometimes all paired an
cased pistols tend to be classified as duelling pistols, which is not correc
since they may also be classed as travelling or target weapons.

Some duelling rules included the requirement that the pistols used in
duel should not be provided with rifled barrels, hair-triggers and sights c
that the sights should not be adjustable. However, these criteria cannot b
considered as general attributes of duelling pistols, since the various rule
and codes were of local validity only. These requirements appeared in th
later periods only, stemming from endeavours to reduce the accuracy an
effectiveness of the weapons and so diminish the chance of a tragic outcom
to the duel. Duelling pistols were not richly decorated as a rule, but som
simple ornamental engraving on the lockplate and modest carved or er
graved decoration on other parts may sometimes be found. For a gentlema
only pistols could be considered as duelling weapons, although some due
using rifles, carbines or revolvers took place.

Although the main duelling era ended in the mid-19th century, duels sti
occurred in the second half of the century and even in the 20th century
This holds true particularly for countries where the ruling classes preserve
significant positions in economic and social life and also in the officer clas
in Russia and Austro-Hungary. In various periods and countries duels wer
banned. Some European 19th-century penal codes do not mention duels a
all, in others causing death in a duel is classified as murder and causing injur
as inflicting bodily harm. Penalties were far from being uniform –

sometimes severe, in certain countries rather lenient. There were instances when criminal proceedings following a duel were stopped on the orders of Emperor Franz Joseph I. It is no wonder therefore that even the early 20th-century catalogue of Prague's Novotný gunmaking enterprise reads as follows: 'With regard to duelling pistols, we will provide a special offer if so desired,' or, 'two or three pairs of duelling pistols are usually available out of stock.'

In the 19th century firearms with the appearance of a cane walking stick appeared intended primarily for personal defence. The hollow body of the cane served as a barrel while the firing mechanism was located in the handle. Originally these shooting canes were percussion weapons; later on they used cartridges.

357   Gaulois pistol, French patent by P. Blachon and E. Mimard, 1893, produced by Manufacture Française d'Armes et Cycles Saint-Étienne. Magazine for five rounds fired by pressing home the sliding palm section. The weapon is loaded from above, the magazine cover having been shifted forwards; the opening at the same time serves for ejecting spent cartridges.
(Bottom:) Protector revolver, design (1882) and production by Jacques Edmond Turbiaux, Paris. After unscrewing the right-hand plate of the casing the seven-round magazine can be removed (there are also 10-round specimens).

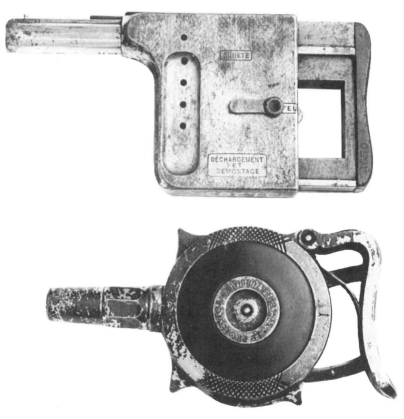

358 Gun concealed in a walking-stick, Germany, end of 19th century. The weapon can be loaded after the ca.. handle has been screwed off, the action is cocked by pulling out the handle a little, the firing-pin behind the barr actuated by coiled spring, the muzzle covered with a removable spike.

Some special types of weapons which could have been included in th.. chapter have already been mentioned above, where they, at least partiall. belong, such as blunderbusses or signal pistols. Therefore only some curios remain to be mentioned here, such as miniature firearms. Pistols and gur reduced to minute dimensions yet fully functional were being produced a early as the 16th century, even though they were a proof of their maker skill rather than actually being used as weapons.

FIREARM ACCESSORIES

Some accessories were essential for the functioning of the weapons; others were employed for maintenance and repairs. Some items were in use over long periods of time, others were intended for specific weapons, or connected with a precisely limited period related to technological progress in firearm development.

Over the entire muzzle-loader period, shooting was impossible without the ramrod. The earliest ramrods were made of wood, with just the tip of iron, non-ferrous metal, bone or horn. From the 16th century onwards, the ramrod was almost universally inserted into the forestock under the pistol or gun barrel. However, there were cases where the ramrod was carried separately from the weapon, as with some jaeger guns and many Balkan weapons or cased pistols. A broken ramrod rendered the weapon unusable and for this reason military weapons used iron ramrods from the mid-18th century. In order to prevent the loss of this important part, numerous models of 19th-century army pistols were fitted with ramrods permanently linked to the weapon at the muzzle. Most percussion revolvers, too, featured attached loading levers fitted alongside the barrels or under them as an integral, inseparable part of the weapon. Pepperboxes often had the ramrod housed at the centre of the barrel cluster.

Each firearm user had to have a sufficient supply of ammunition at hand. Originally, gunpowder was most probably kept in a leather pouch, but from the 16th century on powder flasks of diverse shape and material were used. No other firearm accessory item shows such variety as powder flasks do. The Renaissance period favoured fork-shaped staghorn flasks. Along with these, wooden flasks were among the earliest ones; later on flasks of iron, copper, brass and other materials were common. Powder-flask shapes are equally diversified. In addition to the original natural horn shape there appeared round-, barrel-, pear-shaped and other powder flasks. Musketeers' powder

359 Percussion pistol with captive ramrod and shoulder stock, tubular priming-cap magazine alongside the barrel, mid-19th century. Detachable shoulder stocks enabled pistols to be used as carbines and have been known since the 16th century. They became more widespread only in the 19th century.

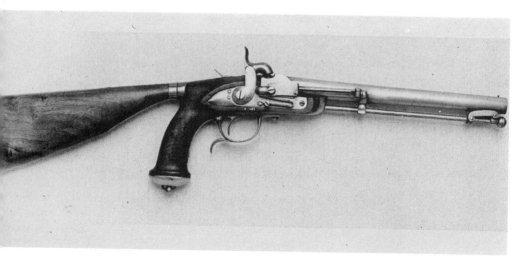

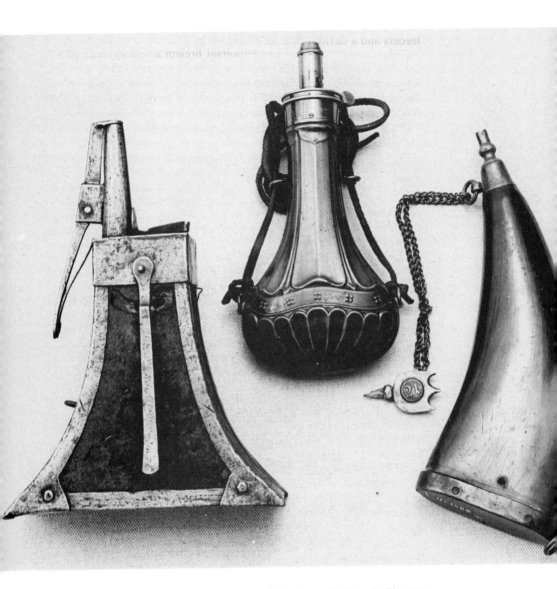

360 Musketeers' trapezoidal wooden powder flask, early 17th century.
Hunting pear-shaped copper powder-flask, James Dixon & Sons, Sheffield, mid-19th century.
Army powder-horn of Austrian jaegers, first half of 19th century.

flasks are of trapezoid or annular shape. 18th- and 19th-century servic[e] regulation models often show military symbols; civilian powder flasks ar[e] decorated with engravings, chiselling, embossing and other technique[s]. Later powder flasks were fitted with a nozzle which could be set to pour th[e] desired measure of powder.

Small powder flasks, less common, were intended to hold the finer-grai[n] powder used in the pan. For percussion weapons the small priming-powde[r] flasks were replaced with cap magazines, some provided with self-acting feeders and a device which facilitated pushing the cap over the nipple.

Bullets moulds, too, were an important firearm accessory since, prior to the 19th-century standardization of calibres, each individually produced weapon required projectiles cast in a mould whose dimensions corresponded to the barrel bore. Spherical bullets were cast originally but during the final stage of the muzzle-loader era in the 19th century there originated bullet moulds for casting ogival bullets. The basic shape of bullet moulds remained the same from the 16th till the 19th century, even though from time to time various improvements or different variants emerged, such as moulds for casting more than one bullet at a time. The individual cavities could be of the same calibre — which speeded up casting — or of different calibres in case bullets for different weapons were required. After cartridge-using breech-loaders became the rule, bullet moulds disappeared, but case-reloading tools came into being.

Bullets were initially kept in a leather or cloth pouch, but as early as the 16th century cartridge cases appeared, and from the late 17th century onwards the military generally used cartridge pouches. The 17th-century

361   Barrel-shaped wooden powder-container for *tschinke* guns, Silesia, *c.* 1650.

362   Powder flask of bone, engraved, second half of 16th century.

363   Shot flask, James Dixon & Sons, Sheffield, mid-19th century.
Container to hold glowing tip of the match, 17th century.
Balkan pistol ramrod, 18th century.
Wheellock-spanner (with different spindle diameters) combined with a screwdriver, 17th century.

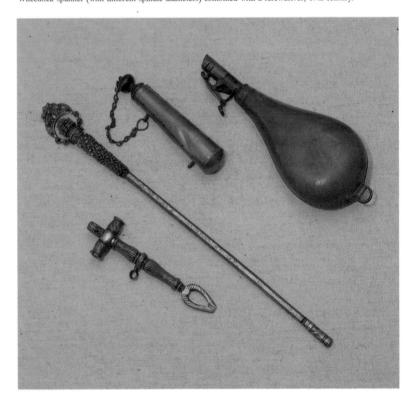

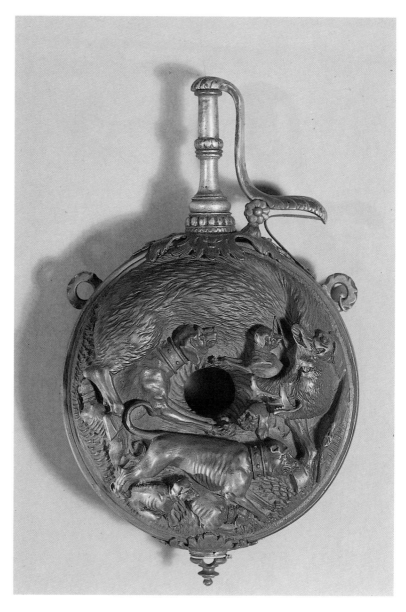

364   Powder flask of wood decorated with carving, Central Europe, second half of 17th century.

musketeer's equipment included the bandoleer — a belt crossing the shoulder from which wooden or metal containers were suspended, each holding the measured charge of powder required for one shot. Sportsmen, too, carried their lead-shot in leather pouches.

19th-century ammunition is immensely varied, due not only to tech-nological development such as paper cartridges, Lefaucheux pin-fire car-tridges, rim-fire or central-fire cartridges, but also to a whole range of

Examples of some bayonet types

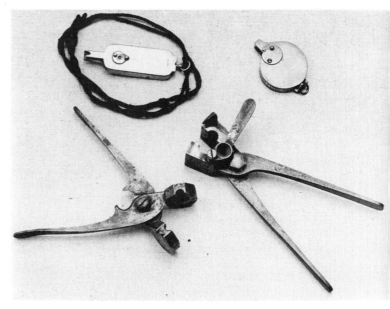

365 Mould for casting balls (left) and ogival bullets (right). Two magazines for percussion caps.

Socket bayonet with cross-shape, four-sided with deep concave sides, cross section of blade (Russia, Model 1867)

Hunting plug-bayonet (dated 1700)

Socket cutting bayonet with sabre-style blade (Model 1795 for Austrian Jaegers)

Yataghan blade (France, Model 1866)

Saw back-edge blade (Prussian pioneer falchion, Model 1871)

Knife-type blade (Italy, Model 1891 TS)

short-lived transition designs. There were also a wide range of weapons, each requiring its own specific type of cartridge. Cartridges were produced by numerous makers so that even in the same cartridge category there existed a wide and diverse assortment of types. The cases are of different outlines, too — cylindrical, tapered or necked. Other distinctive features are the cartridge base, either rimless or rimmed, the material used or the varied dimensions of the bullet.

The bayonet became a vital accessory of most regulation service weapons from the second half of the 17th century. The earliest 17th-century examples were actually daggers whose hilt could be pushed into the gun muzzle — in much the same way as a cork into the neck of a bottle: hence the term plug bayonet. Along with the military kinds, there existed civilian, hunting bayonets in the 17th and early 18th centuries.

Towards the end of the 17th century there appeared the socket bayonet, which spread all over Europe within a short time. The socket was slipped over the outside of the muzzle. Bayonets of various models and origin differed in such detail as blade length and cross-section (two-edged dagger

366   Two powder-testers shaped as flintlock pistol (*c.* 1760) or percussion pistol (*c.* 1840). The instrument was fired in the usual way (without the bullet) and the pressure developed was recorded by the scale on the wheel.

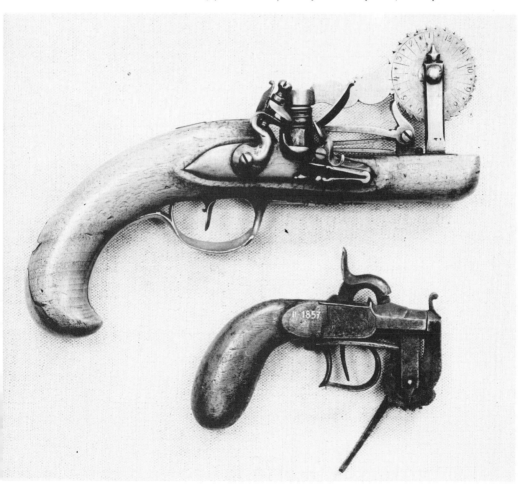

367 Cartridge-box,
or patron c. 1600.

type, triangular or four-sided blades), the way they were fixed to the barrel and in other details. Sword bayonets were designed so that they could be used both for cutting and thrusting. Originally they were used by skirmishers in the 18th century, but later on other special units were equipped with them and sometimes the general infantry as well.

The French bayonet Model 1840 became a pattern for another bayonet group — with the yataghan blade in contrast to bayonets which featured a straight blade. Attachment to the barrel was secured by means of a spring clip in the grip. Bayonets of the knife type appeared towards the end of the 19th century and were most common in the periods to follow. In various countries and at different times other types of bayonet emerged, e.g. with an unusual shape of the blade or with the bayonet permanently fixed to the barrel. Spring bayonets had already appeared on Swedish muskets in the second half of the 17th century; the Prussian jaeger gun of 1854 was fitted with a retractable pike-shaped blade bayonet. Some special army units, pioneers and others, were equipped with bayonets provided with a saw-back edge.

Other firearm accessories may be met less frequently either because they were in use only for a specific period or were associated only with one particular weapon. The wheellock required a key to span the action; it could be permanently attached to the weapon, or designed as a separate item and sometimes combined with the powder flask. Air-operated guns as well had their mechanism spanned by a key or a lever. Matchlock guns sometimes had a match case to protect the glowing end of the match from wind and rain. The fork-like rest was used by musketeers to support the weight of the heavy musket while aiming and firing it. Soldiers who had completed their sentry duty, and sometimes civilians, needed to unload their firearm and so

368 Percussion revolver cased with accessories, A. V. Lebeda, Prague, c. 1854. The weapon was made for the explorer Baron Petz and decorated following the pattern by the painter Josef Mánes (1820—71). Ctirad and Šárka (a story from ancient Bohemian tales) carved on one ivory butt-plate, Mazepa (Ukrainian Cossack hetman, 1664—1709) on the other.

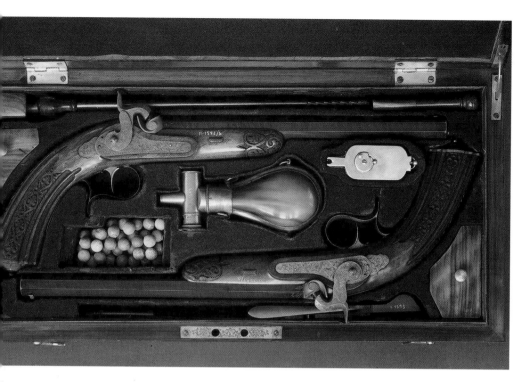

369 Cased pair of percussion pistols with accessories (loading mallet, powder-flask, bullet-moulds, percussion-cap magazine etc.), A.V. Lebeda, Prague, *c.* 1850.

the bullet had to be extracted from the barrel. The worm, a corkscrew-type device attached to the ramrod, served for this purpose.

The quality of the gunpowder could have a significant influence on accuracy and effect. For this reason various powder testers appeared from the 16th century onwards. Most frequently during the 18th and 19th centuries they were made in the shape of a flintlock and later on a percussion pistol. Wad-cutters could influence the results of firing, since a uniform size of cloth or leather patches was vital for accuracy.

Weapon cases were used to protect firearms against dirt and accidental damage, especially during transport. The cases were made of leather, cloth, wood or even metal. Leather holsters and wooden cases were most common. Used mostly for pistols and revolvers, they can also be found with shoulder guns. Cases usually contained the weapon, accompanied with more or less extensive accessories including as a rule the ramrod, a tongue-like bullet mould, a powder flask, a supply of shot and wadding and, for rifled weapons, a mallet for driving the bullet into the muzzle. In the case of percussion weapons a capping magazine and extra nipples were common. There were also various tools in the case — a screwdriver, an aid for placing the cap over the nipple, a nipple wrench, a needle for cleaning the touch-hole, and tools for dismantling the weapon or adjusting the sights. Later on various oil cans and other cleaning or conserving items were included. Pistol cases may sometimes contain detachable shoulder stocks.

Professional gunmakers used further special tools and equipment for repairing weapons, and there also exists a whole range of other objects loosely connected with the world of soldiers, hunters and marksmen such as targets, cups, prizes, emblems, etc.

DECORATION OF FIREARMS

Decoration of weapons, of the unmarked specimens in particular, is an important identification element, enabling a more accurate estimation of the date and provenance of weapons.

In the 14th and 15th centuries, when firearms were an exclusively military weapon, there was either no decoration at all, or just some restrained decorative elements on the barrels. This situation changed radically in the early 16th century when firearms were commonly used for hunting, target shooting and personal protection. The firearm, in addition to its functional and other merits, also became a prestige object, a symbol of the owner's power and wealth. The most diverse decorative techniques, applied before to edged weapons and armour, were gradually adapted to firearms.

Even the finish of metal parts taken over from the armourers' trade and serving as a protection against corrosion became a decorative element. From the 16th century on, the barrels of civilian weapons were blackened or blued. A darker blue shade was typical of Spanish products while there was a lighter tone on the French ones. Somewhat later, the browning of barrels appeared, spreading more extensively from the 18th century thanks to the English gunmakers. Browning and blackening of barrels also appeared on some regulation army models of firearms.

Starting with the 16th century, metal firearm parts were decorated with engraving and chiselling and from the second half of the century also with carving. From the 16th century on, the stock was inlaid with ivory, bone, mother-of-pearl or woods of different colour. The stocks of the 16th-century luxury specimens were often completely overlaid with plates of bone or other materials decorated with carving or other techniques. From the 17th century on, wood stocks, too, were carved and in the 17th and 18th centuries inlaid with ornaments of iron or silver wire. Fruit wood (pear- or plum-trees) were the most frequent material for stocks and butts; later on it

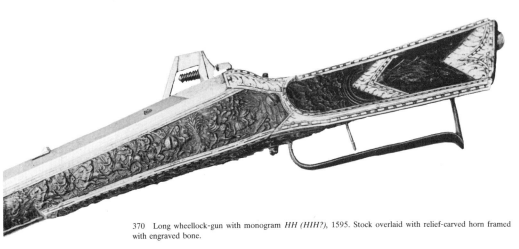

370 Long wheellock-gun with monogram *HH (HIH?)*, 1595. Stock overlaid with relief-carved horn framed with engraved bone.

301

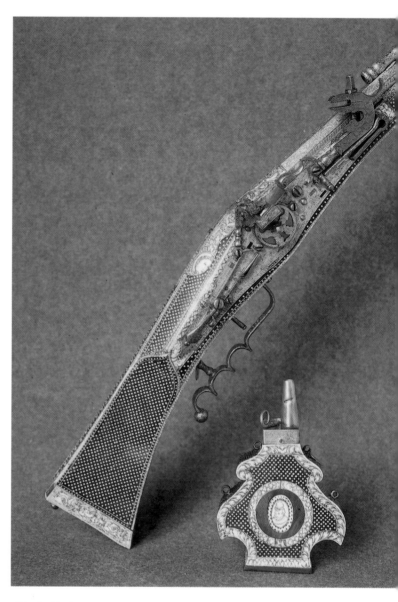

371 Combined snap- and wheellock gun and a powder flask (once belonging to Karl of Waldburg), Augsburg or Nuremberg, South Germany, c. 1570. Richly decorated with gilding and engraving, the stock of ebony decorated with ivory studs. The powder flask belonging to the weapon was decorated in the same manner.

was mostly walnut; in some cases even the root wood or other kinds of imported exotic wood (ebony etc.) were used.

Decoration gradually affected almost all firearm components, not only the most spacious ones like the stock and the barrel or the lockplate, which were particularly suitable for decoration, but smaller parts of the furniture (side-plate, trigger-guard, and butt-plate). Engraving or carving were the

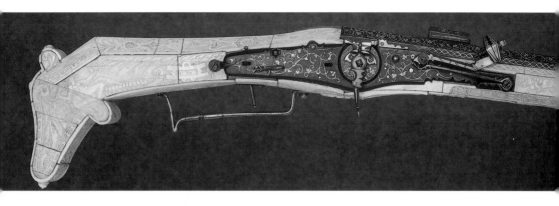

372 Wheellock gun once belonging to Cosimo I Medici, Duke of Tuscany, South Germany, 1544. The owner's name on the barrel, the Medici coat of arms underneath the barrel and the stock. On the right, wheel-spanner set on the wheel-spindle. Gilt ornaments on black background on the barrel and lockplate. The stock with particular butt-type entirely overlaid with ivory, relief-carved with ornamental motifs.

most usual decorating techniques, but chiselling, etching, incrustation or inlay, and to a lesser extent painting, enamelling and other creative techniques found their place in firearm decoration. As to the materials, gold, silver, precious stones, ivory, brass, mother-of-pearl, antler, horn, bone and other materials were used for decoration.

The origins of firearm decoration fall within the Renaissance period, and the character of decoration changed together with the transformation of aesthetic views and interchange of styles. It was the Baroque in particular with its taste for rich ornamentation which contributed to spreading decora-

373 Wheellock gun, the barrel marked with initials *PD* and a snake motif (Peter Danner), the lock marked with *GH* initials and a heart, Nuremberg, end of 16th century. The stock overlaid with green-coloured bone and mother-of-pearl.

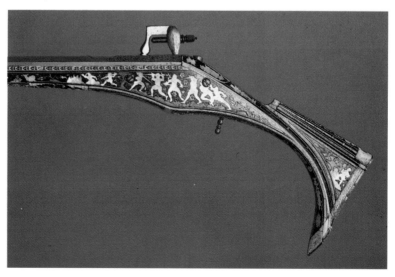

tion over practically all guns or pistols. Even gunmakers' marks, often gold- or silver-encrusted on the barrel, became a decorative element. In the first half of the 18th century the firearm furniture was frequently of gilt brass and a number of diverse decorating techniques were used even on a single weapon. Neo-Classicism of the late 18th century preferred a more restrained style of decoration in which fine engraving prevailed; moreover, particularly in England, at the turn of the 18th and 19th centuries, more emphasis was put on functional perfection than on decoration, and the latter attracted less attention. The sober English style then exerted an influence upon the decoration of firearms even on the Continent. This, however, was connected with the fact that in the 19th century hunting was gaining ground among the middle classes. This group was, as a rule, not in a position to pay as much money to procure a gun as the wealthy noblemen of the 17th and 18th century. They also preferred functional reliability to prestige decoration. In the second half of the 19th century the traditional manufacture of firearms was superseded by industrial machine production and most firearms ceased to be artistic or craft product. However, industrial production did not mean the end of decoration, which was still applied to more expensive civilian weapons and to individually decorated luxury pieces. It goes without saying that later military weapons would seldom be found with much decoration except on some officers' personal weapons such as pistols, revolvers, or on presentation pieces.

The foremost creative artists of the period sometimes participated in the decoration of firearms, personally working on orders by sovereigns and

374 Pair of wheellock pistols by Giovanni Battista Francino, Brescia, c. 1640. Carved and pierced furniture typical of 17th-century Italian weapons.

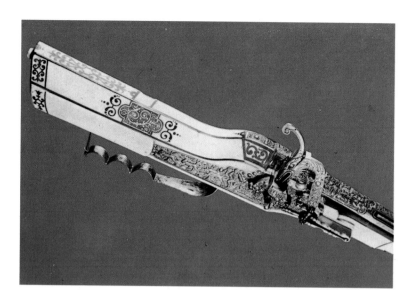

375 Wheellock rifle, barrel and lock by Daniel Sadeler, stock by Hieronymus Borstorfer, Munich, 1630. Metal parts decorated with carving, stock overlaid with bone (ivory?) and inlaid with ebony and horn.

magnates. More frequently their graphic patterns were executed on weapons by professional engravers. In 17th-century France there were published a number of pattern-books for the decoration of guns and pistols. François Marcou, Thuraine and Le Hollandois, Jean Baptiste Bérain and Claude

376 Wheellock rifle by Martin Gummi, Kulmbach, Germany, 1650. Stock and brass gilt lock and furniture decorated in carving.

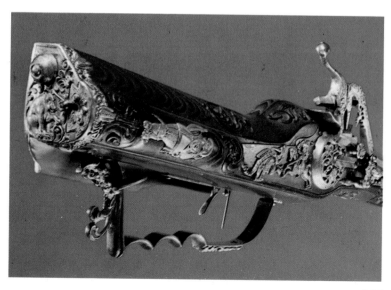

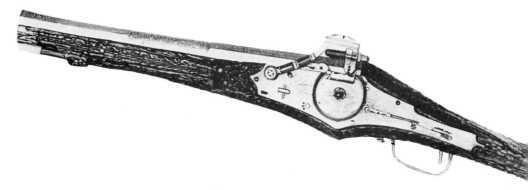

377 Pistol with a left-hand lock, South Germany, 1551. Stock of staghorn.

Simonin were among the well-known pattern-book authors. About 1700
firearm-decoration pattern-books were also published in Germany and the
Netherlands and in the first half of the 18th century further pattern-books
by new authors appeared in France. Pattern-books spread abroad, too,
where they served as models for the decoration of firearms and as a consequence motifs presented in a French pattern-book can be met on weapons
produced in Italy, Central Europe and elsewhere. Pattern-books for the
decoration of firearms were published in the 19th century, too, e.g. Charles
Claesen, Liège, 1856. The upsurge of romantic styles in the second half of
the 19th century affected this form of art as well and resulted in diverse
Neo-Gothic motifs and other elements.

Art styles crossed frontiers freely and undisturbed and the manufacturers
adopted well-attested decoration techniques and motifs; often the same

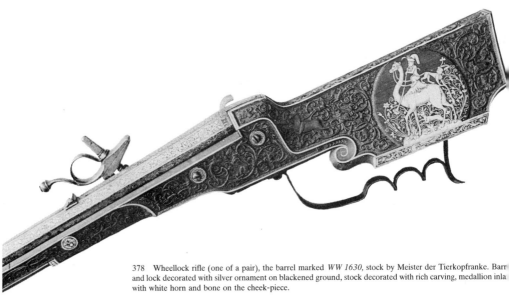

378 Wheellock rifle (one of a pair), the barrel marked *WW 1630,* stock by Meister der Tierkopfranke. Barrel
and lock decorated with silver ornament on blackened ground, stock decorated with rich carving, medallion inlaid
with white horn and bone on the cheek-piece.

pattern-books were used in various countries. In this sense we can, to a certain degree, talk about the international character of arms decoration manifested by identical features in a number of European countries. Yet, over specific periods some countries and even smaller territories preserved characteristic elements typical of their origin. Richly pierced iron furniture is typical of Italian weapons produced in 17th-century Brescia. As a rule this decoration was not limited just to individual items of furniture, but even covered a part of the stock. Numerous firearms from 18th-century central Italy feature lockplates richly ornamented with figural motifs in relief, sometimes of a grotesque nature. The cocks of these weapons were often shaped into human form carved in relief. Weapons from 17th-century Silesia had stocks richly inlaid with geometric and plant motifs of white bone, complemented with animal and figural scenes. This ornamentation is common on *tschinke* guns, but also on other wheellock and flintlock shoulder guns originating in this area as well as on the axe and pistol combination called a *fokosh*. The Cheb (Eger) style of inlay was used especially on 17th-century jewel-boxes, escritoires, cupboards and other types of furniture, although the relief carving on the stocks of guns was equally typical. Side by side with this style of carving, the decoration of lockplates with engraving or the pierced carving of dense floral motifs was typical of the 1665–80 style of decoration. The Karlovy Vary gunmakers of the first half of the 18th century often employed furniture of gilt brass, even gilt barrels, even though in the 18th century this trend was far from being restricted to the Karlovy Vary region only. The butts of 17th-century Dutch pistols were sometimes carved in the form of a human head. This is typical of weapons produced about 1660 in Maastricht which feature butts in ivory. A number of other examples from various parts of Europe could be mentioned here as well.

379 Wheellock rifle (one of a pair), with initials *MP*, Central Europe, second half of 17th century. Stock entirely overlaid with staghorn.

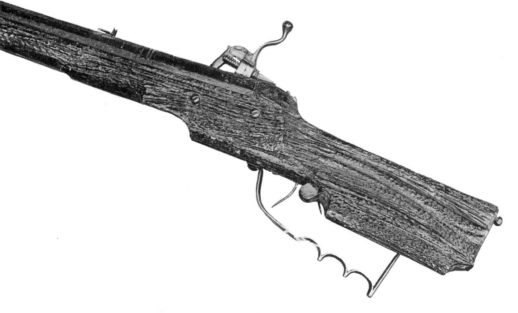

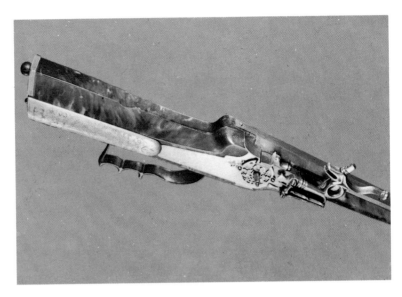

380 Wheellock rifle, stock overlaid with tortoiseshell, Central Europe, first half of 17th century.

381 Painted decoration on firearms is exceptional. Heavy wall-gun, calibre 32 mm, overall length 178 cm, provided with matchlock is adorned (both barrel and stock) with white and red stripes, coat of arms of Janovský of Janovice nad Úhlavou, noble family on the butt, Bohemia, 17th century.

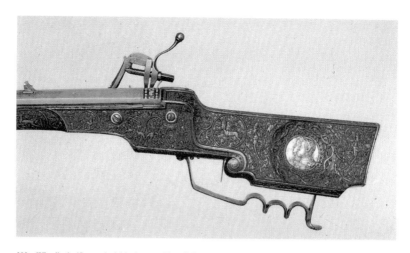

382 Wheellock rifle, stock richly decorated in relief carving. The specific style of decoration gave the unknown author the title of Meister der Tierkopfranke (Master of scrolls with animal heads). Medallion depicting a man and a woman with REX BOHE inscription inlaid in the butt. The weapon was apparently a gift for Ferdinand III (1608—57, crowned Bohemian king 1627), on the occasion of his marrying (1631) Maria Anna, daughter to Philip III, King of Spain.

383 Wheellock gun, Ch. Herold, Dresden, 1669. Lockplate and cock decorated with gilt carving, coloured enamel on the wheel-cover.

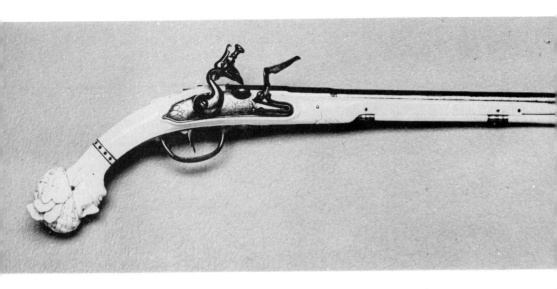

384 Pistol with French-style flintlock by Jacob Kosters, Maastricht. Stock of ivory, butt-end shaped as Turk's head. Pistols of this type were produced in the Netherlands, first of all in Maastricht, in the second half of 17th century. The weapons depicted was a gift for Augustus the Strong, King of Poland and Elector of Saxony in 1705

Attention should be paid to the fact that the evolution of weapon decoration in the Balkans was following a pattern different from that of Christian Europe. In the same way as in other territories under Islamic rule, depiction of the human form was not allowed, and for this reason decoration centred on rich geometric ornamentation. Stocks of Balkan firearms were richly inlaid with white or coloured bone, overlaid with chiselled silver or brass plate; coral and semi-precious stones were used for decoration, too.

As already suggested, individual periods favoured specific decorating techniques. The etching of metal parts was prevalent in the 16th century but later on it occurred less often. The 16th- and 17th-century stocks were inlaid with both ornamental and figural motifs of white bone. The 18th-century stock was first of all decorated with carved Baroque and Rococo ornamentation or inlaid with motifs of metal wire. These prevailing trends however, cannot be regarded as definitive. A number of diverse decorating techniques were employed on a single specimen. Side by side with ostentatious, richly decorated pieces, weapons of high technology and functional standards with only moderate decoration appeared throughout. Beside expertly executed examples we can find specimens whose decoration betrays a not too well trained hand. The latter can be compared with works by the later naive painters.

In much the same way as the blueing, blackening or browning of barrels, certain functional improvements of the 18th and 19th centuries can be considered decorative elements: Damascus barrels produced by various techniques were used on a large scale. Forge-welding iron and steel rods or bands — either twisted or straight — result in a material of not only greater strength and hardness, but of improved resilience and durability as well. The Europeans encountered damascus work on both edged weapons and firearms in the Orient, and their first use on European firearms came in the 17th and 18th centuries when Damascus barrels seized from the Turks were fitted with new stocks and locks by Austrian and other Central European gunmakers. Already in the 18th century Damascus barrels were produced by European makers and various methods and techniques in their production were developed in the early 19th century. Different types of Damascus were named either after the method of manufacture (twist, band) or after the motif (e.g. rose) on the barrels produced by processing heterogeneous material. The inventor's name might be used, e.g. Bernard Damascus, in the case of N. Bernard, a Paris gunmaker whose son Léopold in particular became famous for the production of Damascus barrels. Due to their quality, the popularity of these barrels increased considerably and imitations occurred — the surface of barrels produced in the traditional way was provided with a finish imitating the Damascus look.

In the 19th century other types of special finish were developed — although to a lesser extent—, e.g. the marble-look finish of the lockplates. To a degree the hatching on the neck and forestock of shoulder weapons or on pistol butts can be considered a decorative element, although this, too, was again a case of functional improvement aimed at a better grasp of the weapon by its owner.

The motifs appearing in decoration are as diverse as the decorating techniques. Besides plant and geometric ornaments, various hunting scenes depicting both the game and the hunter are among the most frequent themes. Various military and historical scenes, themes from ancient mythology and the history of Christianity are numerous, and even themes influenced by the events of the period appeared in the decoration of firearms. Target shooting motifs can be found, too, though their occurrence is rela-

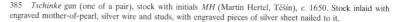

385 *Tschinke* gun (one of a pair), stock with initials *MH* (Martin Hertel, Těšín), *c.* 1650. Stock inlaid with engraved mother-of-pearl, silver wire and studs, with engraved pieces of silver sheet nailed to it.

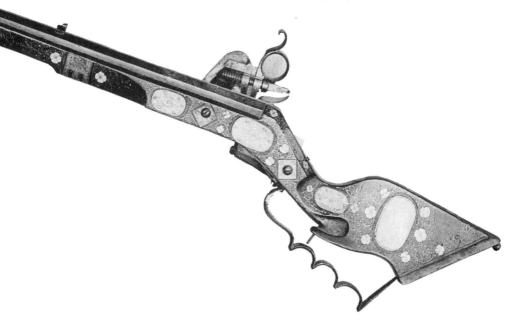

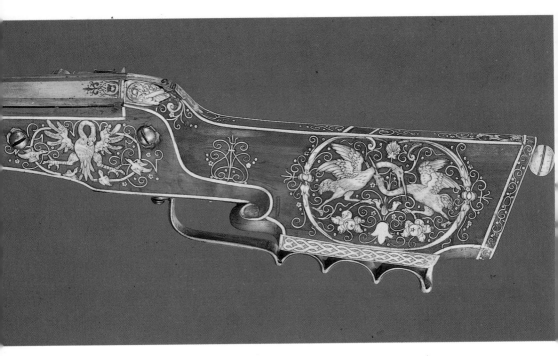

386 Wheellock rifle, Saxony, 1615. Stock inlaid with motifs of plant and bird ornaments, decoration according to the *Ornamentstiche* by Theodor Bang issued in Nuremberg in 1610.

387 Single-barrelled gun with French-style flintlock, Central Europe, first half of 18th century. The weapon decorated with engraving, chiselling and other techniques, blackened barrel inlaid with gold, stock of root-wood Thumb-plate with the owner's monogram on the wrist of the stock.

388 Gun with French flintlock, barrel marked *CV*, Silesia, end of 17th century. Barrel decorated with silver ornament on blackened background. Stock inlaid with bone, mother-of-pearl and white horn (scrolls, points, hunting motifs) in Silesian style.

tively rare compared with that of hunting motifs. Besides real types of game the engravings often depict diverse mythical animals, monsters and dragons; mascarons represent a frequent decorative element. The list of motifs can be complemented with diverse heraldic themes and symbolic depictions. Antique firearms were — leaving aside the not too numerous exceptions —

389 Pair of wheellock rifles, Hans Keiner, Cheb (Eger), *c.* 1670.
Cheb-style decoration with relief carving of the stock.

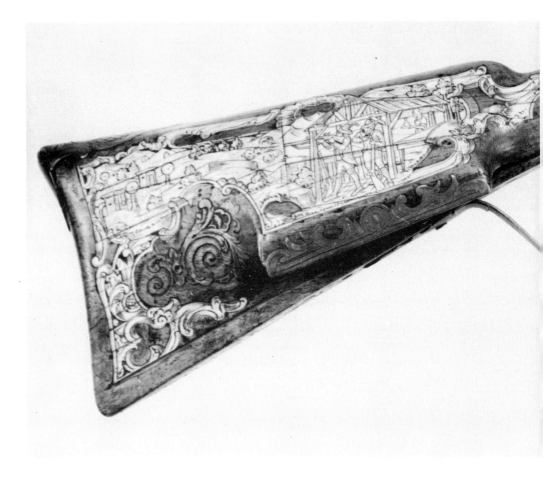

390 Rifle for left-hander, originally flintlock weapon converted to percussion system, Joseph Planer, Vienna (master in 1775). Butt decorated with motif of shooting range.

intended for men, and thus it is not surprising that erotic motifs can be found in their decoration from time to time. In the same way we find different decorating techniques on a single specimen. The multi-thematic decoration of a single firearm can often occur.

Since it was mentioned at the beginning of this chapter that the style of decoration can help when attempting to date a weapon, attention should also be drawn to certain pitfalls in such an approach. The new style was always most popular in the country of origin before it was adopted by other countries after varying delays. There could also be some lapse of time between the town and the countryside. Another problem is presented by the fact that in some areas the traditional way of decoration continued to be observed over long periods. Finally, although isolated instances only are involved, we can find weapons whose decoration just does not correspond to the style of the period. A pistol is known to the author which, as indicated by its serial number, was produced in the 1850s, yet its overall style and

391 Wheellock rifle, barrel with monogram *HP* (Hans Paumgartner, Graz), 1591, lock with initial *TM*. Bone detail of inlaid humorous hunting motifs on stock of hare sounding a horn and riding a dog.

392 Wheellock rifle by Maximilian Wenger, Prague, *c.* 1630. On butt inlaid motif of three stags with one common head.

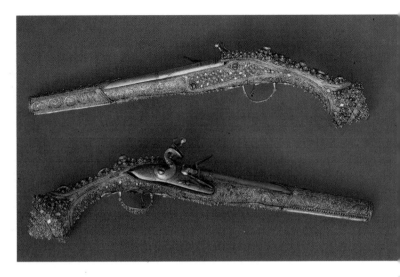

393   Two French flintlock pistols with typical Balkan decoration of silverwire, beads and filigree with orange and red stones.

decoration class it as at least twenty years older. It corresponds neither to fashion trends nor other arms by the same craftsman of the 1850s. Most probably it is a case of a firearm produced in a style following a customer's specification.

MARKS ON FIREARMS

Marks on the weapon can sometimes be of great significance for its identification. True, there exist firearms (sometimes even quality specimens) on which no marks can be discovered. Much more frequently, however, shoulder arms and pistols bear gunmakers' marks. On hand-held firearms the first marks appeared as early as the 14th century and in the subsequent periods their number grew. It is very important to note exactly what kind of mark is involved and to interpret its meaning correctly, as the most diverse marks and inscriptions can be encountered on firearms.

Marks can be found on practically all parts of firearms. Most often they appear on the barrel or on the lockplate but various marks may be discovered on the butt, on furniture such as the butt-plate, trigger-guard, side-plate and elsewhere and, on more modern weapons, on the breech. Sometimes marks are found only after the weapon has been dismantled, as they may be situated on the inside of the lockplate or beneath the barrel and inspection of the external appearance cannot reveal them. In the case of a firearm provided with several marks, their correct interpretation can furnish a remarkable amount of information on the weapon's history.

Gunmakers' marks are among the most important identification features. The mark represented the gunmaker's privilege through which he attested the quality either by his mark or his name on the weapon. Gunmakers' marks appeared on firearms as early as the 14th century, but in the early period it was a case of simple motifs (crosses, stars, etc.) and their original owners are quite unidentifiable today. From the mid-16th century, master gunmakers' initials began appearing on firearms, sometimes alone, but mostly accompanied by a pictorial mark. This could be represented just by a simple figure but gradually, however, marks depicting various plants, animals, tools, figural motifs and others appeared. In some cases the gunmaker's mark is small but complex. There was no uniform way of punching or engraving these marks, even though, in some cases, in certain areas identical approaches were traditionally observed. The marker's initials may appear in a square or a rectangular form, in a heart-shaped or oval field. From the 17th century some gunmakers started using marks consisting of three letters instead of two-letter initials. It must be pointed out that interpretation in such cases may vary. Initials of the first, the middle and the family name can be involved, e.g. *ICK* = Johann Christoph Kuchenreiter, or initials of the Christian and the family name plus another letter from the middle of a longer family name (*HBF* = Hans Breitenfelder). In yet another variant the three letters can stand for the gunmaker's initials and the initial

Examples of maker's marking

$M \cdot F \cdot I 691$

Monogram MF (wheellock rifle, 1691)

Thomas Addis, London (gun with snaphaunce lock, end of 16th century)

Matthias Muck, Brno (single-barrelled smooth-bore gun with French-style flintlock, first half of 18th century, so-called 'rebus mark' (Mücke means mosquito in German)

Chassier, Paris (single-barrelled smooth-bore gun with French flintlock, second half of 18th century)

Auguste Francotte, Liège (a 19th-century company; executions of the mark may slightly differ from the depicted variant)

The same weapon, mark on butt-plate

Salvador Zenarro (Cenarro), Madrid (single-barrelled smooth-bore gun with Catalan lock, second half of 18th century (mistake in spelling — Savador instead of Salvador)

of the town where he was working (GZZ = Georg Zellner, Zell am Wallersee). We do not know the name of many makers nowadays, but a number of the marks have been deciphered, although not always without some doubt and sometimes with possible different interpretations.

Marking the full gunmaker's name and the locality where he worked on firearms began — possibly in Italy — in the 16th century, and from the mid-17th century it was commonly used all over Europe. Even though gunmakers were already marking their weapons with full names, a number of them kept using symbols side by side with the name; in the 19th century company trademarks developed from this style of marking. It must be pointed out that a gunmaker himself could change his mark in the course of his career, or, which is a more frequent case, he could use the identical basic symbols in different forms. There are also instances when the son took over his father's mark along with the business. Yet another letter can sometimes be found following the maker's full name; if it is an *F*, it usually stands for *fecit* (made). (In Britain it can also stand for 'Foreigner'.) In other cases it is an initial of the town where the maker operated (e.g. in the inscription *Hans Keiner E.* the *E* stands for Eger, the German name of the town of Cheb).

As already mentioned, the subject of gunmakers' marks is very complex. One example of the problem is the so-called 'rebus marks' where the symbol represents the maker's family name. Gunmaker Hubert Storch had a stork for his symbol, gunmaker Jelínek used a stag (*jelínek* means 'little stag' in Czech). Some members of the well-known Klett family used one or three burdocks (*Klette* means 'burdock' in German). A number of similar cases could be mentioned, and they are typical of the period of individual gunmaking; today the symbol of the rearing horse has been used over a long period on arms by the Colt company and could be considered a 'rebus mark'.

The maker's entire name was initially engraved or stamped on the barrel; from the 17th century it also appeared on the lockplates. Various types were used — both capital letters, italics and script. If on the barrel, it was as a rule situated on the upper surface, on the lockplate in the middle, but as the latter was often used for decoration, the marking sometimes appeared in places where it would not disturb the artistic concept, such as on the lower lock-plate edge, behind the cock or under the pan. Alternatively, the gunmaker's name was directly incorporated into the decorative pattern. Initially the maker's names were engraved. In the 18th and to certain extent also in the 19th century they were, in considerable numbers, inlaid with gold or silver, particularly on the barrels.

Spanish gunmakers, too, started marking their products with names in full in the 17th century, but in a distinctive manner. In two or even three lines the name was located in a rectangular field on the barrel where previously only the gunmaker's initials had been placed. The graphic mark with the maker's name was supplemented with a pictorial mark in a square field and a number of decorative signs (pomegranates, lilies, roses and others) and also a cross. Spanish shotgun barrels were renowned for their quality and were exported to other European countries and under these circumstances the Spanish type of mark was used by many gunmakers working in countries far away from Spain. This was the case with the Austrian Hapsburg monarchy whose noble families had numerous contacts with Spain, but it was also true of other European countries, too.

Long arms and pistols, apart from exceptional pieces purposely kept in their original state, were utility objects which often served their original owners over a long period of time, and their descendants in succeeding generations as well. For this reason they were repaired and modified as specified by their owners of the time, a fact which must be taken into account each time a weapon and its marking are to be evaluated. Older high-quality barrels were commonly fitted with new stocks and locks. The original name remained on the barrel while the lockplate would bear the name of the new gunmaker often living long after the time when the barrel was made. Flint-lock weapons were converted to the percussion system in large numbers; either minor alternations of the lock mechanism took place in the process while the original marking was preserved, or, in other cases the complete lockplate could be replaced.

The approach to methods of marking was very diverse and the gunmaker did not always mark both the barrel and the lockplate with identical inscriptions including his name and the place where he worked. Some firearms featured the maker's name on the barrel and his place of work on the lockplate. On paired long arms or pistols the gunmaker's name could be on one weapon and the name of the town on the other. If additional modifications were carried out on such weapons, or if only one of the pair has been preserved, we may now find incomplete marking on a weapon (e.g. just the locality without the maker's name).

Some further remarks regarding the gunmakers' marking should be added. As a rule it consists just of the name of the maker and of his place of business, sometimes supplemented with other particulars when the makers claimed they were royal or princely suppliers. The Viennese gunmaker Keiser, who lived to a great age, marked his later production with his years. At other times the marking consists of a whole sentence announcing that the said maker produced the firearm, that he was the inventor of the design employed or the like.

Marking firearms was not always carried out in the maker's mother tongue. French was the language of diplomats and also the language of communication for noblemen in most European countries, and it is therefore not surprising that firearms were marked in French even outside France. Latin, too, had the character of a universal language and there

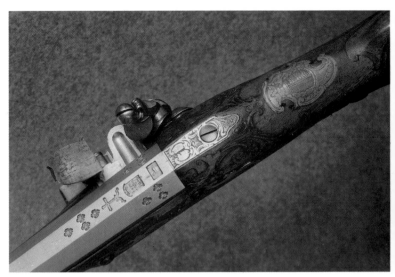

395 Single-barrelled (smooth bore) flintlock gun by Jan Čermák, Ústí nad Orlicí, Bohemia, 18th century. Spanish style of marks. On the neck thumb-plate bearing the original owner's coat of arms.

exist weapons with Latin inscriptions, or just quoting the name of the locality in Latin. In areas with mixed population, the language used in the marking is more likely to disclose the nationality of the client than that of the gunmaker. As an example, products by the Prague master gunmaker A. V. Lebeda are known to have been marked in Czech, German and French, but also in Hungarian.

It may be difficult for today's reader to understand that the name of the same gunmaker can appear on his products in different spellings, but even in the 18th century there still was nothing extraordinary about it. Family names, which from the viewpoint of history had been established only shortly before, in many instances were not yet fixed firmly. Different variants of a name can be found not only in the records of the period where the spelling was up to the scribe, but in the marking of weapons, too, where for once we would expect a higher degree of consistency. Thus the same gunmakers or members of the same family can be found in various documents entered as: Breitenfelder-Braydenfelter-Breidfelter-Preitenfelder, etc.; Brixi-Brykcy-Prizi-Pritzi; Bloch-Floch-Ploch-Flag; Geidel-Geudel-Jaidtl-Jeitl, etc. Similar deviations, even though not to such an extent as in written sources, also appear in the marking of weapons.

In the 19th century, when the significance of tradition was duly appreciated, a new owner — no matter whether a family member or an outsider — would run the business under his predecessor's name and also preserve

◄ 394 Single-barrelled (smooth-bore) gun with miquelet lock, lockplate and barrel marked *IOA/QUIM/ANT/DAS* (Ioaquim Antdas) barrel also *ARCENAL REAL DO EXERCITO 1792*. The grooved steel is typical of miquelet locks.

the marking used on weapons until then, which was a guarantee of quality and sound sales. In other cases the new proprietor used his name in the marking where at the same time he mentioned the previous owner. Johann Springer, who married Matthias Novotny's sister, having taken over Novotny's business, marked his products as follows: *Joh. Springer vorm. Nowotny in Wien* (Johann Springer, formerly Novotny in Vienna). Later on he used just his name and became a well-known gunmaker of such fame that after his death his firm marked their firearms *Joh. Springers Erben* (Joh. Springer's heirs). Sometimes the family connection with the original proprietor whose products had gained high repute was included in the marking. This happened most frequently in a firm taken over by a son or sons of the gunmaker, but other cases can also be found. After the death of A. Ch. Kehlner, a Prague gunmaker, his business was taken over by his nephew named Petzold, but the weapons produced there were as a rule marked: *A. Ch. Kehlner Neveu*, or, less frequently *A. Ch. Kehlners Neffe*.

A firearm was seldom the product of a single craftsman, even though generally only the gunmaker's marks can be found on it. Craftsmen of related skills also participated in its creation and their name, monogram or mark may be discovered on a long arm or a pistol. Originally it was the case of stockmakers producing wooden stocks and butts, but in the early period of craft production the strict division into gunmakers and stockmasters did not always exist, so that sometimes even the stockmaker assembled firearms and sold the complete product. Some craftsmen specialized in the production of barrels or locks only and provided the respective parts with their marks. As a result, in addition to gunmakers' marks indicating who assembled and sold the weapon, barrelmaker's marks or the marks of makers of other parts may be found on the weapon, as well as the marking by the creative artist or engraver who designed or executed the decoration. Finally, the fact must be mentioned that the inscription on the weapon may be the name of the dealer who sold it, without having anything in common with its production. This is typical above all of the 19th century when craftsmen started facing competition from industrial production and were forced to look for less expensive, industrially produced barrels for their weapons. Later they completely abandoned their own production and devoted themselves only to selling, repairing or individual modifications. The fact that the weapon was marked by the seller and not by the maker was not restricted just to the 19th century. Instances are known from earlier periods when a trader or a military entrepreneur supplied weapons provided with their marking but manufactured by someone else.

The mass-production of weapons, especially of military ones, began much earlier than in many other branches of industry. The 17th- and 18th-century manufacturers, as well as the later state-owned or private arms works, used makers' markings and often included the place of production, the name of the proprietor and, in the 19th century, the company name. In some manufactures the individual craftsmen marked the pieces they had made with letters; the 19th-century arms works, particularly the large ones, sometimes had their 'sub-contractors', who supplied trigger guards, barrel-mounts and other parts. However, the meaning of marks on the individual details is very seldom known to us — just exceptionally in the case of larger enterprises specializing in the manufacture of barrels. Both manufacturers and industrial enterprises could mark their products using either the full name or just abbreviations; the latter are decipherable to a substantially greater extent than in the case of individual makers from earlier periods. As examples of

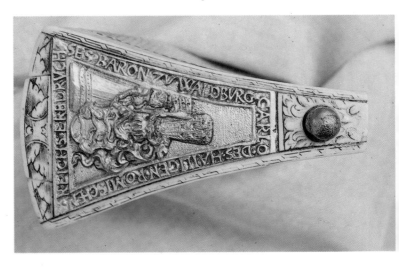

396   Detail from gun with combined snap- and matchlock, South Germany, *c.* 1570. On the butt, coat of arms, name and rank of the original owner (Baron Karl of Waldburg, Dapifer Hereditary of the Holy Roman Empire).

similar marks we can mention the following abbreviations: *IIGVW* (Johann Joseph Graf von Waldstein = Count Wallenstein, proprietor of the Duchcov manufacture 1713—19), *S. et D.* (Splittgerber and Daun, a marking on 1722—74 products of the Potsdam manufacture), on Russian weapons *T. O. Z.* in Cyrillic alphabet (Tulsky Oruzheiny Zavod = Armoury Works of Tula), *AF* topped by a crown (Auguste Francotte, a well-known 19th-century Liège company), *ML* topped by a crown (Manufacture Liégeoise d'Armes à Feu, an arms works in Liège founded in 1866), *OEWG* (Österreichische Waffenfabrik-Gesellschaft, Austrian arms works in Steyr).

As already mentioned, the maker's mark was a guarantee of quality and firearms by renowned gunmakers were considerably more expensive than products by their more or less unknown colleagues or weapons without any marks. For this reason the falsification of some makers' marks occurred both by their contemporaries, who wanted to increase the selling price of their lower-quality weapons, and later on when an additionally engraved mark of a well-known gunmaker would increase the value of the weapon as a collector's item. On a large scale the Cominazzo mark, belonging to well-known 17th- and 18th-century Italian makers, was imitated, but so was that of Israel Segalas, a London gunmaker, and others. Even among factory-produced weapons of the second half of the 19th century instances of falsified marking occurred which were intended to mislead the customer and make him pay a higher price for an inferior weapon. In Liège, Belgium, also in Spain and elsewhere, the local products were sometimes marked as 'Colt system' or with an English inscription recommending use of 'Smith and Wesson cartridges' to make the inexperienced customer believe that revolvers made by well-known U.S. companies were involved. A similar practice was adopted even with regard to some European products which had gained renown, e.g. the Austro-Hungarian revolver Model 1870 by the Viennese Gasser company and its Montenegro variety in particular, were manufactured by other producers with just a slightly altered maker's marking. On Balkan weapons an inscription consisting of a group of

397 Lancaster double-barrelled rifle, end of 19th century. Silver plate with the owner's (Prince Colloredo-Mansfeld) monogram inserted into the butt from underneath.

398 Gun with miquelet lock by Joseph Mendizabal, Placencia, 1814. On the barrel, gold-inlaid mark with name of the maker, name of his workplace (*EN PLACENCIA* — rear part of the inscription covered with rear sights), date of production *(AÑO DE 1814)* and quality of material used for production of the barrel (*DE HERRADURAS* — of horseshoes).

Barrels made out of horseshoes were considered the best quality. (Nicolas Bis, a Madrid gunmaker who was producing such barrels about 1700, is considered to have been the first.) About 1700 also the habit originated in Spain of marking the name of the maker, his workplace and date of production on three upper surfaces of the edged barrel.

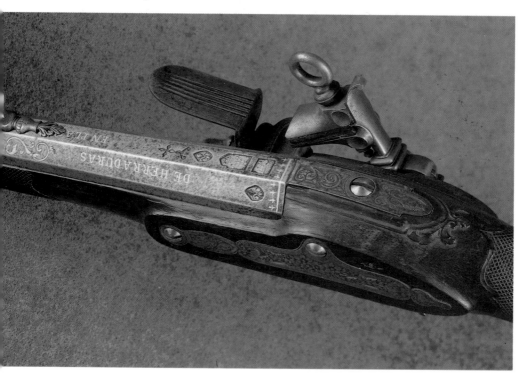

399 Pair of flintlock pistols by Michael Bayer, Würzburg, *c.* 1760. One weapon marked with the master's name, the other with the place where he worked.

Roman characters can sometimes be found which makes no sense. The reason behind it is evident for, as a rule, the customer was illiterate or perhaps he could read Arabic characters only and the cluster of Roman characters was just to create an impression of a maker's mark.

Makers' marking has been accorded considerable attention here, since an important identification element is involved, but apart from it a number of other marks can appear on a weapon. The name shown on the weapon does not always indicate the maker; it can be the owner's name as well. Owners' marks used to be less frequent than the maker's marking and usually differed from the latter both in appearance and position on the weapon, so that no doubts should arise as to which sort of mark was involved. In the earlier periods coats-of-arms could appear on noblemen's arms; later on the owner's monogram was generally used. This can often be found particularly on weapons of Central European provenance. In the case of a merchant owner the mark consisted of his initials and, if a nobleman was involved, the monogram was complemented with a crown, the shape of which corresponded to the owner's rank — a closed crown for a prince, a 9-pearl crown for a count, a 7-pearl crown for a baron, and a 5-pearl crown for a knight.

In the 18th and 19th centuries the owner's monogram was most often engraved in a metal plate inserted into the upper part of the wrist of the stock or into the upper part of the butt; at times it was called a 'thumb plate', as the thumb of the right hand is placed here while shooting. However, the owner's initials could be positioned elsewhere, too — either on a metal plate inserted in the butt or in the forestock from underneath or they could be decoratively executed on another part of the weapon, perhaps on the trigger-guard or buttplate. Sometimes the owner's name was included in full as it was on sharpshooters' weapons which had the name of the sharpshooter corps member shown on the side-plate. The owner's monogram appeared only quite exceptionally on spaces reserved for the maker's marks (barrels or lockplates).

At the time when the army was considered the sovereign's exclusive property, owners' marks can be found on military weapons, too. The sovereign's initials were situated on the thumb-plate in Prussia, Russia and other countries; English military weapons had an abbreviation on the lockplate consisting of the initials of the sovereign's name and the letter R (*rex, regina* in Latin).

Proof marks are of considerable significance, too. Shortly after firearms first appeared it was considered necessary to verify their safety. As early as the 14th century firearms were subjected to test-firing using an increased charge of gunpowder. However, compulsory testing of weapons by test-shooting did not appear until the 16th century, and then only in some towns. The meaning of marks found on some weapons originating in those earlier periods is not quite clear. They may be view-marks attesting to external inspection of the weapon and its acceptance to the town armoury rather than proof marks confirming the fact that test-firing had been undergone.

Proof-houses originated in the large centres of gun manufacture as early as the 16th century (St. Étienne in France, Placencia near Eibar in Spain) and particularly in the 17th century (Liège and London) and later, but testing remained mostly voluntary. Only in the 19th century was the testing of all firearms made compulsory by legal regulations, but only in some countries (e.g. France in 1869, Germany and Austria-Hungary in 1891). The testing of weapons in other European countries was either not enforced at all, or was left at the manufacturer's discretion. A system of marking was

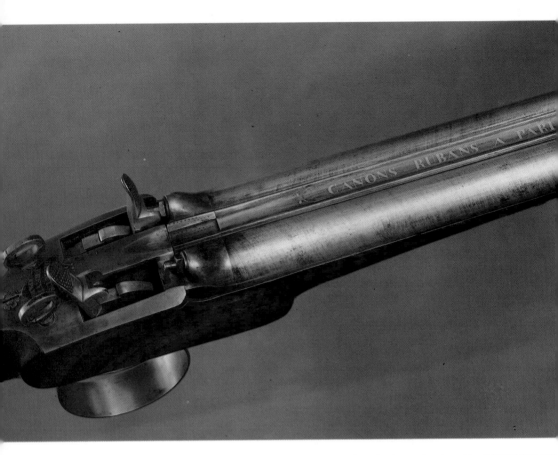

400 Percussion double-barrelled gun, *c.* 1835. On flat surface between barrels, marking *CANONS RUBANS A PARIS* (band-barrels from Paris; ruban —- Damascus band), on lock-casing the inscription *INV^N /POTTET/ DELCUSSE/BREVETE/A PARIS/* (invention Pottet-Delcusse, Parisian patent).

developing within the individual proof-houses, and the proof marks changed as at certain dates, so that today they sometimes reveal not only the provenance of the weapon, but its date of manufacture as well. It is of particular significance in cases when, based on local practice, proof marks were accompanied by the date of the test.

Armies, too, created their own inspection and control systems. Within arsenals or private or state manufacturing enterprises turning out firearms for military use, army inspectors or inspection committees stamped the 'passed' weapons with the appropriate test and acceptance marks. Some other marks may be found on military weapons in particular, such as an indication of the model and the user of the weapon. It does not hold true for all European armies, and even in those armies which adopted this marking there was no uniform practice and many ways of marking were employed. A military model specification was most frequently determined by the year when the weapon was officially adopted. French military guns were already so marked on the breech-plug projection in the 18th century (M 1777 = Model 1777). With regard to French weapon in the course of the French Revolution a new calendar was introduced in 1793, in which the first day of the new era was September 22nd, 1792, when the Republic was proclaimed. As a result, weapons from the Revolutionary and Napoleonic period bear unusual model marks: *M an 9* (Model of the year 9, i.e. the period between September 1800 and September 1801), *M an 13* (Model of the year 13, i.e. 1804 — 05). The revolutionary calendar was abolished in December 1805, and from then on French weapons again showed the model year in Gregorian style.

Model indication sometimes included not only the year of adoption, but also the official denomination of the weapon, usually in an abbreviated form. On military breech-loaders the model indication was mostly located on the breech-sleeve, for example, the following marks can be found on Prussian needle-guns: *ZG Mod. 62* (Zündnadelgewehr Model 62, i.e. needle-gun Model 1862), *ZPG M. 69* (Zündnadel-Pioniergewehr Model 69, i.e. Pioneer needle-gun Model 1869) and others. Similar abbreviations occurred also on English weapons from the turn of the 19th and 20th centuries (*S^{HT} L. E.* = Short Lee-Enfield, i.e. Lee-Enfield short rifle). Another British system did not show the year of official adoption but the serial numbers of the individual types (*Mk I, Mk II*), while minor improvements and modifications within the same type were indicated by the added symbol of a star (*Mk I**).

It should be pointed out with regard to military weapons that in the case

401 Pistol with combined flintlock and percussion lock by Johann Baptist Strixner, Vienna, *c.* 1830. In percussion operation the touch-hole from the pan was covered by a screw-on cover and the lower jaw of the cock struck the cap placed over the nipple. The weapon, rather interesting from the technical point of view, has the barrel provided with production marks and inscription *Aus Gusstahl gebohrter Lauf* (barrel of cast steel).

Sovereign's monogram on
military weapons (marking on
the thumb-plate of a Russian
army pistol — Nicolas I, Tsar
1825—55)

Model on military weapons
(French pistol 1763, mark on
the projection of the barrel
tang)

F.R. 35
8.123

Identification marks on military weapons (on butt-plate of
Prussian fusilier gun Model
1860 — fusilier regiment No.
35, company No. 8, weapon
No. 123 in the company)

Proof-house (testing mark
used in Liège 1811—93)

of a later official conversion to another model the original model marking may have been preserved. The Prussian *Mod. 54* may indicate both the original jaeger gun Model 1854 and the pioneer gun U/M adapted from the former when it was shortened by 15 cm and provided with different rear sights.

The model can be indicated also on firearms for civilian use produced in large numbers, but in Europe this practice caught on only in the 20th century. In the U.S.A. it already existed in the 19th century.

In the 19th century some armies introduced markings enabling identifica-tion of the user of the weapon. Abbreviations consisting of several letters and numerals indicated the army branch which had been issued with the weapon (infantry, cavalry, artillery), specified numbers or denominations of the respective unit (regiment, battalion, company, battery, squadron) and the serial number of the weapon in the unit. According to this marking, military authorities could identify the soldier to whom the particular weap-on belonged; for example, such a marking on the bayonet which every soldier was obliged to carry when off duty, had, among other things, the function of a military identity card. Today this marking, linked with data concerning the history of the unit, helps to indicate in which garrisons, campaigns and battles the weapon saw service.

Dating ranks among very significant data which enable an exact classif-ication of a weapon in time. Although the production year appeared on some firearms in the 16th century, dating never became a rule and can be found on only a small proportion of the preserved weapons. The production year is most often shown at the maker's initials or name, but may be found in a number of other places as well, e.g. on the butt-plate, integrated into the decoration and the like. Sometimes it cannot be discovered by an inspection of the external appearance, since it is located on the inner surface of the lockplate or on the bottom surface of the barrel hidden behind the forestock — to be found only after the weapon has been dismantled.

The date when a weapon was made can sometimes be determined exactly, using the maker's marks and the known data concerning his career. Nicolaus Dreyse used to mark his weapons — both for army and civilian use — with the initials *ND*. Later, having been elevated to the nobility, with *NvD* (Nico-laus von Dreyse). If we know he was raised to nobility in 1864, then it is evident that his weapon marked *NvD* must have originated between 1864 and 1867, the year of his death. The gunmaker Heinrich Barella was work-ing in Magdeburg between 1844 and 1865. In 1860 he settled in Berlin, to where he transferred his operation completely in the mid-1860s. Weapons showing 'Magdeburg and Berlin' as his workplace consequently originated between 1860 and 1865.

Dating appears not only on civilian weapons, but on a lot of military guns, where it can be found on various parts including the barrel, lockplate, breech-sleeve and elsewhere. It specifies the year of production, which is very important for weapons marked with the model, as some types of milit-ary weapons were produced over a long period. The production year is mostly shown in full (*1822*), but also in the form of the last three or two digits (*856* = 1856, *67* = 1867).

The year marked on the weapon need not mean the year of production in each instance. It may also indicate the year of repair or modification, presentation and the like. Prussian army needle-guns are marked with two years; the earlier indicates the production year while the later the year when an army unit was actually issued with it. The weapons were

Proof-house (testing mark used in Vienna from 1892 onwards)

stockpiled in dumps and only after a sufficient number had been accumulated for rearming a larger part of the army were they distributed to units. There also occur cases when the year marked on the weapon evidently corresponds to neither its design nor decoration, and unless it is supplemented with an explanatory inscription it is difficult to determine its significance.

Occasionally firearms were marked with production or serial numbers in the 18th century, but more commonly in the 19th century. Even earlier paired pistols and long arms had been marked 1 and 2 — mostly on the breech-plug projection. Identical hunting guns produced for the same customer were often numbered from 1 to as many as 12. In large-series production of military guns, initially 1-digit, 2-digit and at most 3-digit numbers were used in marking all the basic parts of the same weapon.

In the 19th century some gunmakers numbered their products in a single ascending series, irrespective of the type or system of weapon. Even if no written evidence of their activity is known today — which is the case in the majority of instances — some dated specimens can help establish a quite accurate date of origin for undated pieces with close production numbers. With the expansion of industrial production of army weapons and, somewhat later, of arms for civilian use, a new system was gradually gaining ground in which each weapon had a separate numbering of its own. In some cases the production numbers follow a single ascending series from 1 up to the last produced weapon of the same model; in other instances, on military weapons in particular (these being produced in huge numbers), the numbering went from 1 to 9999 for each individual lot, which was moreover marked with letters (e.g. A, B, C) in addition to the number. Production numbers were always stamped on all basic parts of the weapon and often on numerous other parts as well. On less important details such as barrel mounts or places where there was not sufficient space for showing the number in full (bolts, screws etc.), a shortened variant may be found such as, for example, the last two or three digits.

As early as the 17th century, and in the 18th century, too, isolated instances of inscriptions on weapons are found claiming the gunmaker to be the inventor of a technical concept or design innovation. After patent protection for inventors was introduced, a growing number of inscriptions appeared claiming that principles or solutions protected by a patent had been used on the weapon. In contrast to the United States, where indicating both the number and the date of the granted patent was a custom, such a practice was rather exceptional in Europe, even though here, too, some weapons showed the date or the number of the patent. As a rule the weapon was just marked *Patent*, or, in French-speaking regions *Breveté*; some weapons were marked *Invention*, or, in an abbreviated form, *Inv^n* or *Inv^{on}*. In Germany the abbreviations *D. R. P.* (Deutsches Reichspatent — German Empire Patent) or *D. R. G. M.* (Deutsches ReichsGebrauchsmuster — German Empire Registered Design) were used. The fact that the patent had been applied for and not yet granted could be stated on weapons — *Patent pending*, or, in German *Patent angemeldet*, which was also used in the *Patent angem.* abbreviated form.

In connection with innovations in production and technology becoming widespread, particularly in the first half of the 19th century, some gunmakers inscribed their products in order to call attention to a better-quality material used or to special production techniques. This, of course, served to improve publicity and sales. On the barrels we can find an inscription informing us

329

that they have been produced from cast steel (*Gusstahl* or *Acier fondu*), or about special techniques used in producing them such as information about various types of Damascus barrels (inscription *Damas Anglais* — English Damascus, *Canons Rubans* — barrels from Damascus band, *Canon Tordu* — barrels from twisted material).

In the second half of the 19th century inscriptions which were to guarantee the owner's safety began appearing on weapons. These indicated what cartridge was to be used or showed the amount and occasionally even the type of gunpowder. Sometimes the latter concerned the type and amount of gunpowder used by the proof-house while test-firing.

Not even this quite extensive coverage has dealt all the variations of marking. There are also other ways of marking, either applied to the weapon in the course of production or to completed ones, attesting to the history of the weapon. As regards the former category, Prussian needle-guns provide an example: starting from Model 1860 they were produced in two sizes differing in length by 19.5 mm so that soldiers of different height could choose a longer or a shorter weapon. The guns were consequently marked on the right side of the stock either *K. A.* (*kurzer Anschlag,* i.e. shorter butt) or *L. A.* (*langer Anschlag,* i.e. longer butt). The position of the safety catch on modern wapons is usually indicated by a letter or in full; on shotguns

402 Butt of a Lefaucheux double-barrelled rifle, by A.V. Lebeda, Prague, 1866, barrels by A. Francotte Co., Liège. According to the owner's monogram probably a weapon once belonging to Prince L. Rohan.
In the second half of the 19th century some sportsmen started marking their trophies. On the band at the butt-plate types of game were inscribed; oval metal plaques on the butt indicate years and the studs the number of game shot. Trophy records on the weapon depicted cover the period from 1866 to 1886; 1003 pieces of game had been killed by the weapon by 1878.

„ALS BESTE GEGEBEN HERR GRAF ARTUR POTOCKI AM 13 JULI 1873 AUF DER SCHIESZSTÄTTE ZU WITTINGAU."

403 Barrel of a target rifle with falling-block action, Josef Plaschil, Napajedla, Moravia. Prize at shooting competition in Bohemia town of Třeboň (Wittingau in German) of 1873. Patent, producer's name and presentation inscription on barrel.

with choked barrels there is a warning not to use ball cartridges — 'Not for Ball', 'Non pour Balle' in French and 'Nicht für Kugel' in German.

As to additional inscriptions on weapons, their extent is considerable. They may be various presentation inscriptions, records of types and numbers of game killed, inscriptions concerning repairs of the weapon or information that the sovereign or another important person shot with it. Specimens which were included in important antique weapon collections may carry the marking of the collection and the corresponding serial number.

All the most frequent and important sorts of marking have been discussed, although it is not possible to mention all the unusual variants. In the field of antique firearms instances when marking was intended to mislead were rare; in practice it was just the case of falsified maker's marks as already mentioned here. The situation in the 20th century has been somewhat more complicated, because in various countries not only coded makers' names have been introduced but coded production years as well, and sometimes even the model has been deliberately marked by a number not corresponding to the year when the army has been issued with it.

Markings on weapons are of great importance for their identification, and correct deciphering of marks can in some cases provide us with significant information about the history of the weapon in question. A weapon should always be evaluated in a complex manner and the information provided by marks must be in accordance with the overall character of the weapon, its design concept and decoration in particular.

331

COMBINED WEAPONS

We have already discussed dual-purpose edged weapon. The advanced 16th-century type of halberd is in fact a combination of two weapons — the pike and the battle-axe.

In a similar way, although on a different level, a crossbow coupled with a pistol, a combination of a missile weapon with a firearm, doubles the chance of hitting the target. In the first quarter of the 16th century the invention of the wheellock provided the possibility of designing a fairly manageable and comparatively short weapon — the pistol. Lack of confidence as to the potential of the new weapon may have caused experimentation with the pistol and crossbow combination. The reason behind it was to enable effective use of one weapon in case of the other's failure.

Probably the earliest combination of this type comes from about 1510 and is to be found in the Doge's Palace in Venice. The weapon is provided with an iron stock in whose front part the pistol barrel is mounted with the muzzle over the bow. All the parts of the wheellock are situated on the side of the stock.

Another such combination of a crossbow and a pistol with an early form of wheellock, featuring the so-called sickle spring, is of Central European origin. This time the pistol barrel is mounted on the upper side of the wooden stock. Information available suggests that it was a present for Archduke Ferdinand from Anne Jagiello in the year of 1521.

Crossbow and pistol combinations were always exceptionally rare since the wheellock pistol quickly proved suitable for solo use. The isolated specimen of crossbow and pistol from the 1560s was, to a large extent, already an anachronism. From the 1540s combinations of an edged weapon with a pistol were becoming common.

A special group is the English Morgensterns from the second quarter of the 16th century, with several barrels fitted into the head and ignited by the match. One of them, a three-barrelled specimen, is associated with Henry VIII.

A number of lance and one or two wheellock pistol combinations probably originated in Germany. Halberds or partisans can be found among them, but they were mostly hunting weapons. The feasibility of firing a shot in case the wild boar had not been killed by the point of the spear could play a vital role in saving the hunter from being attacked by the wounded prey. Such long lances appeared, not only in Germany, from the 1540s and throughout the 16th century. As an example, an early 17th-century two-spiked halberd with the wheellock-pistol barrel situated in between (probably French) can be mentioned. The French naval pike (enterpike) of 1809 combined with a flintlock pistol, of the Charleville manufacture, is also an isolated case.

A separate group consists of maces and hatchets in combination with wheellock pistols. Mostly they were cavalry commanders' weapons, relatively frequent particularly in Central Europe, even though a Spanish specimen dated 1551 is known. Most combination weapons of this type probably originated in Augsburg workshops as attested by the rich ornamental decoration etched on a blackened background. An early 17th-century hatchet combined with a pistol and provided with both wheellock and snaplock was probably of German origin, too. In Central or Eastern Europe hatchets of this type could be found even at the end of the 17th century and perhaps in the early 18th century. At that time they were already fitted with flintlocks. The barrels were as a rule embedded in the wooden shaft often richly inlaid with bone, white horn and mother-of-pearl in a way resembling the Silesian style of decoration on stocks of the light tschinke guns. Sometimes a thin dagger was inserted from the rear into the shaft in such a manner that its hilt served as a grip for the hatchet. A hatchet and flintlock pistol combination was even introduced into the Swedish navy in the early 18th century.

Side-arms combined with pistols are known in various parts of Europe. In the second half of the 16th century it was most often a combination of a sword or a rapier with a wheellock pistol — often originating in Germany, but also in Spain, and after the mid-17th century there were flintlock variants from France. About 1600, weapons with curved blades appeared — sabres combined with wheellock pistols.

In the 18th century mainly hunting falchions were used in combination with firearms, particularly in Central Europe, where the French-type flintlock was the common igniting device. In Southern Europe, too, in Spain and perhaps also in Italy, combinations of this kind were produced, since combination weapons including miquelet pistols are known.

In the 19th century, particularly, after the mid-1850s and later, diverse combinations of pistol and knife appeared in England and America. However, a sabre of German provenance coupled with a Lefaucheux-system revolver (the combination datable to the 1860s) is a remarkable oddity.

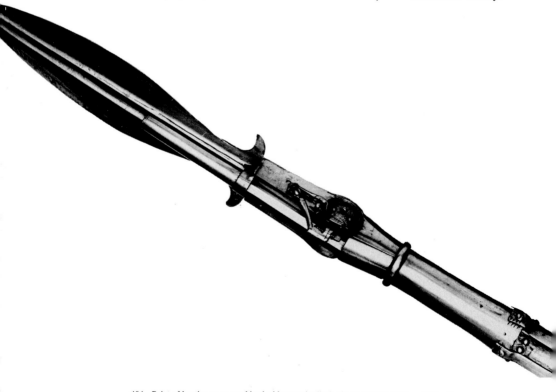

404 Point of hunting spear combined with two wheellock pistols, Central Europe, 1540—60.

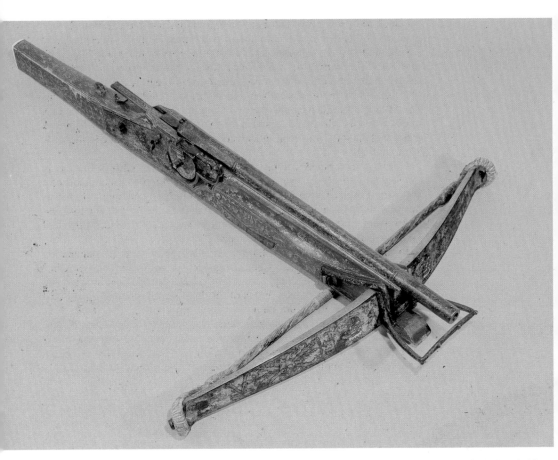

405 Crossbow combined with wheellock pistol, probably a wedding present of 1521 by Anne Jagiello to Ferdinand Hapsburg.

406 Battle-axe hatchet combined with a flintlock pistol and a dagger. Handle encrusted with bone, white horn and mother-of-pearl in Silesian style.
Hunting falchion combined with flintlock pistol, Central Europe, first half of 18th century.

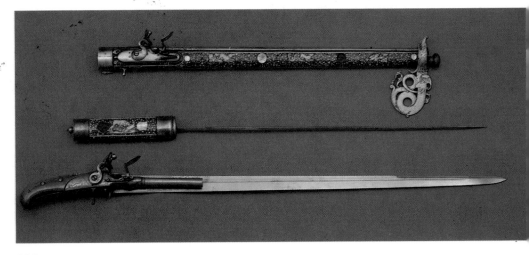

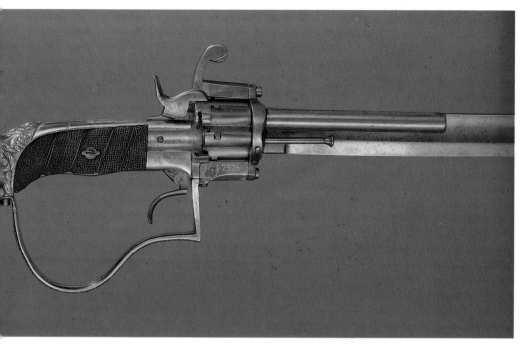

407 German sàbre combined with Lefaucheux-system revolver, Germany, 1865–75.

AIR-OPERATED WEAPONS

There are shoulder guns and pistols whose outer appearance is identical with that of firearms, yet they do not belong to this category, since projectiles are not propelled out of their barrels by energy generated by gunpowder, but by air pressure. Air-guns were developed on a large scale only in the 19th century, but their origin is much earlier. They fall into the two basic groups: air-guns where the air is compressed at the moment of firing, and air-guns in which the air is compressed beforehand into a special reservoir constituting a part of the gun. Both these categories can be further subdivided according to different design concepts.

From the chronological point of view the earliest air-guns were preceded by blow-pipes, tubes from which a missile is propelled by a blast and for which human lungs serve as the air reservoir. Blow-pipes are most frequently associated with the native peoples of the Asian and American continents, but there is also evidence attesting to the use of these weapons in Europe for shooting birds and rabbits (France, the Netherlands and Spain in the 14th – 16th centuries), and later on, in the 18th – 19th centuries but mainly for hobby-shooting only.

The earliest preserved air-guns come from the end of the 16th century and they are also documented in the written records of the period. They were piston-type air-guns whose mechanism was mostly cocked by means of a chain wound round the wheel spindle; from the outside these weapons look like standard wheellock guns. Piston-type air-guns were also produced in the course of the 17th and 18th centuries, but only infrequently and they did not become widespread till the 19th century.

In the 17th and 18th centuries the reservoir-gun became pre-eminent among air-guns. In these guns the air was compressed beforehand into a pressure reservoir which was a part of the gun and whose volume was sufficient for a large number of shots. The air was compressed using a hand-pump, which could be set in the butt, but was often a separate item. Pump air-guns can be classified according to the different types of reservoir, which could either be detachable or an inseparable part of the weapon.

Pump air-guns with a pressure reservoir around the barrel are the earliest type. Written records attest to such a weapon constructed by Marin le Bourgeoys from the French town of Lisieux (who was also considered to be the inventor of the French-type flintlock) and demonstrated for Henry IV, king of France, at the beginning of the 17th century. There is additional written evidence of similar reservoir-guns (with the reservoir in the butt) from France and Italy during the first half of the 17th century; the oldest preserved examples are datable no earlier than the 1640s. Guns with an air-reservoir in the form of a cylinder placed around the barrel proper employed two valves — a suction one to let the compressed air in, and an outlet valve to release the required volume of air into the barrel after the trigger had been pressed. Wind-guns of this type were still produced in the 18th century, but at that time other designs were already dominant.

At the end of the 17th century, throughout the 18th century and in the first half of the 19th century, guns with a spherical reservoir were being produced. The reservoir was designed as a detachable hollow ball screwed on to the breech part of the barrel, beneath, above or on the side, and using one valve only for both intake and release of the air. Weapons of this type were most common in England, but were also used in Germany, Denmark and elsewhere.

From the first quarter of the 18th century, members of the Bossler gun-making family in Darmstadt as well as other German gunmakers were producing guns with an air reservoir in the butt. The air reservoir, permanently fitted into the wooden butt, had two valves. Some written evidence indicates the existence of this particular wind-gun as early as the 17th century. In the second half of the 18th century guns of this design occurred sporadically, having been replaced with a more efficient system of air-guns with a detachable (screw-on) hollow butt reservoir. Weapons of this type appeared as early as the beginning of the 18th century, but became widespread particularly in the second half of the century and in the first quarter of the 19th century. The metal pressure-reservoir used one valve only and on the early examples it was enclosed in the detachable wooden butt. The following development proved the wooden stock to be dispensable and its function was completely taken over by the screw-on metal reservoir with leather or cloth covering. This served as thermal insulation when handling the weapon in extreme cold, for the metal would have felt chilly and the reservoir became hot due either to the sun or to rapid pump action in the course of filling the reservoir.

Air-guns in which the air reservoir was shaped as a screw-on gun or pistol-butt spread throughout almost all Europe in the late 18th and early 19th century. From the design point of view, the only pump air-gun used by the military, the Austrian air-gun Model 1780 designed by B. Girandoni, should also by included into this category. It was a repeater with a tubular magazine for 20 balls situated alongside the barrel. Tests carried out showed its effective range to be 135 m after the first 10 shots, 110 m after 20 shots and 90 m after 30 shots, the range decreasing along with the air pressure in the reservoir.

Bellows guns were produced from the mid-18th century till the first quarter of the 19th century. When the trigger was pulled, the leather bellows in the butt was snapped shut by two iron springs (exceptionally by just one spring) forcing the compressed air into the barrel. All weapons of this design were breech-loaders whose breech could be tilted up a little as a rule. The effective range of these air-guns was by no means impressive (10 − 15 m); they were used for practice or hobby shooting indoors or in the garden and as they shot darts, breech-loading was essential. Bellows guns come almost exclusively from Austria, Bohemia or South Germany.

The piston-type air-guns already mentioned at the beginning of this section and which appeared sporadically during the 17th and 18th centuries, began featuring new design elements in the first half of the 19th century. The pressure cylinder is provided with two opposite spiral springs (concentrically conical if released). The spring action was cocked by a detachable lever.

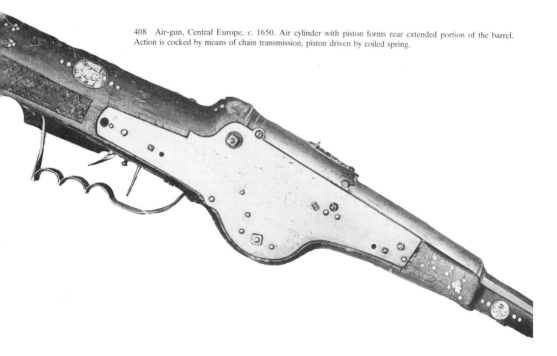

408   Air-gun, Central Europe, c. 1650. Air cylinder with piston forms rear extended portion of the barrel. Action is cocked by means of chain transmission, piston driven by coiled spring.

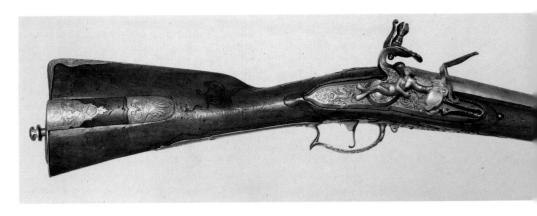

409 Air-gun with pressure-reservoir around barrel and pump in butt (pump protruding from butt-plate), Reismüller, Bautzen, c. 1730. Trigger-mechanism fashioned as French-style flintlock.

410 Air-gun with pressure reservoir around barrel and pump in butt, Central Europe, end of 17th century. Trigger mechanism shaped as wheellock.

411 Detail of foregoing air-gun. End of pump protruding from butt-plate. On cheekpiece, oval plate with engraving of a man loading a muzzle-loader.

412 Air-gun with detachable screw-on spherical pressure-reservoir, end of 18th century.

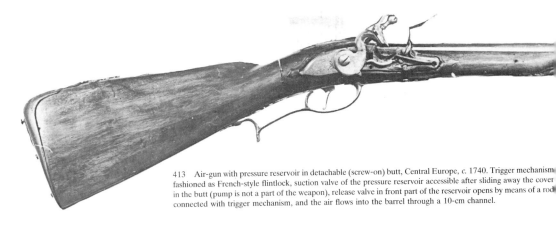

413 Air-gun with pressure reservoir in detachable (screw-on) butt, Central Europe, *c.* 1740. Trigger mechanism fashioned as French-style flintlock, suction valve of the pressure reservoir accessible after sliding away the cover in the butt (pump is not a part of the weapon), release valve in front part of the reservoir opens by means of a rod connected with trigger mechanism, and the air flows into the barrel through a 10-cm channel.

Some later specimens feature the lever permanently attached to the gun. The appearance of the earlier types resemble bellows guns — the pressure cylinder with the piston is situated in the butt where the bellows was previously, the action is cocked at the rear part of the butt, and the barrel, too, can be tilted up a little. Later the pressure cylinder moves right behind the barrel. Air-guns of this type, too, are known first in Central Europe. The action was originally cocked by means of a pinion in mesh with the rack on the piston rod. This was very labour-intensive in production, and after the mid-19th century this arrangement was replaced with cocking by means of a lever (Wil

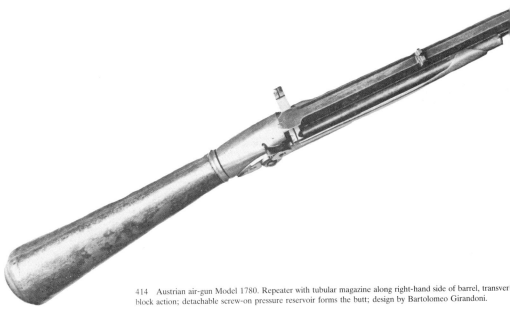

414 Austrian air-gun Model 1780. Repeater with tubular magazine along right-hand side of barrel, transvers block action; detachable screw-on pressure reservoir forms the butt; design by Bartolomeo Girandoni.

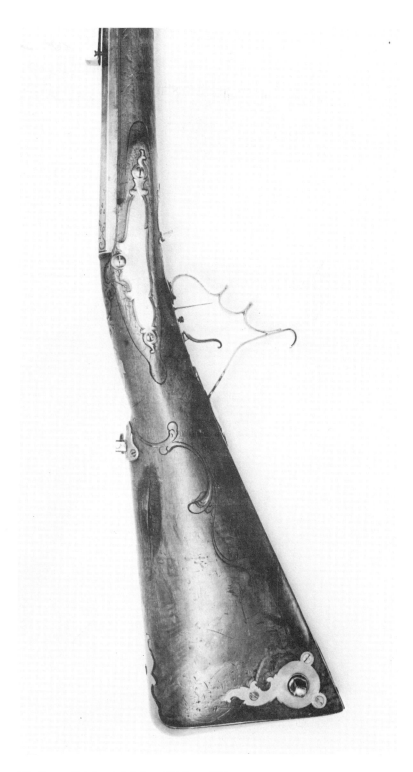

415 Air-gun with bellows in butt, Anton Pell, Linz, *c.* 1800.

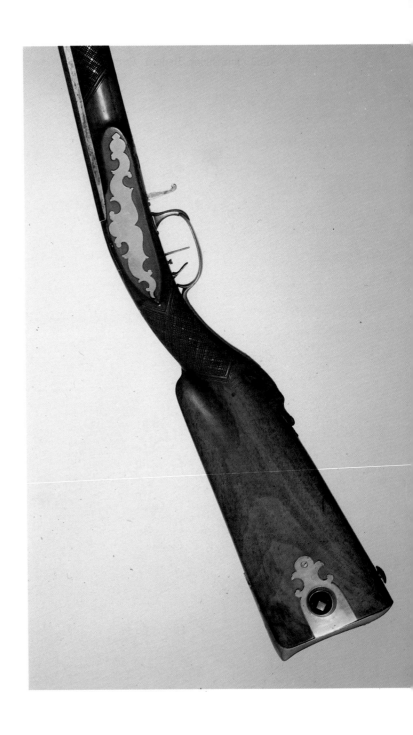

416   Air-gun with two opposite coiled springs, Josef Rutte the Elder, Česká Lípa, *c.* 1820.

from Zella St. Blasii) and the lever became the trigger-guard at the same time (Flürsheim, Baden). From the 1870s a number of new designs appeared in the U.S.A. and somewhat later in Europe, too, and production increased considerably.

417 Air pistol, A. V. Lebeda, Prague, *c.* 1866. Monogram of the owner (Count Franz Clam Gallas) on the butt. Behind the barrel, air cylinder with two opposite coiled springs, spanning lever on right-hand side. The casing also includes cleaning rod and wooden box for 12 darts.

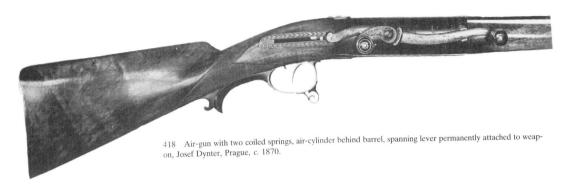

418 Air-gun with two coiled springs, air-cylinder behind barrel, spanning lever permanently attached to weapon, Josef Dynter, Prague, *c.* 1870.

In the second half of the 19th century there also appeared another type of gun with the pressure cylinder under the barrel and the pump permanently attached to the weapon. Paul Giffard procured a patent covering this weapon in the 1860s and weapons of similar design were turned out under the Bamco and Excellent trademarks in early 20th-century Sweden. The air was compressed in the pressure reservoir by few strokes of the pump, but it was necessary to repeat the procedure before each shot. Paul Giffard redesigned his wind-gun into a gas-gun which was then produced in France at the end of the 19th century. The pressure reservoir, containing carbon dioxide instead of air, was mounted under the barrel. Neither guns with the pressure

419 Gas-gun, bolt-action breech, pressure reservoir for carbon dioxide mounted under barrel. Design by Paul Giffard, produced by Manufacture Française d'Armes et Cycles de Saint-Étienne, *c.* 1895. Released hammer strikes a rod which opens outlet valve of pressure reservoir for a short burst.

reservoir under the barrel, nor gas-guns enjoyed much success, though, since they appeared in the period when numerous air-gun designs with a piston in the air cylinder had already started to emerge. Their diverse designs differed chiefly in the cocking of the mechanism.

Besides air-guns, air pistols appeared on a large scale in the 19th century — initially reservoir types and later on piston-type air-guns. In a way similar to firearms, some air-guns were designed to resemble walking sticks.

The same way as today, in the past some air-guns served for training purposes because their operation was considerably less expensive than that of firearms, and they were also used for indoor shooting. However, many air-guns equalled their firearm counterparts in power and were often used as hunting and sporting arms, and in an already mentioned instance as a military weapon. Among antique air-guns good-quality examples both as regards execution and the applied material and decoration can be found. In certain designs the value of the weapon was further increased because of the relatively complex mechanism.

The barrels of air-guns are more frequently smooth-bore, but specimens with rifled barrels are also known. Some air-guns are provided with a safety catch enabling them to release the cocked mechanism without letting out any air from the pressure reservoir. This was practical in cases in which the weapon had already been prepared for shooting, which was then not required. Silent operation (or at least a substantially reduced noise in comparison with firearms) was among the air-gun's virtues, too, the game not being roused when the sportsman was out shooting. Air-guns could also function better and with reliability in bad weather, since rain was a considerable problem in flintlock shooting. Air-guns were simpler to load and had a possible higher rate of fire, etc. Among the drawbacks, apart from the higher price and complex mechanism, the not always perfect obturation and the resulting possibility of leakage of the compressed air must be mentioned, because the latter rendered the air-gun incapable of use or less effective. However, the worst accidents were caused by the rupture of the reservoir either because of over-inflation or increased pressure in the reservoir caused by a considerable change of temperature. This was the principal reason behind the limitations and bans on air-guns production and use.

The external appearance of many antique air-guns closely resembles a common firearm of the period, including the non-functional wheellock or flintlock, and in a few cases only dismantling the weapon will reveal that an air-operated gun and not a firearm is involved.

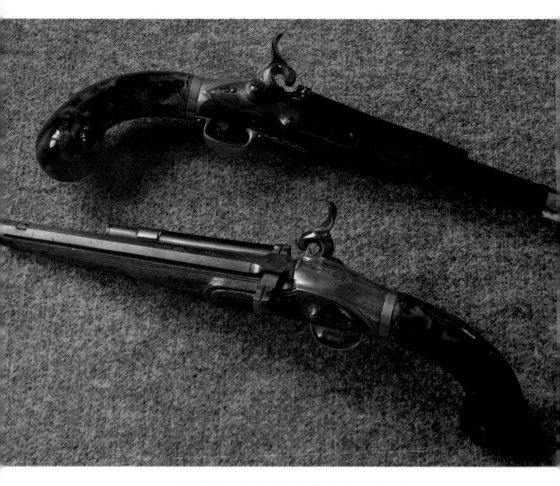

420 Pair of repeating air-pistols using Girardoni's system, Joseph Lowentz, Vienna, *c.* 1810. Screw-on pressure reservoirs fashioned as butt, finished with red/black lacquer in tortoiseshell effect.

BIBLIOGRAPHY

There exist vast numbers of books on arms and new ones are constantly being published both of a general and a narrowly specialized nature dealing with just a few weapon types or a specific period. For this reason the following list represents a choice of the most significant publications, although many others, not listed here, are important, including those by some 19th-century scholars, a number of which having been reprinted lately. Attention should also be drawn to the fact that most important weapon collections have issued printed catalogues either complete or on a selective basis. Antique arms are also discussed in specialized magazines issued in many countries. From this category, only some more significant periodicals published in Europe have been included in our list.

Publications:

Atkinson, J. A., *Duelling Pistols*, London 1964

Bearse, R., *Sporting Arms of the World*, New York 1975

Blackmore, H. L., *British Military Firearms*, London 1961

Blackmore, H. L., *Guns and rifles of the World*, London 1965

Blackmore, H. L., *Hunting Weapons*, London, s. a.

Blair, C., *Pistols of the World*, London 1968

Blair, C., *European and American Arms c. 1100—1850*, London 1962

Boccia, L. G., *Nove secoli di armi da caccia*, Florence 1967

Boudriot, *Armes à Feu Françaises. Modèles Réglementaires*, 4 parts, Paris 1961, 1963, 1965, 1967

The Complete Encyclopaedia of Arms and Weapons (Ed. L. Tarasuk—C. Blair), London 1982

Demmin, A., *Die Kriegswaffen in ihren geschichtlichen Entwickelungen...*, 4th edition, Leipzig 1893

Denisova, M. M.—Portnov, M. J.—Denisov, E. N., *Russkoe oruzhie XI—XIX vekov*, Moscow 1953

Dolínek, V.—Durdík, J.—Šáda, M., *Vzácné zbraně a zbroj* (Rare Arms and Armour), Prague 1986

Dolleczek, A., *Monographie der k. u. k. österr.-ung. blanken Handfeuer-Waffen...*, Vienna 1896

Duchartre, P. L., *Histoire des armes de chasse*, Paris 1955

Dunlap, J., *American, British & Continental Pepperbox Firearms*, San Francisco 1964

Durdík, J.—Mudra, M.—Šáda, M., *Alte Handfeuerwaffen*, Prague 1977

Eckardt, W.—Morawietz, O., *Die Handwaffen des brandenburgisch-preussisch-deutschen Heeres 1640—1945*, Hamburg 1957

Ezell, E., *Handguns of the World*, Harrisburg 1981

Faktor, Z.—Gargela, J., *Zeichen auf Handfeuerwaffen*, Hanau 1985

Gaibi, A., *Armi da fuoco italiane*, Busto Arsizio 1978

Gaier, C., *Quatre siècles d'armurerie liégeoise*, Liège 1977

George, J. N., *English Guns and Rifles*, Plantersville 1947

George, J. N., *English Pistols and Revolvers*, London 1961

Götz, H. D., *Militärgewehre und Pistolen der deutschen Staaten 1800—1870*, Stuttgart 1978

Hartmuth, E., *Die Armbrust*, Graz 1975

Hayward, J. F., *The Art of the Gunmaker*, vols. I—II, London 1962—63

Hayward, J. F., *Die Kunst der alten Büchsenmacher*, vols. I—II, Hamburg—Berlin 1968—69

Heer, E., *Der Neue Stöckel*, vols. I—III, Schwäbisch Hall 1978—82

Hoff, A., *Feuerwaffen,* vols. I—II, Brunswick 1969

Hoff, A., *Windbüchsen und andere Druckluftwaffen,* Hamburg—Berlin 1977

Kiesling, P., *Bayonets of the World,* vols. I—IV, Zaandam 1973—76

Kist, J. B.—Puype, J. P.—van der Sloot, R. B. F., *Dutch Muskets and Pistols,* London 1974

Lavin, J. D., *A History of Spanish Firearms,* London 1965

Lenk, T., *The Flintlock,* London 1965

Lenk, T., *Steinschloss-Feuerwaffen,* vols. I—II, Hamburg—Berlin 1973

Lugs, J., *Handfeuerwaffen,* vols. I—II, 3rd edition, Berlin 1970

Lugs, J., *Das Buch vom Schiessen,* Prague 1968

Lugs, J., *A History of Shooting,* Prague 1968

Lugs, J., *Firearms Past and Present,* vols. I—II, London 1956

Martin, J., *Armes à feu de l'armée française 1860 à 1940,* Paris 1974

Müller, H., *Historische Waffen,* Berlin 1957

Müller, H., *Gewehre, Pistolen, Revolver,* Leipzig 1979

Müller, H.—Kölling, H., *Europäische Hieb- und Stichwaffen,* Berlin 1981

Muster, H. P., *Revolver Lexikon,* Dietikon—Zurich 1976

Myatt, F., *Modern Small Arms,* London 1978

Petersen, J., *De norske vikingesverd,* Kristiania 1920

Pollard's History of Firearms (General Editor C. Blair), 1983

Rankin, R., *Small Arms of the Sea Service,* New Milford, USA, 1983

Robson, B., *Swords and the British Army,* London 1975

Russian Arms and Armour (Ed. Y. Miller), Leningrad 1982

Schedelmann, H., *Die grossen Büchsenmacher,* Brunswick 1972

Schöbel, J., *Prunkwaffen,* Berlin 1973

Schöbel, J., *Jagdwaffen und Jagdgerät des Historischen Museums zu Dresden,* Berlin 1976

Seitz, H., *Blankwaffen,* vols. I—II, Brunswick 1965

Smith, C.—Curtis, C., *The Pinfire System,* San Francisco 1983

Smith, W. H. B.—Smith, J. E., *Small Arms of the World,* 10th edition, New York 1973

Tarasuk, L., *Starinnoe ognestrelnoe oruzhie* (Antique Firearms), Leningrad 1972

Taylerson, A.—Chamberlain, W., *Adams' Revolvers,* London 1976

Wagner, E., *Hieb- und Stichwaffen,* 2nd edition, Prague 1978

Wagner, E., *Ars bella gerendi,* Prague 1980

Wagner, E.—Drobná, Z.—Durdík, J., *Tracht, Wehr und Waffen des späten Mittelalters,* Prague 1957

Westley, L., *Air-Guns and Air-Pistols,* 7th edition, London 1979

Wilkinson, F., *Edged Weapons,* London 1970

Winant, L., *Early Percussion Firearms,* London 1961

Winant, L., *Firearms Curiosa,* New York 1955

Zygulski, Z., *Broń w dawnej Polsce,* Warsaw 1975

Periodicals:

Armi Antiche (Turin)
Deutsches Waffen-Journal (Schwäbisch Hall)
Diana Armi (Florence)
Guns Review (London)
The Journal of the Arms and Armour Society (London)
Livrustkammaren (Stockholm)
Schweizer Waffen-Magazin (Zurich)
Střelecká revue (Prague)
Waffen- und Kostümkunde (Munich)

INDEX OF ARMS MANUFACTURES AND DESIGNERS

Page numbers in *italic* indicate captions to illustrations.

350